# A Study of Conflict in Innovation Teams in the Chinese Context

T0293243

www.royalcollins.com

# A Study of
# Conflict in Innovation Teams in the Chinese Context

Gao Hong

*Books Beyond Boundaries*

ROYAL COLLINS

A Study of Conflict in Innovation Teams in the Chinese Context

Gao Hong
Translated by He Li, Ayinuer Yiganmu, Xu Yan, and Feng Lei

First published in 2023 by Royal Collins Publishing Group Inc.
Groupe Publication Royal Collins Inc.
BKM Royalcollins Publishers Private Limited

Headquarters: 550-555 boul. René-Lévesque O Montréal (Québec) H2Z1B1 Canada
India office: 805 Hemkunt House, 8th Floor, Rajendra Place, New Delhi 110008

ISBN: 978-1-4878-1150-1

To find out more about our publications, please visit www.royalcollins.com.

# About the Author

Gao Hong (1986–), female, from the city of Kunshan in Jiangsu Province, associate senior editor, graduated from Hohai University with a doctor's degree in technical economy and management, and is a postdoctoral researcher in the discipline of Library Information and Archive Management of Nanjing University (still as a member of the workstation). She is now the Director of the Media Communication Studios of the Journal Department of Hohai University, and also the Deputy Editor-in-Chief of Journal of Hohai University (Philosophy and Social Sciences) and Journal of Economics of Water Resources.

Over the years, she has focused on the development of innovation teams and academic journals, published more than 20 high-quality papers, presided over the sub-project of China Science and Technology Journals Excellence Action Plan for the Selection and Cultivation of High-level Talents, the philosophy and social science projects of Jiangsu Province's colleges and universities, the basic scientific research business fees of central colleges and universities, and participated in many national, provincial and ministerial projects. She was awarded the honorary titles of "Excellent Editor of Social Science Journals in Chinese Higher Education Institutions," "Jiangsu Journal Pearl Award ⊠ Excellent Editor," "Excellent Executive Editor of Jiangsu Journal Publishing and Research," "Excellent Essay Award on Editorial Science," etc.

# Abstract

At a time when the world economy is in a long-term downturn and is struggling to seek growth drivers, the COVID-19 pandemic is spreading around the world at a stunning rate, which has brought a strong impact on the world and triggered sharp fluctuations in various markets. Global macroeconomic governance has stepped into unknown areas, and social distribution has witnessed a continuous widening of the income gap, and digital and intelligent technologies are accelerating the effect of the new industrial revolution. In particular, the high penetration of information technology has led to profound changes in the forms of market entities in various industries, and the spatial layout and codes of conducts of industrial organizations and economic activities have been reconstructed. In the face of the great changes in the post-pandemic era, China will embark on a new journey to build socialist modernization with Chinese characteristics on the basis of building a moderately prosperous society in all respects. Macro-economic and micro enterprises are actively exploring effective paths for high-quality transformation and upgrading. With the urgent need for industrial upgrading and transformation and the growing complexity of product technology, the innovation team integrating various human resources is gradually becoming an important organizational form of innovation activities. With the implementation of the innovation-driven strategy, the innovation ability of the innovation team is gradually placed in a more important position, becoming an important embodiment of the country's composite national strength and core competitiveness.

The innovation team emphasizes the exertion of individual creativity and the collaborative work of the team as a whole. By using the wisdom of the group and the interaction between members to innovate, it can be more flexible and responsive in the complex and changing knowledge-based economy environment. At present, academia has conducted extensive research on how to improve team effectiveness, among which team conflict, as one of the important variables in the team interaction process, has received more and more attention. The reason is that, compared with individual actions, the operation process within the innovation team is more complex, and the interdependence between members is stronger. As the most common interaction between people, conflict is inevitable in the team operation process. Moreover, the impact of conflict on team effectiveness has great uncertainties. With different types and different levels, and in different situations, the role of conflict is completely opposite. To this end, this book takes innovation team conflicts as the research object, starting from the three stages of "input-process-output" of team operation, and comprehensively uses qualitative and quantitative research methods, aiming to make a systematic study on the antecedent variables of innovation team conflict, the conflict relationship between members, and the impact of team conflict on team effectiveness.

First of all, the antecedents of team conflict are studied by constructing the conflict brittleness model of the innovation team. In the "input" stage of team operation, the complex system brittleness is applied to analyze the brittleness of innovation team conflict, and a four-level innovation team conflict brittleness model is constructed, which includes brittleness factors, brittleness events, relationship structure and brittleness results. The brittleness factors are classified to guide the research on the antecedent variables of team conflict. Based on this experience, it verifies the applicability of the two-dimensional model of innovation team conflict (task conflict and relationship conflict) in China. Then, the antecedent variables of task conflict and relationship conflict are studied by literature analysis, questionnaire and Ridit analysis.

Secondly, a "team-individual and team-individual and individual" research model of the conflict relationship among members of the innovation team is constructed. In the "process" stage of team operation, the conflict relationship among members of the innovation team is comprehensively studied from three levels of "team-individual and team-individual and individual." At the level of "team," combined with the social network theory, an innovation team conflict network is built and analyzed from the perspective of the whole innovation team, and the implementation steps of the team conflict network are put forward; at the level of "individual and team," using the content of brittle source level judgment for complex systems, the model provides a method to judge the impact of innovation team members on the conflict network; at the level of "individual and individual," taking the specific conflict interconnection among members as the ultimate goal, this paper proposes an assessment method for the conflict interconnection of innovation team members based on the brittle relevance of complex systems and the catastrophe progression method. After that, the research contents of the three levels are combined to form a "team-individual and team-individual and individual" research model of the conflict relationship among members of the innovation team.

Thirdly, the paper constructs the relationship model between the innovation team conflict and team effectiveness. In the "output" stage of team operation, we mainly designed new situations to study the impact of team conflict on team effectiveness, that is, considering the moderating effect of team emotional intelligence and team conflict network density in the relationship between team conflict and team effectiveness, according to the content of emotion theory and conflict network. Through small sample testing, a large-scale questionnaire and data statistical analysis, the relationship model between innovation team conflict and team effectiveness is constructed.

Finally, Matlab software is used to simulate the conflict brittleness model of innovation team, and corresponding countermeasures and suggestions are proposed according to the above research contents and results, in order to effectively deal with and manage the conflict of innovation team.

**Key words:** Chinese context; innovation team; team conflict; conflict network; team effectiveness

# Contents

# List of Tables

# List of Figures

# CHAPTER 1

# Introduction

## 1.1 Research Background, Purpose and Significance

### 1.1.1 Research Background

At present, the knowledge innovation system and innovation ability have become an important basis for determining the economic and social development of a country or region, and are the key factors affecting competitiveness. In order to meet the requirements of scientific and technological innovation and enhance the ability of independent innovation, it is imperative to build a scientific and comprehensive national innovation system. The national innovation system, which integrates innovation subjects (individuals and teams), innovation environment and innovation mechanism, can reasonably allocate and efficiently utilize various innovation resources, promote coordination and interaction among innovation institutions, and is an organizational system that fully reflects the national innovation will and strategic objectives. Because of the extensive need for knowledge support for innovation and the increasingly complex and specialized innovation tasks, the traditional way of relying on excellent individuals to complete innovation can no longer meet the organization's needs. The emergence of innovation teams conforms to the trend of knowledge innovation, and has become a new management model to meet the needs of the knowledge economy. Innovation teams emphasize the exertion of individual creativity and the collaborative work of the team as a whole. They achieve innovation using collective intelligence and interaction between members, so they can be more flexible and react more quickly in the complex and changing knowledge economy environment. The *OECD SME and Entrepreneurship Outlook 2021* report shows that during the COVID-19 pandemic, small and medium-sized enterprises and entrepreneurs were hit hard.[1] Although the impact was great, the available data shows that start-ups in most OECD countries have been emerging and showing innovation dynamics rather than a wave of bankruptcy. However, government support is less effective in helping self-employed people, smaller and younger companies, women and ethnic minority entrepreneurs.[2]

In addition, according to *China's Youth Entrepreneurship City Vitality Report (2021)*, more than 44 million new start-up companies were established in China from 2011 to 2020. Artificial intelligence, big data and other hardcore technology and cultural creativity are the preferred choices for youth entrepreneurship.

With the wide application of innovation teams in practice, how to gather team strength and improve team effectiveness has become the focus of many scholars, and is also one of the research focuses of management and organizational behavior. Looking at the existing literature, the research perspectives on innovation team effectiveness can be summarized into three aspects: first, take team effectiveness as the outcome variable, analyze the factors that affect team effectiveness and their specific impact mechanisms, and the antecedent variables involved are organizational structure characteristics, team task characteristics, team heterogeneity, team trust, team learning, team atmosphere, knowledge sharing behavior, psychological contract, emotional intelligence, leadership behavior and social capital. The second is to evaluate team effectiveness, mainly by building an indicator system and selecting evaluation methods to achieve effective evaluation. The third is to discuss the problems existing in the innovation team from a relatively macro perspective and propose countermeasures to improve the team effectiveness as a whole. No matter what the perspective of the research and practice is, the ultimate goal is to help the members work more effectively and the team achieve better efficiency. In the first research perspective of innovation team effectiveness, most of the literature follows the basic model of "input-process-output" proposed by McGrath in 1964, which mainly analyzes the impact of individual members, team factors and environmental factors on the outcome variables of team through the team

---

[1] https://read.oecd-ilibrary.org/industry-and-services/oecd-sme-and-entrepreneurship-outlook-2021_97a5bbfe-en#page1

[2] http://zqb.cyol.com/

interaction process.

As one of the important variables of the team interaction process, team conflict is crucial for understanding team effectiveness, because innovation teams do not always produce synergy as "1+1+1>3." Compared with individuals fighting alone, the internal operation process of an innovation team is more complex, and the interdependence between members is stronger. As the most common way of interaction between people, conflict cannot be avoided in the process of team operation. At the same time, the impact of conflict on team effectiveness is highly uncertain. The influence of conflict of different types, different levels of conflict, and different situations, will be completely varied. Therefore, more and more scholars study team conflict from different perspectives. The fundamental purpose of this book to study the conflict of innovation teams is to improve the effectiveness of innovation teams from a new research perspective and promote collaboration among members through the study of this variable.

### 1.1.2 Purpose and Significance

The existing literature has made a lot of useful attempts to study team conflict, most of which are based on the team conflict theory or conflict management theory to qualitatively or quantitatively explore the concept, type, antecedent variables, mode of action and results. Although fruitful achievements have been made, there is still much room for discussion in this field. For example, are the antecedents of different types of conflict in the team the same or different? How did the conflict develop in the whole team? How to measure the conflict relationship between members? Under the influence of different regulatory variables or intermediary variables, how does team conflict affect team effectiveness? In order to better analyze the conflict problem of innovation teams, based on the theory of complex system brittleness, this book aims to look at innovation team conflict from a relatively new theoretical perspective, and start with the three stages of "input-process-output" in the team operation process, respectively analyzing the antecedents of innovation team conflict, the conflict relationship among members and the impact of team conflict on team effectiveness; therefore, enriching the research content in this field and reflecting a certain practical management significance, so as to reduce the negative impact of conflict at the source, comprehensively manage the conflict during its processing and ultimately improve the effectiveness of innovation teams.

Through this research, the book is expected to expand the research content in the field of team conflict in theory and propose practical countermeasures in practice. In terms of its theoretical significance, the first is to analyze systematically the antecedents of team conflict in a qualitative and quantitative way according to the team conflict brittleness model of innovation teams and the relevant content of brittleness factors. This is slightly different from the existing research perspective, thus enriching the research on the antecedents of team conflict. Second, based on the social network theory and the complex system brittleness theory, the conflict relationship between members is systematically analyzed from the three aspects of "team-individual and team-individual and individual." This is relatively new for the research of team conflict, which can not only strengthen the understanding of the internal conflict of innovation teams, but also treat this "black box" from a broader and more diverse perspective. Moreover, it can promote the conceptualization and instrumentalization of complex system brittleness theory and social network analysis in this research field. The third is to consider the moderating effect of conflict network density and team emotional intelligence on the relationship between task conflict and team effectiveness from the team level, which can not only enrich the existing research conclusions of task conflict effect, but also explore the moderating effect of conflict network and emotional factors in the relationship between team conflict and team effectiveness. More importantly, this book systematically analyzes the antecedents of team conflict, so that innovation teams can avoid or reduce the negative impact of conflict at the source, grasp the overall situation of team conflict at the macro level, have a more comprehensive understanding of team conflict, and specifically consider the conflict relationship between each member and others at the micro level, so as to develop targeted conflict management methods and measures.

## 1.2 Related Documents

### 1.2.1 Research on Innovation Team Conflict

There is less research literature on innovation team conflict, and the research contents can be roughly divided into two aspects: one is about the management strategies of innovation team conflict; the second is about the relationship between innovation team conflict and other variables.

For example, Zhou Ruichao and others mainly studied the conflict management methods of innovation teams conducting scientific research, and proposed that reasonable conflict resolution should start from the team level and individual level. At the team level, the team should establish a common vision and goal, strengthen the cultivation of cohesion, and create a good atmosphere. The individual level focuses on the strategic choice of specific research members[1]. Lin Li and others believed it is extremely normal for conflicts to occur during the operation of an innovation team. Conflicts can bring new ideas and opinions. However, if conflicts are allowed to develop freely, they may sabotage the innovation team's work and undermine the team's performance. Therefore, certain strategies, such as decisively stopping the destructive conflicts, establishing effective communication mechanisms, cultivating a good team atmosphere, etc., should be adopted to grasp and resolve conflicts and transform their negative effects into positive ones[2]. In Gao Xiaoqing's view, the conflict risk faced by the enterprise innovation team mainly has two levels: internal and external. The conflict between individuals, the conflict between individual goals and team goals is an internal conflict of the team; the conflict between the team and external individuals, and the conflict between different teams is the external conflict of the team. In terms of conflict management, first of all, we need to recognize the nature of the conflict, eliminate destructive conflicts by coordinating the relationship between the two parties to the conflict, and guide conflicts that have constructive values[3].

As for the relationship between innovation team conflict and other variables, Men Yazhen has shown through research that relationship conflict has a significant negative impact on innovation performance, and the impact of task conflict on innovation performance has yet to be verified. But as a mediating variable, relationship conflict has a partial mediating effect on trust and innovation performance[4]. Han Fei et al. studied the relationship between conflict and performance of corporate science and technology innovation teams. The results showed that when members adopted competitive conflict management behavior, the more significant the conflict with positive correlation with performance will be, and the more significant the conflict with negative correlation with performance will be; when members adopt cooperative conflict management behavior, the more significant the conflict with positive correlation with performance will be, and the less significant the conflict with negative correlation with performance will be[5]. Yin Huibin built a multi-level fuzzy comprehensive evaluation model by combining fuzzy comprehensive evaluation and hierarchical analysis on the causes, states and strategies that affect the level of knowledge conflict, and realized the quantitative evaluation of the level of knowledge conflict[6].

## 1.2.2 Concept and Type Division of Team Conflict

With regard to the concept of team conflict, Jehn's view is typical and widely used, that is, team conflict is the difference between the two sides in their perception of each other's values, interests and preferences, and the inconsistency in the perspective and method of looking at problems[7]. Rahim believes that team conflict is the discussion and debate about work tasks and work processes among team members or small groups of stakeholders[8]; in De Dreu's view, team conflict is the generation process of the perception that team members are incompatible or mutually exclusive[9]. Most Chinese scholars believe that team conflict is a conflict within a team. It is a discussion on possible conflicts among members at the team level[10], and it is also a common perception of differences among most members during team interaction[11].

### (1) Types of Team Conflicts

Jehn et al. divided team conflict into relationship conflict and task conflict according to the source of conflict[7]; Pinkley et al. believed that relationship conflict and task conflict are the most important classifications[12], in which task conflict is the different opinions on the pursuit of organizational goals and the existing conflicts of interest, the core of which is cognition, and such conflicts are inevitable in the team[13]; relationship conflict is the pressure and depression caused by individual differences (beliefs, values, personality and preferences) of members, including emotional factors, such as mutual hatred, hostility, aversion, etc.[14]. In 1996, Amason divided conflict into cognitive conflict and emotional conflict; The former is the inconsistency of members' cognition and opinions on task objectives, task execution methods and others related to the work. The latter reflects the disharmony of interpersonal relations, which stems from mutual suspicion or hostility among members[15]. This dichotomy is a very common and widely accepted method to divide the types of team conflict. In 2001, Jehn et al. classified team conflict into relationship conflict, task conflict and process conflict from the perspective of team interaction and cooperation, task allocation and implementation process. The process conflict arises from the process of work execution, that is, when there are different opinions on how the work should be completed and implemented, on the work and responsibility and resource allocation, and when the team has differences on the responsibilities that a member should assume[16]. Chinese scholars have also considered classifying team conflict into these three categories. Process conflict refers to the conflict among members about how to complete tasks, and is more related to resources and responsibilities[17].

Although scholars have proposed different ways to divide team conflict from different research perspectives, they are very similar in nature. Because task conflict and process conflict are task-oriented when compared in a broad sense, except that the former emphasizes differences in task content and objectives, and the latter emphasizes differences in views during task completion. So far, the two-dimensional division method of team conflict has been widely recognized, and most scholars have adopted Jehn's division method of task conflict and relationship conflict, or Amazon's division method of cognitive conflict and emotional conflict when conducting empirical research.

### (2) The Relationship between Task Conflict and Relationship Conflict

The relationship between task conflict and relationship conflict is a hot issue in the field of team conflict research. Many researchers point out that the two conflicts have a positive correlation. For example, Simons' research shows that task conflict will lead to relationship conflict under specific circumstances, with an average correlation coefficient of 0.47[18]; The meta-analysis results of 23 teams by De Dreu et al. revealed that the average correlation coefficient between them was 0.52, and task conflict could explain 27% variance of relationship conflict[19]; based on the Chinese cultural background, Lang et al. found that due to misunderstanding of the causes of conflict, members tend to have negative emotional reactions, which turn task conflict into relationship conflict[20].

There is a correlation between task conflict and relationship conflict because rationality and emotion cannot be completely separated in the process of conflict interaction[21]. Quarrels often occur when members have different perceptions of tasks. When inappropriate verbal expressions appear in the debate process, task conflict and relationship conflict may occur at the same time[22]. Amason proposed that the correlation between the two is due to the fact that the objection to the perception of the task may be interpreted as personal emotional conflict[23]. Some scholars use attribution theory to explain the relationship between the two, that is, when others deny their ideas, members tend to make an external attribution, that is, they are not responsible for other people's denial, and this negative attribution will inevitably stimulate relationship conflicts between members[24].

### 1.2.3 Antecedent Variables of Team Conflict

The causes of team conflict are very complex. Scholars have studied the antecedents of conflict from different perspectives and aspects. For example, Bsino held that the root causes of conflict include biosocial type, personality communication type, structural type, cultural concept type and complex type[25]; Forsyth divided the sources of conflict into competing for limited resources, adopting controversial influence strategies, and personality traits and behavior types of both parties of the conflict[26]; Steven et al. thought that the incompatibility and difference of goals, the interdependence of tasks, shortage of resources, vague regulation and communication problems were the main causes of conflicts[27]; Cronin et al. pointed out that the diverse functions of the team have increased the divergence of members' perception of tasks. In addition, some empirical studies have listed in detail the antecedents of team conflict, mainly concentrated at the task, team, organizational, and personal levels[28].

### (1) Task Characteristics

Task conflicts usually have a strong correlation with the team task. If the task is too simple, members tend to think they have fully understood the essence of the problem and the solution, so task conflict is more likely to occur[29]. Consistent with this view, Olson et al. found that when dealing with routine tasks, task conflict and team output are significantly negatively correlated; When the task is unconventional, there is a significant positive correlation between the two[30]. Jehn et al. pointed out that the clearer the task objective is, the more likely it will lead to task conflict. When the task is uncertain, various disputes will arise when confirming the scope of the problem, which is conducive to good communication and interaction among members[31]; Van Der Vegt's research showed that the higher the task dependency, the closer the collaboration between members and the higher the conflict level[32].

## (2) Organizational Characteristics

In terms of organizational characteristics, previous studies have focused on the impact of cultural norms and executive team compensation structure, that is, if organizational culture is team-oriented and compensation design is team-based, there is a significant impact relationship between the two and conflict[33]. At the same time, a complex team organizational structure will increase the frequency of team conflict, thus affecting team innovation efficiency[34].

## (3) Team Characteristics

Team-level factors, such as scale, heterogeneity, previous performance, synergy, cohesion, group pressure, group norms, trust, atmosphere, behavior integration, communication level and leadership style, are considered to trigger team conflicts. Relevant research shows that the larger the team size and the more complex the structure, the lower the level of communication and trust among members, and the frequency of conflict will increase significantly[35]; when a new member enters the team, the cognitive inconsistency between members on tasks and emotions will be more prominent[36]. Team surface-level diversity refers to the demographic diversity that could be directly observed, which is positively related to relationship conflict and task conflict[37]. Team deep-level diversity refers to differences in attitudes, values, knowledge, skills, abilities, etc., that cannot be directly observed, which will increase conflicts within the team[38]. In addition, by studying the relationship between conflict and negative performance feedback, Peterson found that the more negative the performance feedback, the higher the conflict level[39]; Michalisin et al. showed that team cohesion and team conflict were significantly negatively correlated[40]. Jehn et al.'s research on the impact of team atmosphere on conflict showed that openness is conducive to forming a benign conflict model within a team[41].

### (4) Personal Characteristics

In terms of individual characteristics of members, Kriedler et al. pointed out that differences in personal needs, values or beliefs are the sources of conflicts[42]; Eisenhardt believed that internal differences in goals, ideals, values, motivations, beliefs, etc., at the individual level will lead to conflicts[43]. Jehn proposed that differences in demographic variables such as gender and age are positively correlated with relationship conflict, while cognitive level and functional background diversity are positively correlated with task conflict[31]. In addition, Chatman found that different educational backgrounds of team members will increase conflict related to tasks[44], and interdependence between members is also the basis for conflict, because interdependence means that members have a certain power over each other. Specifically, this power is not a vertical power generated by different levels of the organization as commonly understood. It is an advantage caused by the team members' control over different resources or exclusive possession of a certain professional knowledge[45].

### 1.2.4 The Role of Team Conflict

Regarding the role of relationship conflict, the research conclusion is consistent: relationship conflict is harmful, always reduces team effectiveness and has a negative impact on members' work attitudes. However, as for the role of task conflict, research conclusions have yet to reach a consensus, and even results that are completely opposite have emerged.

### (1) The Role of Relationship Conflict

In various research situations, researchers agree that relationship conflict is harmful. For example, the research results of Jehn et al. showed that relationship conflict is significantly negatively correlated with member satisfaction, identity and emotional acceptance[7]; further research by Jehn found that no matter whether the task is conventional or unconventional, relationship conflict is always negatively related to team performance[46]; the meta-analysis conducted by De Dreu et al. found that the average correlation coefficient between relationship conflict and various team outputs was r=−0.27 and significant at 0.001 level[15]; Langfred believed that the reason why relationship conflict is harmful is that it destroys members' self-management process[47]; Mortensen et al. also showed that interpersonal tension caused by relationship conflict would hinder the development of cognition, thus damaging task-related efforts[48].

## (2) The Role of Task Conflict

(1) The harmful theory of task conflict: Camevale found through experiments that members' divergent thinking can generate more creative ideas in situations with very low conflict levels, while members' creativity decreases a lot in situations with high conflict levels[49]; Friedman believed that task conflict can intensify members' pressure, divert their attention, and thus bearing a negative impact on the team's final performance [50]; Sonnentag's survey of 291 white-collar workers showed that employees who perceive high-level task conflict have lower job performance[51]. The information processing theory explains the reasons for the negative impact of task conflict: once a task conflict occurs, it will bring overwhelming information and excessive cognitive load, which will interfere with the normal task processing of members[52]. In addition, Wang Guofeng's research also found that the increase of task conflict will lead to the emergence and increase of relationship conflict[53], and relationship conflict is often considered as a mediator between task conflict and team performance[54].

(2) The beneficial theory of task conflict: some scholars have found that task conflict is beneficial through qualitative or quantitative research. For example, Kurtzberg believed that members learn more from each other after task conflict occurs, which is conducive to generating new ideas and improving team efficiency[55]; at the same time, task conflict is also a useful means to avoid negative effects caused by collective thinking[56]. The reason why task conflict has a positive effect is that it can integrate various cognitive resources. This process of analyzing information is often better than that of an individual, thus making the team more effective.

(3)  A more complex view of the role of task conflict: now, more and more scholars try to explore the dual effects of task conflict in different situations, and take into account the role of various moderating variables or intermediary variables. With regard to the relationship between task conflict and team performance, studies have shown that the relationship among task conflict, decision quality, and decision commitment should be inverted U type[57], that is, a moderate level of task conflict is conducive to team performance for some types of tasks[58]. For example, De Dreu's research showed that moderate task conflict will improve team innovation, because members' collective learning awareness and ability are the best during that time, which can best promote the development of innovation ideas[59]. In addition, Kurtzberg et al. found that the role of task conflict on team performance is different in teams at different developmental stages. For example, for teams at a more mature developmental stage, the higher the level of task conflict, the higher their performance[60]. Some scholars attribute the inconsistent effect of task conflict on team performance to differences of research situations, that is, varied moderators or mediators exist.

### 1.2.5 Management of Team Conflicts

Blake et al. first proposed five different types of conflict management[61]; Singh et al. further described these five types as withdrawal type, mitigation type, mandatory type, compromise type and problem-solving type[62]. Based on the two dimensions of conflict management, Thomas et al. divided the conflict handling mode into five styles: competing style, collaborating style, compromising style, avoiding style and accommodating style[63]. Among them, the most representative is the conflict handling model proposed by Thomas, which proposes five conflict management strategies based on the two dimensions of "care about others" and "care about themselves"[64]. It can be seen from the analysis that the common point of the above conflict management methods is the emphasis on the need to take corresponding solutions according to the causes of conflicts.

### 1.2.6 Conflict Research in Other Fields

Conflict is a universal and eternal phenomenon both between and within societies. As a basic form of interaction in human society, the range of conflict is extensive. In addition to the internal conflict of a team, scholars have conducted corresponding research on the disputes between individuals at the micro level, the confrontation between groups and organizations at the middle level, and the conflicts between countries at the macro level. For example, international conflict is the most prominent manifestation of various complex relationships between countries with different levels of strength in pursuit of their own interests[65], the product of sharp contradictions between international political entities, and the situation of friction, confrontation and struggle between conflicting parties in pursuit of their own interests or to achieve specific policy goals[66]. Because the contradictions among countries are universal and the interests of countries cannot be converged, international conflicts are unavoidable. There are many kinds of international conflicts, which can be divided into different categories from different angles, such as political conflict, economic conflict, military conflict, diplomatic conflict, cultural conflict, etc. Western scholars believe that there are three levels of causes of international conflicts, namely, international structural, social and psychological interpretation, and migration[67]. Specifically, the causes of international conflicts involve the collision of national interests, the rampant hegemonism and the outbreak of nationalism. In addition, social and public conflicts are also common[68].

From the research results of the conflict in other fields, conflict research involves a wide range of fields, but the core problem is still to explore the causes, manifestations, effects and solutions of conflict. Although scholars study conflicts in different fields, the universality of conflict phenomena, the complexity of conflict causes and the diversity of conflict results are all widely discussed.

## 1.3 Relevant Concepts, Theoretical Basis and Research Framework

### 1.3.1 Related Concepts

#### (1) Innovation Team

Innovation team has always been a hot issue for researchers. Scholars at home and abroad have extensively discussed the characteristics, components, life cycle, performance, existing problems and countermeasures of innovation team. Before studying the concept of "innovation team," we should first clarify the relevant concepts of "team," because the research of innovation team starts from the research results of the team, and the latter is the organizational form and guarantee for the former to realize innovation; at the same time, "team" is also the upper concept of "innovation team." Through the comprehensive analysis of research results, the widely accepted concept of "team" refers to a formal group composed of individuals with complementary talents and interdependence for common goals, standards and responsibilities. "Innovation team" is a team formed for innovation, whose value and significance are to achieve innovation. The understanding of "innovation" is crucial to the conceptualization of "innovation team." Joseph Schumpeter was the first to bring "innovation" into the theoretical system as an economic category. He proposed that to innovate is to "establish a new production function and apply a combination of production factors and production conditions to the production system as never before"[69]. Peter Drucker is the most representative of the research on "innovation" in the field of social management. He pointed out that innovation is "a systematic work that can be organized and needs to be organized," "a practice that needs knowledge accumulation as a backing," and "a behavior that endows resources with new ability to create wealth."[70] Therefore, an innovation team should not only have the characteristics of a team, but also provide conditions to meet the requirements of innovation, that is, to complete "a systematic work that needs knowledge as a backing" in the form of a team.

Through the review of the concept of team, the tracing of innovation meaning, innovation motivation and innovation rules, and the combing of existing literature based on content analysis, this book believes that an innovation team is a team that, in a certain environment or platform, achieves specific innovation goals through mutual supplement of knowledge and skills, division of labor and cooperation, resource sharing, responsibility sharing, and the team is formed by the collaboration of knowledge talents who mainly engage in innovation activities and have team spirit and good cohesion.

## (2) Innovation Team Conflict

Conflict is a very complex and diverse phenomenon. According to different research perspectives and research priorities, scholars have different opinions on the definition of conflict, but the common points of conflict can be extracted: first, it contains two or more conflict subjects; second, there are differences between the conflict subjects. The innovation team conflict studied in this book refers to the conflict among the innovation team members. It is the discussion of possible conflicts among members in the working context of the innovation team, which belongs to the research concept at the team level.

This book defines innovation team conflict from the perspective of conflict process analysis, and believes that innovation team conflict refers to the inconsistent or opposite interaction process caused when there are incompatible and difficult-to-coordinate goals, cognition or emotional factors among innovation team members.

Although various scholars put forward different types of team conflict from different research perspectives, their contents are very similar in nature. So far, the division of task conflict and relationship conflict proposed by Jehn is widely recognized and applied. This book also follows this division method, and believes that innovation team task conflict is an opposite or inconsistent interaction process caused by different views of innovation team members on task-related issues (including purpose, main decisions, procedures and choice of best action), and the relationship conflict is the interaction process of opposites or inconsistencies between members due to emotional opposition, interpersonal friction, etc.

### (3) Effectiveness of Innovation Team

The concept of innovation team effectiveness is mostly developed from the perspective of team performance or team effectiveness. This book follows Hackman's definition of team effectiveness[71], and believes that innovation team effectiveness is the result of the final activities of the innovation team, which can be evaluated from three aspects: output results, which refers to the creative tangible or intangible products and results produced by the innovation team must meet or exceed the indicators specified by the organization, namely business performance, which is the performance of the innovation team in terms of the degree of completion and compliance with the task target; the satisfaction of members, which refers to the satisfaction of all aspects of the needs of members brought about by the activities of the innovation team; sustainable development capability, which refers to the ability of innovation team members to work together to achieve sustainable development of the team.

## 1.3.2 Theoretical Basis

### (1) The Brittleness Theory of Complex Systems

Previous studies have shown that complex systems are characterized by openness, complexity, nonlinearity, hierarchy and emergent evolution[72]. Chinese scholar Jin Hongzhang first proposed the concept of brittleness of complex systems and pointed out that brittleness is also a basic feature of complex systems and an objective existence[73].

1) The definition and characteristics of brittleness

The dictionary interprets "brittleness" as "the property that objects are easy to break when subjected to tension or impact" and "the property of plastic deformation that materials do not detect before fracture." Jin Hongzhang and others extended the term brittleness in the mechanics of materials to the study of the characteristics of complex systems and gave a linguistic description of the brittleness of complex systems: for an open complex system, a collapsed subsystem (not a soliton) will exchange matter and energy with other subsystems, so its collapse will destroy the ordered state of the subsystem that exchanges matter and energy with it, and finally collapse. Recursively, with the increase of the number and level of collapse subsystems, the entire complex system will eventually collapse. This behavioral characteristic of complex system is called brittleness[73].

The state vectors of several subsystems of a complex system are denoted by $x(t) = \{x_1(t), x_2(t), \cdots, x_n(t)\}$ , $x_i(t)$ is the state vector of the $i$ th subsystem. When the system is running normally, there is a set $K \subset R^n$ , $\forall x_i(t) \in K, 1 < i < n, n \in N, \forall t \geq 0$ . Disturbance $r(t)$ acts on the subsystem at moment $t$ and causes its collapse; When $t > t_0 + T$ , $\exists n_0 < n$ , $x_j(t) \notin K, j = 1, 2, \cdots, n_0$ , at which time the whole complex system collapses, and these $n_0$ subsystems are called key subsystems of the whole complex system[74].

Brittleness is the basic attribute of complex systems. The basic characteristics of brittleness are as follows: concealment, that is, brittleness of complex systems can only be shown when they are subject to interference with sufficient strength; the diversity of action results, that is, brittleness has different effects on the system; interlocking: when a subsystem collapses, other subsystems related to it will also collapse due to the effect of brittleness; Integration. If only one subsystem is considered, brittleness cannot be reflected, meaning that it is an attribute of complex system as a whole. The non-cooperative game between subsystems is a source of brittleness of complex systems. Brittleness makes the entropy of subsystems increase continuously. In order to reduce its entropy value, a non-cooperative game will be conducted between subsystems to compete for negative entropy[73].

2) The process of complex system collapse

The collapse process of a complex system[74] is shown in Figure 1-1.

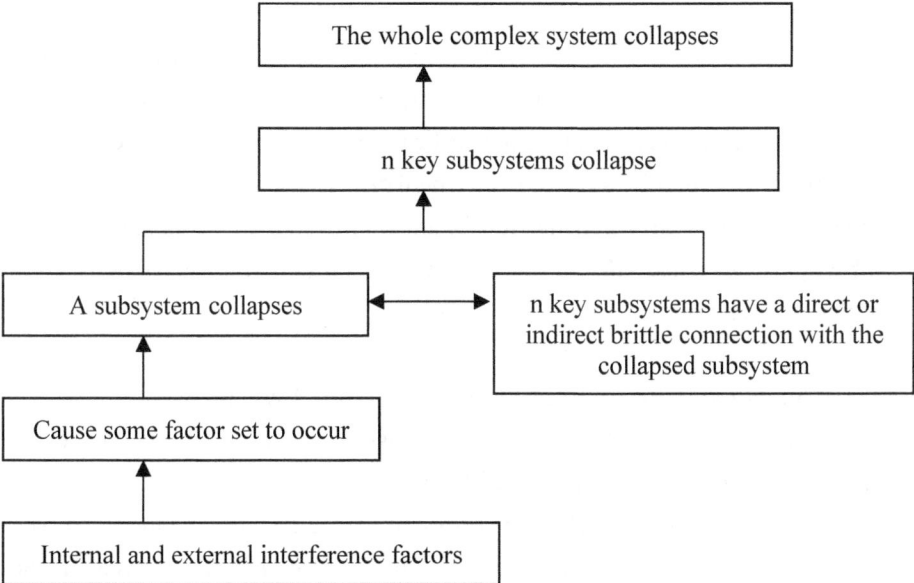

**Figure 1-1 Collapse process of complex system**

It can be seen from Figure 1-1 that when a complex system is disturbed by internal and external interference factors, a subsystem will collapse. Because this subsystem has direct or indirect brittle links with all subsystems in a set of key subsystems, the collapse of the entire complex system will eventually occur.

3) Brittle element

The chain reaction process of collapse between subsystems is the result of the activation of the brittleness of complex systems. The brittleness element is the smallest unit in the chain reaction process, which is composed of brittleness source, brittleness receiver and brittleness relevance. The relationship between the three is shown in Figure 1-2.

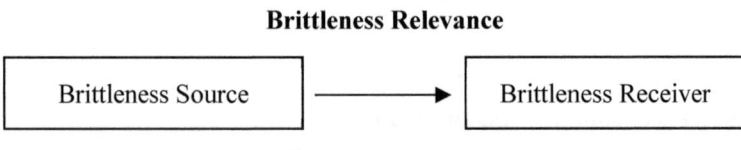

**Brittleness Relevance**

Figure 1-2 Brittle element

Brittleness source is the part (subsystem) that first collapses when a complex system is disturbed by internal and external boundaries. It can be divided into direct brittleness source and intermediate brittleness source according to different action modes[75]. All subsystems are intermediate brittleness sources except for the direct brittleness source and the subsystem that eventually collapses. The part (subsystem) collapsed due to the collapse of other parts (subsystems) is a brittleness receiver.

4) Graphical description of the brittle effect of complex systems
According to the characteristics of brittleness of complex systems, there are generally four graphic descriptions of them[76]:

First, the domino model. Each subsystem in the system is represented by a domino. The distance between each domino represents the degree of the brittleness relevance between subsystems. The smaller the distance is, the stronger the brittleness relevance is. The larger the distance is, the weaker the brittleness relevance is. The distance between two dominoes is related to the energy that can be transferred to the next domino when one domino falls, and whether the other domino falls also depends on the energy that can be transferred to it from the surrounding fallen dominoes. The domino model is shown in Figure 1-3.

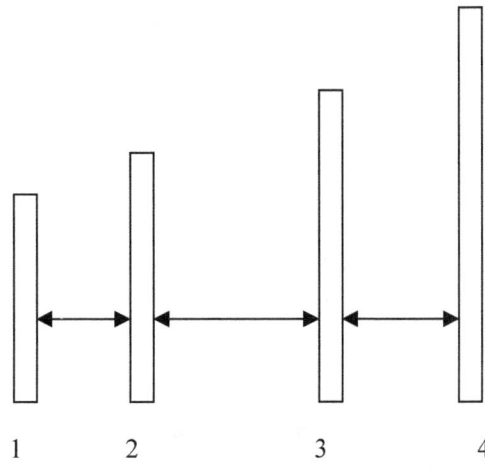

**Figure 1-3 Domino model**

Second, the pyramid model. This model refers to when a larger subsystem located in the upper layer collapses due to interference, the system brittleness will spread from top to bottom. The number of subsystems collapsing from top to bottom will increase just as the system brittleness does. The pyramid model is shown in Figure 1-4.

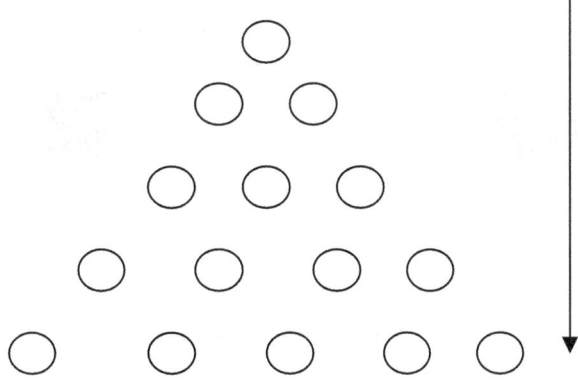

**Figure 1-4 Pyramid model**

Third, the inverted pyramid model. This model means that when a smaller subsystem located in the lower layer collapses, the brittleness of the complex system will spread from bottom to top, leading to more and more subsystems collapsing. The inverted pyramid model is shown in Figure 1-5.

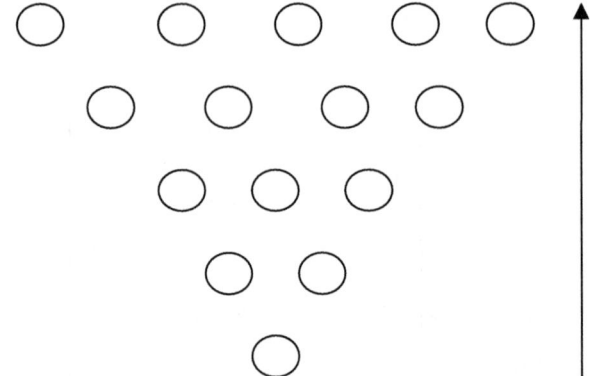

**Figure 1-5 Inverted pyramid model**

Fourth, the cellular automata model. The above three models reflect the brittleness relevance between subsystems of the same level and different levels in a complex system, but the brittleness relevance between subsystems has specific directionality. If a subsystem is regarded as a cell, when the cell collapses under the interference or impact of the internal and external boundaries, cells in other directions adjacent to it will be affected. Von Neumann's and Moore's types of two-dimensional cellular automata are more famous, as shown in Figure 1-6.

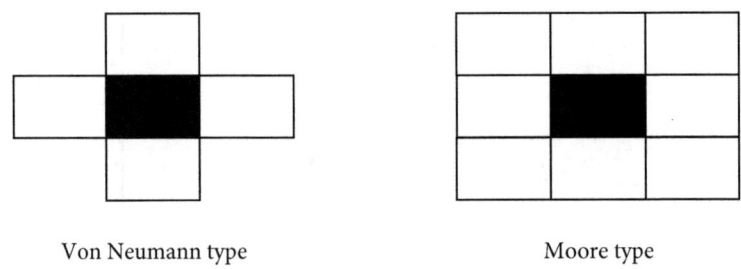

Von Neumann type                                     Moore type

**Figure 1-6 Cellular automata model**

5) Brittle connection function

Four commonly used methods exist to study the brittleness of complex systems: brittle link function, set pair analysis, brittle link entropy and non-cooperative game. This book mainly analyzes the brittle link function. Will the collapse of a subsystem in a complex system under the influence of internal and external interference factors affect other subsystems? This issue can be analyzed using the brittle link function between subsystems, through which the concepts of brittleness identity, degree of opposition, fluctuation and brittleness change rate can be established[73].

Suppose that there are three subsystems $X, Y, Z$. Subsystem $X$ is described by the state vector $X = \{x_1, x_2, \cdots, x_n\}$, $1 < i < n$; subsystem $Y, Z$ are described by state vectors $Y = \{y_1, y_2, \cdots y_j \cdots, y_n\}$, $Z = \{z_1, z_2, \cdots z_j \cdots, z_n\}$, $1 \leq j \leq n$ respectively. There are $n$ states in the set of state vectors of the subsystems $Y, Z$. The change degree of these $n$ state vectors under the action of internal and external factors will play a key role in the whole subsystem. If subsystem $X$ collapses under the interference of internal and external factors, and at least one of the state vectors of the associated subsystem $Y$, $y_j (1 < j < n)$, changes due to the influence of brittleness relevance, the subsystem $y_j$ is said to be brittle identical to subsystem $X$; other unaffected state vectors are brittle opposites to subsystem $X$; with the change of time, some states sometimes tend to be the same and sometimes tend to be opposite, then these states are brittle fluctuations with subsystem $X$. Assume that the brittleness weight coefficient vector $\beta = \{\beta_1, \beta_2, \cdots \beta_j, \cdots, \beta_n\}$ is respectively relative to each state vector of the subsystem $Y$, indicating the degree of influence on the whole subsystem when each state vector of the subsystem $Y$ collapses alone when the subsystem $X$ collapses. When $y_i$ is brittle identical to subsystem $X$, the weight coefficient is 1; when $y_i$ is brittle opposite to subsystem $X$, the weight coefficient is 0; when $y_i$ is brittle and has fluctuations with subsystem $X$, the weight coefficient is between 0 and 1. The degree of transmission and amplification of brittleness between subsystems is related to the brittleness link function between subsystems. The brittleness link function can be measured by the brittleness identity, brittleness opposition and brittleness fluctuation between subsystem states.

According to the above analysis, the brittleness identical degree of the subsystem $Y$ at the moment $t$ is $a = \sum_{j=1}^{k} \beta_j(t), 1 < k < n$, if there is no state vector identical to the subsystem $X$, then $a = 0$; The brittleness opposition degree of the subsystem $Y$ at the moment $t$ is $b = \sum_{j=1}^{h} \beta_j(t), 1 < h < n$, if there is no state vector

opposite to the subsystem $X$, then $b = 0$; The brittleness fluctuation degree of the

subsystem $Y$ at the moment $t$ is $c = \sum_{j=1}^{n-k-h} \beta_j(t)$, if there is no fluctuation between

the state vector and the subsystem $X$, then $c = 0$.

The brittle link function $F$ between subsystem $X$ and subsystem $Y$ is:

$$F = f(a,b,c) \quad \text{Equation (1.1)}$$

Wherein, $a, b, c$ are the identity degree, opposition degree and fluctuation degree of brittleness between the two subsystems, and they are functions of the moment $t$. With the evolution of time, the change rate of brittle link can be expressed by $\dot{F}$ as follows:

$$\dot{F} = \frac{\partial F}{\partial a}\frac{da}{dt} + \frac{\partial F}{\partial b}\frac{db}{dt} + \frac{\partial F}{\partial c}\frac{dc}{dt} \quad \text{Equation (1.2)}$$

The change rate of brittle link reflects the change degree of brittle link between subsystem $X$ and subsystem $Y$.

### (2) Conflict Management Theory

The conflict management theory mainly resolves or transforms conflicts from the perspective of process management by analyzing the causes of conflicts and exploring the process of conflict development. It covers the following contents: first, cognition of conflicts. The theory of conflict management holds that conflict, as one of the basic forms of human interaction, inevitably and objectively exists in any society and at any time. Conflict cannot be "eliminated," but can only be "managed." Therefore, through conflict management, the harmfulness and destructiveness of conflict can be limited to a certain extent, scope and level. Second, the duality of the role of conflict. Corse believes that conflict has both negative and positive functions. The theory of conflict management is to find and guide the positive effects of conflict and curb the negative effects[77]. Third, conflict management theory treats and manages conflicts from a dynamic and procedural perspective. Pondy views conflict as a process that consists of 5 stages – latent conflict, perceived conflict, felt conflict, manifest conflict and conflict aftermath[78]. Therefore, conflict management should be a systematic process. Different levels of conflict prevention, resolution, disposal and transformation play different roles in different stages[79]. Fourthly, actors' reaction to conflict determines the development and outcome of conflict to a large extent. According to the conflict management theory, there are two processes of conflict management: one is the constructive process, which responds to conflicts in a positive way and regards conflicts as opportunities; the second is the destructive process, which holds a negative and aversive attitude and behavior towards conflict and regards conflict as dangerous. The former often leads to positive outcomes of conflict, while the latter usually leads to negative ones[80]. Fifth, the path of conflict management shows a diversified development trend. Because the causes of conflicts are diverse, the conflict management theory proposes to adopt different paths according to the specific situations of conflicts. Reimann distinguishes three conflict management paths-conflict management, conflict resolution, and conflict transformation – from the perspective of results, processes, and structures. The three conflict management approaches have their own perspectives and priorities, and have different applicability in different stages of conflict development[81].

Based on the conflict management theory, to effectively resolve and manage conflicts, first of all, we should have a more comprehensive understanding of conflicts; secondly, conflict management should not only rely on multiple forces to seek solutions and mitigate the consequences of conflicts, but also be committed to improving cooperation capabilities; finally, we should use the conflict transformation path to manage conflicts, not only to resolve and supervise conflict events, but also to prevent them in advance and follow up and monitor them afterward.

## (3) Social Network Theory

Thanks to the development of multiple disciplines and schools, social network theory emerged in the 1930s. This is a new sociological research paradigm, which emphasizes the interpretation of social phenomena by interpersonal relationships, relationship connotation and social network structure. It can quantitatively analyze various relationships, and at the same time, it can see through various uncertain constraints and opportunities implied in specific social connection models. The quantitative analysis is supplemented by qualitative data and graphic data.

1) Basic concepts

Social network: a social network is a collection of actors and their relationships, containing multiple points and connections between these points[82].

Actor and node: the actor can be all individuals and organizations in the social network, including not only specific individuals, but also groups, enterprises, countries and other organizations analyzed as a whole[83]; the position of each actor in the network is called a node.

Relation: relations are also called relationship ties or edges, which represent the mutual relations between actors. Relations are usually indicated by connecting lines, representing the communication and collaboration of individual members. Relations can be divided into undirected ones and directed ones. Symmetrical relations are called undirected relations, and asymmetrical or directional relations are called directed relations[84].

Sociogram and matrix algebra method: sociogram and matrix algebra method are two mathematical expressions of social networks[85]. In social network analysis, the graph composed of points and lines is called the sociogram, which represents the relationship between members of a group. This method is applicable to describing the relationship form of small groups, and can intuitively express the structural characteristics of the network and the relationship between nodes; Matrix algebra is a method to list all factors corresponding to the problem into a graph in the form of matrix, and then analyze them according to their characteristics to determine the key points[86].

2) Research orientation

Generally speaking, social network an alysis is mainly conducted from two perspectives: one is the analysis of self-centered social network formed by individuals, and the other is the analysis of the overall social network focusing on the broad characteristics of the network. The former takes the individual network as the focus, studying how individual behavior is affected by its interpersonal network and how the individual affects network construction, and focusing on individual characteristics and connections; The latter takes all actors in the whole social network as the object to analyze the relationship between the whole social actors.

3) Measures

Size: size refers to the number of all actors in the social network. In the sociogram, it is the number of nodes. Large size means that the network structure is more complex, and the internal differences and the inequality of resource circulation will also be greater.

Nodal degree: nodal degree refers to the number of connections directly associated with a node, indicating the popularity or influence of the actor in the network. The greater the value, the more nodes are connected to it in the whole network. In a directed graph, nodal degrees are divided into point in degrees and point out degrees. The former refers to the total number of points directly pointing to the point, and the latter is the total number of other points directly pointed to by the point[87].

Density: this indicator is important in the analysis of the overall social network structure. It represents the strength and degree of interaction between members. In graph theory, it can be expressed as the ratio of the number of connections actually owned to the number of lines most likely to have[86]. The internal structure of a network can be close or distant.

In a non-directional network, its expression is:

$$Density = \frac{2L}{g(g-1)} \quad \text{Equation (1.3)}$$

In a digraph, its expression is:

$$Density = \frac{L}{g(g-1)} \quad \text{Equation (1.4)}$$

Wherein, $L$ represents the number of lines and $g$ represents the number of nodes.

Centrality: centrality is an indicator of the structure and position of a person's network. It often evaluates whether a person is important, the superiority or privilege of his or her position, and social prestige. It can also evaluate the degree of centralization of the entire network. Generally speaking, the centrality of social networks has three forms: degree centrality, closeness centrality and betweenness centrality[88].

Cliquishness and cohesive subgroups: there exist the following situations in many networks: node A is connected to node B, and node B is connected to node C, so node A is likely to be connected to node C. This property is called clustering or transitivity. In this case, the aggregation coefficient C is used to measure[89]. Another definition of clustering coefficient was proposed by Watta & Strogatz (1998)[250]. Its value is the average value of the local clustering coefficient:

$$C = \frac{1}{n} \sum C_i \quad \text{Equation (1.5)}$$

Where $C_i$ is the local clustering coefficient of the network. $C_i$ = the number of triangles containing node i/the number of three-point groups centered on node i. This value indicates the degree of small grouping in the network. When the relationship between some actors is close enough to form a subgroup, a cohesive subgroup ("small group") appears. The density of cohesive subgroups can be used to measure whether the "small group" phenomenon is serious, and its value range is [- 1,1][90].

Path length: The average shortest distance between node pairs in an undirected network with n nodes is:

$$l = \frac{1}{\frac{1}{2}n(n+1)} \sum_{i \geq j} d_{ij} \quad \text{Equation (1.6)}$$

$d_{ij}$ is the shortest distance from node i to node j, including the distance from each node to itself (0). There is a problem with the definition of $l$ for a network that contains more than one node. For this reason, the general practice is to make the shortest distance between this node pair infinite, so that the value of $l$ is also infinite. To avoid this problem, define the shortest distance of "harmonic mean" between all node pairs, that is, the reciprocal of the reciprocal average:

$$C_i = \frac{2E_i}{E_i(E_i - 1)} \quad \text{Equation (1.7)}$$

The path length of a network measures the "distance" between network nodes[223].

Structure holes: Burt put forward the concept of "structure hole" for the first time. For example, A maintains direct contact with B and C respectively, while B and C have no direct contact. They establish an indirect relationship through A as an intermediary, so that there is a relationship gap between B and C, which is a "structure hole." The reason why "structure hole" is important is that "structure hole" constitutes the "valve" of information refraction and resource flow in the network. The initiative and means of refraction and flowing are all controlled by the actors occupying the "structure hole."

The more "structure holes" are occupied, the greater the structural advantages of actors, and the higher the possibility of obtaining rewards through these advantages.

### 1.3.3 Research Framework

Through the study of existing literature on team conflict and in-depth reflection on the reality, this book finds that there is room for exploration in this field.

First, research on the antecedents of team conflict. The antecedents of conflict in existing literature studies generally use two methods: one is to qualitatively list a large number of antecedents, and the other is to select one or several antecedents for quantitative analysis. The first method can reveal many antecedent variables at the same time. However, due to the large number, it is unable to conduct in-depth quantitative research, and also cannot distinguish the influence degree and influence path of a certain antecedent variable on different types of conflicts. Although the second method can deeply analyze the impact of a certain antecedent variable on the two types of conflicts, it can only focus on some factors and not enough on other factors. This book believes that it is extremely important to study the antecedents of innovation team conflict, because it is clear which factors can trigger conflicts, and the specific impact degree and impact path can effectively manage conflicts at the source and prevent them before they happen.

Second, research on team members' conflict relations. In the existing literature, little research focuses on the conflict relationship among team members, which is still a "black box." Because conflict is the product of the interaction between members, analyzing the conflict relationship between members is an unavoidable problem for the in-depth study of team conflict. Only by systematically and comprehensively analyzing the conflict relationship of members can we fully grasp the process of conflict development, better monitor and manage team conflict, and thus reduce negative effects.

Third, research on the effect of team conflict. When discussing the effects of team conflict, the existing literature often discusses the specific effects of different types of conflict, especially the effects of task conflict on team effectiveness. Up to now, the academic community has yet to reach an agreement, and even opposite research conclusions have emerged. Scholars agree that task conflict is a "double-edged sword," which sometimes has a positive impact and sometimes has a negative impact. Therefore, it is very necessary to explore the impact of task conflict on team effectiveness in different research situations. Therefore, this book attempts to study the relationship between team conflict and team effectiveness from different research perspectives and different research situations, so as to better understand and manage conflict.

In order to effectively solve the above problems, this book follows the IPO input-process-output) model of team operation, starts from the three stages of team, and combines the unique research methods and tools in the complex system brittleness theory to achieve in-depth research on team conflict.

Before conducting specific research, the book first clarifies the research thinking of the brittleness theory of complex systems. The brittleness theory of complex system establishes the brittleness model of complex system and decomposes it into a four-layer structure of brittleness risk, system structure, brittleness event and brittleness factor (Figure 1-7).

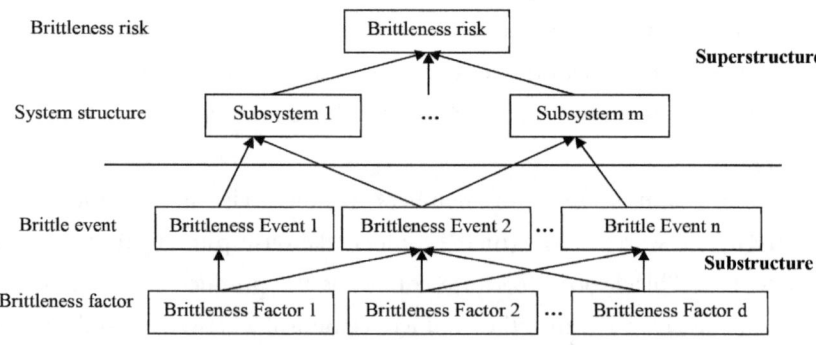

Figure 1-7 Brittle model of complex system

It can be seen from the analysis of the above figure that the brittleness factor and the brittleness event constitute the substructure of the model. The brittleness factor is the internal or external fundamental inducement that causes brittleness of complex systems to be excited. The brittleness event is the medium that the brittleness factor acts on the whole system. The brittleness event acts on the system with a certain probability through various complex coupling relationships. The brittleness of the whole system can be amplified or reduced through the brittleness correlation among subsystems, and finally, the system will collapse with a certain probability.

By combining the team operation IPO model, the book designs a research framework to guide the development of specific content (Figure 1-8).

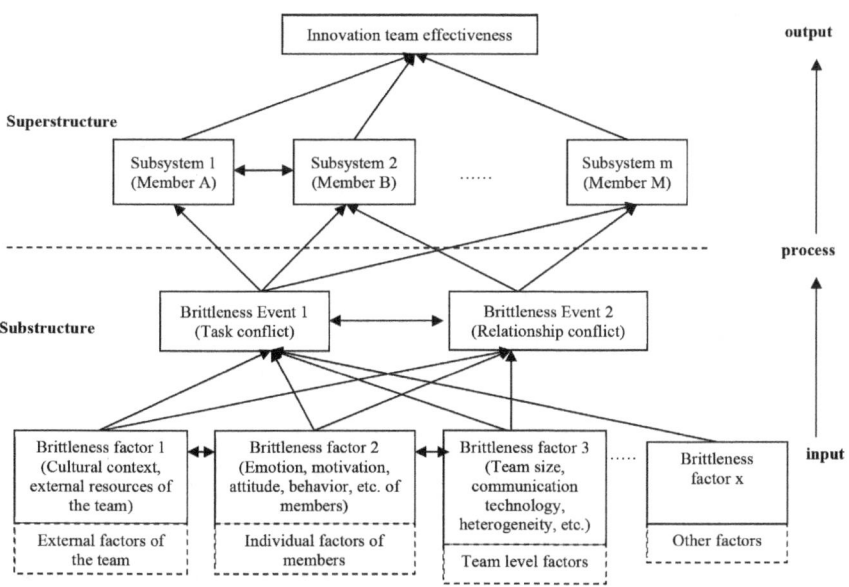

**Figure 1-8 Research framework of the book**

It can be seen from the analysis of Figure 1-8 that: vertically, this book conducts a separate study from the three stages of "input-process-output" of team operation; horizontally, the book refers to the brittleness factor, relationship structure and brittleness risk in the complex system brittleness theory to carry out specific research.

At the same time, the study covers three parts: first, in the "input" stage of team operation, it will study what the main causes of team conflict are and how they are triggered, that is, find out the brittleness factors that cause brittle events according to the internal and external environment of the system; second, in the "process" stage of team operation, it studies how the conflict relationship between members is, that is, analyze the brittle correlation between subsystems; third, in the "output" stage of team operation, the impact of team conflict on team effectiveness is studied, that is, the risk of brittle events leading to the collapse of complex systems is discussed.

# CHAPTER 2

# The Brittleness Analysis and Antecedent Variables of Innovation Team Conflict

The existing literature often uses two approaches to study the antecedents of team conflict: one is to qualitatively list a large number of antecedents, and the other is to select one or several antecedents for quantitative analysis. These two methods are extremely important, but the first method is limited by the complexity of the number of antecedent variables and cannot be studied quantitatively and deeply, and there are differences in the causes of different types of conflicts. This method cannot distinguish the impact of an antecedent variable on different types of conflicts. The second method can deeply analyze the influence coefficient and influence path of a certain antecedent variable on different types of conflicts, but only some variables are concentrated on. In the "input" stage of team operation, it is extremely important to research on the antecedent variables of team conflict, because this will control the negative impact of conflict from the source. In order to achieve this goal, this book starts from a brittleness theory of complex systems, and studies the antecedent variables of team conflict by constructing a brittleness model of innovation team conflict. This part mainly includes the following research contents: first, combining the brittleness theory of complex systems to build a brittleness model of innovation team conflict, and then deeply analyze the evolution of innovation team conflict; secondly, the brittleness factors in the conflict brittleness model of innovation teams are classified to guide the research on the antecedent variables of team conflict; finally, combined with literature analysis, questionnaire survey and Ridit analysis, we specifically studied the antecedents of team conflict. In this way, on the one hand, we can deeply analyze the fragility of innovation team conflict through a unique theoretical perspective, and on the other hand, we can conduct qualitative and quantitative research on a large number of antecedents.

## 2.1 Analysis of the Brittleness of Innovation Team Conflicts

### 2.1.1 Evolution of Innovation Team Conflict

#### (1) The Complexity of the Innovation Team

Research has shown that an innovation team is a complex system: first, innovation behavior and innovation activities themselves are uncertain and complex. The innovation team has innovation tasks and needs to implement the innovation behaviors and complete the innovation activities. The innovation activities and their behaviors are exploratory, uncertain, risky and complex, and members cannot fully perceive the information of the innovation object and the changes in the environment. Therefore, the uncertainty and complexity of innovation behavior and innovation activity itself constitute one of the sources of innovation team complexity.

Second, the complex relationships among members themselves and their internal structure constitute the second source of innovation team complexity. The members of an innovation team have such intelligent characteristics as diversity, self-organization and self-adaptation. They not only have their own characteristics, but also need to actively adapt and evolve under the influence of others and the environment. In addition, members will have various feedback and interactions, forming complex relationships of mutual restriction and interdependence. On this basis, they form different power relationships, role relationships and conflicts of interest within the team.

Third, it is a chaotic creative process for members to rely on their own abilities and their interaction with other members to achieve innovation achievements, which constitutes the third source of the complexity of the innovation team. On the one hand, members need to mobilize their own knowledge resources and experience to carry out innovation activities. On the other hand, they also need to rely on the team platform to obtain the knowledge and skills of other members through the team's knowledge sharing mechanism, shared mental model, etc. This interactive process of achieving innovation results is extremely complex.

Fourth, the nature of the organization, policies and measures, culture, and the broader political, economic, scientific and technological and other external environments in which the innovation team is located are complex and changeable, and the innovation team must maintain constant communication with the external environment in terms of data, materials, information, etc. The complex external environment also has a greater impact on the innovation team, thus constituting the fourth source of complexity of the innovation team.

## (2) The Brittleness of Innovation Team Conflicts

Openness, complexity, nonlinearity, hierarchy and evolutionary emergence are the characteristics of complex systems. Jin Hongzhang, a Chinese scholar, first proposed the concept of brittleness of complex systems and believed that brittleness is also a basic characteristic of complex systems. Jin Hongzhang and others pointed out that the brittleness of a complex system means that in an open complex system, the collapsed subsystem will exchange matter and energy with other subsystems, and its collapse will destroy the ordered state of other subsystems that exchange matter and energy with it, and finally collapse; by analogy, with the increase of the number and level of collapse subsystems, the entire complex system will eventually collapse. This characteristic of complex systems is called brittleness. The definition of "collapse" in the complex system brittleness theory is that in an open complex system, the original order state in the subsystem is destroyed due to internal and external interference factors[73].

From the perspective of the brittleness of complex systems, we can see that for an innovation team, a member who has been involved in the conflict will work cooperatively with other members who have not yet been involved in the conflict. Since the member can transmit the conflict factors and risks through various paths, other members who have collaborative interactions with him will also be involved in the conflict network. With the increase of the number and level of members involved in conflict, the whole team will eventually form a complex conflict network. This characteristic of innovation team conflict is called the brittleness of innovation team conflict. The conflict brittleness of an innovation team is a process of conflict chain reaction among its members. Its simplified evolution process is shown in Figure 2-1 and Figure 2-2.

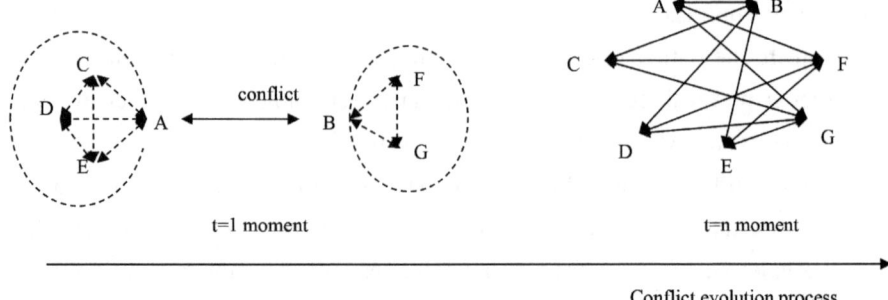

**Figure 2-1 Schematic diagram I of the conflict evolution process**

The double arrow solid line in Figure 2-1 indicates that there is a conflict between the two, and the double arrow dotted line indicates that they are alliances of interests. At $t = 1$ moment, members A and B have conflicts, and members A and C, D and E formed an alliance due to their formal working relationship or personal emotional relationship. Similarly, member B formed an alliance with F and G. As A and B can transmit and spread the conflict factors and risks through various ways, at $t = n$ moment, only the conflict between two members is likely to develop into the conflict between seven members.

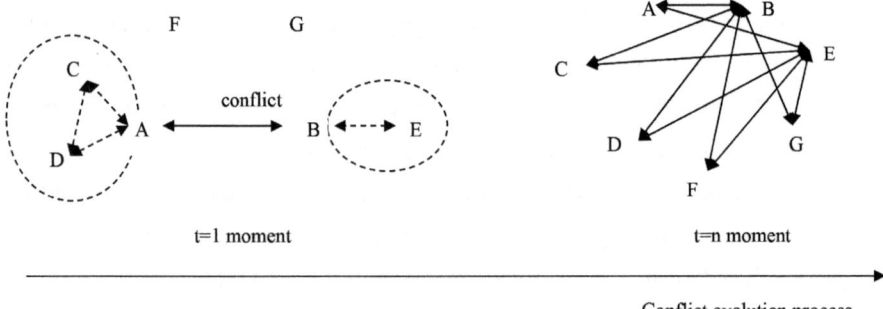

**Figure 2-2 Schematic diagram II of the conflict evolution process**

The double arrow solid line in Figure 2-2 indicates that there is a conflict between the two, and the double arrow dotted line indicates that they are an alliance of interests. At $t = 1$ moment, members A and B clashed; members A, C and D are allies, and members B and E are allies; members F and G are isolated.

As members A and B can transmit and spread the conflict factors and risks through various ways, the conflict between two members may develop into a conflict between seven members at $t = n$ moment. The reason why members F and G join the conflict is due to the role of the principle of balance, that is, a person cannot maintain a good relationship with both sides of the other party for a long time, and he will certainly choose to be close to one side and distant from the other[91].

The existence of conflict fragility in innovation teams and the chain reaction of conflicts among members is explained in the self-categorization theory, which means that individuals tend to divide themselves into members of a specific social group according to certain social standards and always try to clearly distinguish between "insiders" and "outsiders." They think that "insiders" are more attractive than "outsiders"[92]. Figure 2-1 and Figure 2-2 reveal that under the influence of the self-categorization theory, the conflict in which only two members participated has gradually evolved into the conflict in which seven members participated.

## 2.1.2 Construction of Conflict Brittleness Model of Innovation Team and Analysis of Brittleness Factors

### (1) Construction of Brittleness Model of Team Conflict

According to the brittleness model of complex systems (Figure 1-7) and the review of existing research results on team conflict, the book constructs the brittleness model of innovation team conflict (Figure 2-3) as follows.

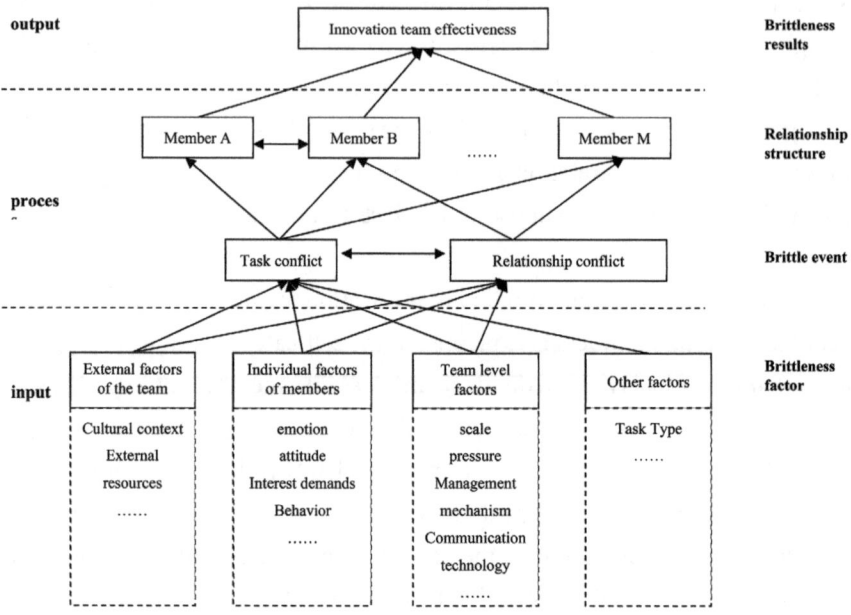

**Figure 2-3 Brittle model of innovation team conflict**

It can be seen from Figure 2-3 that the innovation team conflict brittleness model consists of four parts: brittleness factor, brittleness event, relationship structure and brittleness result. The brittleness factor refers to the internal or external factors that lead to the innovation team conflict; brittleness events refer to team conflicts caused by internal and external factors, which can be further divided into task conflicts and relationship conflicts; relationship structure refers to the complex conflict among team members; brittleness result is the influence of team conflict on team effectiveness.

The development process of conflict brittleness of innovation teams is as follows: first, conflict brittleness factors appear, which are connected in a certain way and disturb the members of innovation teams, causing conflicts; secondly, due to the diversity of conflict relations among members, members who have been involved in the conflict can pass on the conflict factors and risks in various ways, resulting in more and more members becoming conflict subjects, and complex conflict relations within the innovation team; finally, team conflict has a certain impact on the effectiveness of innovation teams.

## (2) Functions and Types of Conflict Brittleness Factors

In the brittleness theory of complex systems, brittleness factor is the internal or external fundamental inducement that activates the brittleness of complex systems, and is described as "internal or external factors that disturb or attack subsystems of complex systems"[93].

Brittleness factors are identified according to the internal and external environment of the system, which can be divided into key brittleness factors and secondary brittleness factors. The former refers to those factors with high occurrence probability, strong association with other factors and high hazard; the latter refers to those factors with low occurrence probability, loose association with other factors and low hazard. Compared with brittleness events, the brittleness factor is more stable and easier to handle and analyze[94]. Therefore, in order to analyze innovation team conflict, the most basic thing is to analyze the causes of the conflict, and identify the key brittleness factors that can trigger the conflict according to the internal and external environment of the innovation team, that is, to study the antecedent variables of team conflict.

As the brittleness factor has various forms and varying degrees of influence, this book classifies it into a signal variable and a signal function[95] and discusses them respectively. According to literature analysis, the brittleness factors of conflict can be divided into five categories as shown in Figure 2-4.

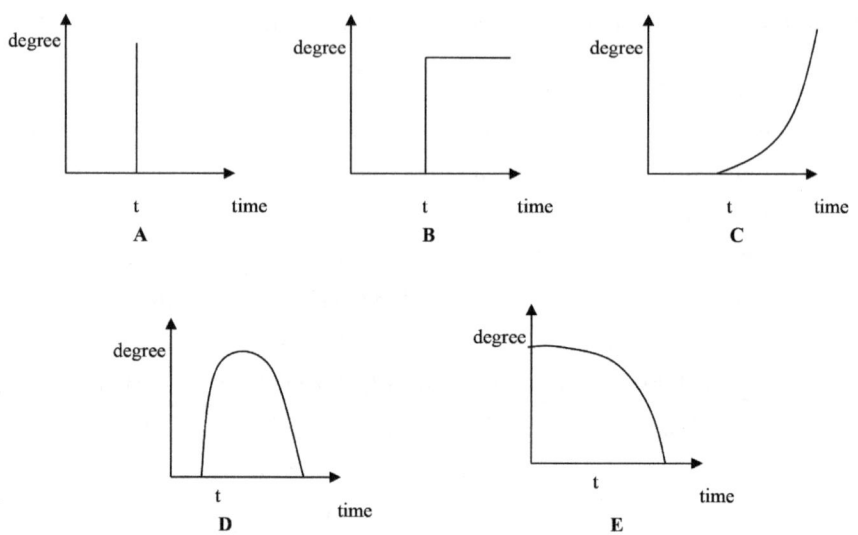

**Figure 2-4 Categories of team conflict brittleness factors**

Figure 2-4 depicts the types of conflict brittleness factors of innovation teams and the impact of different types of brittleness factors on conflict. The first type is linear. The brittleness factor only has a temporary impact at time t. For example, the member's mood is out of control for a while. Although it can cause conflict, it is not a permanent cause of conflict since bad emotions can be pacified or transferred in a short time; the second is the step type, which causes conflicts at time t and can last for a long time. For example, if team leaders change their leadership style and implement abusive supervision within a period of time, relationship conflicts will be significantly triggered[96]; the third type is the enhanced expansion type, which means that the brittleness factor has an impact on the conflict from small to large, from weak to strong. For example, the cultural context of the team's region may not be the main cause of the conflict at the beginning, but with the development and evolution of the conflict, more conflicts are caused by the differences in cultural contexts[97]; the fourth kind of brittleness factor shaped as a curve from weak to strong and then back to weak. For example, task conflict is small in the early and late stages of team development, while reaching the maximum in the middle; the fifth type is the decline type, that is, the conflict can be quickly triggered at the beginning but will slowly disappear after a period of time. For example, the surface heterogeneity of the team can intensify team conflict, but its impact will be gradually reduced in the long-term operation.

The brittleness factor is the internal or external fundamental inducement that simulates the brittleness of complex systems. For the innovation team conflict, the brittleness factor of the conflict is the internal or external fundamental induce-ment that causes the team conflict, and the brittleness factor has different effects on the conflict. Therefore, it is necessary to identify the key brittleness factors that trigger conflicts according to the internal and external environment of the innovation team, that is, to clarify the antecedent variables of innovation team conflicts and their impact.

## 2.2 Determination of Innovation Team Conflict Types and Collection of Antecedent Variables

### 2.2.1 Verification of Conflict Types

Scholars today generally divide team conflict into task conflict and relationship conflict when they study team conflict. The former is caused by members' having different views on tasks, and the latter is caused by members' having oppositional emotions. There are differences in the causes and purposes of team conflict.

This book once again verifies the applicability of the type of team conflict in Chinese situations. The main reason is that Chen Xiaoping pointed out that with the background of Chinese culture, people cannot usually separate people and things from a cognitive level. If a conflict occurs, the parties tend to attribute the task conflict to the relationship conflict[98]; other scholars also pointed out that in case of conflict within the team, the originally distinct task conflict and relationship conflict are often misdirected, which leads to confusion between the two. If the task conflict is not resolved for a long time, the parties will easily mistake the cause of the conflict, leading to escalation of the conflict and interpreting the task conflict as a relationship conflict[99]. Therefore, if team members cannot accurately distinguish different types of conflicts, they will inevitably confuse the causes of different types of conflicts when studying the antecedent variables, leading to deviation in subsequent research. For this reason, this book once again verifies the applicability of the type of team conflict in China.

## (1) Formation of the Questionnaire

This survey uses the scale developed by Jehn, which is mainly used to guide members of innovation teams to evaluate task conflicts and relationship conflicts that they perceive. This scale is used by most team conflict studies and has been modified and tested many times. In this book, the Chinese version of the scale is developed by translation and back translation, and then the questionnaire is formed by referring to the translation of other domestic scholars. See Appendix A for the full version of Questionnaire on Conflict Types of Innovation Teams.

The Task Conflict Scale contains four items, such as "Do members of your team have deep differences in their views?," "Do members of your team have many different opinions on how to complete the work?," etc.; The Relationship Conflict Scale also contains four items, such as "Are there many interpersonal conflicts in your team?," "Are there many tensions between members of your team?," etc. The two types of conflicting measurement items are arranged in a mixed way and measured with Richter's 5-point scale (1 indicates low degree, 5 indicates high degree). In addition, according to the general practice of team conflict research, the control variables were designed as gender, age, education level, member rank, industry, team size and members' tenure in the team.

## (2) Issuance of Questionnaires and Sample Information

The questionnaire used in this survey is relatively mature and widely used, with high reliability and validity. This book skips the process of a test survey, and directly distributes the questionnaire on a large scale for a formal survey. In order to eliminate the sample dependence of the survey results and make the research results universally applicable, this book selected 17 innovation teams in Nanjing, Shanghai, Hefei and Wuhan and issued 400 questionnaires.

A total of 312 questionnaires were collected in this survey, 6 of which were invalid (more than 10% of which were unanswered and all the questions with the same score were considered invalid). Therefore, a total of 306 questionnaires remain with valid callback rate of 76.5%. The survey sample covers colleges and universities, automobile production, pharmaceutical production, software development, transportation planning and design and other industries. The detailed background information of 306 respondents is shown in Table 2-1.

**Table 2-1 Basic information of the sample of conflict types of innovation teams**

| Investigation items | Category | Number of people/persons | Proportion/% |
|---|---|---|---|
| Gender | Male | 193 | 63.07 |
| | Female | 113 | 36.93 |
| Age | 20–29 | 58 | 1.63 |
| | 30–39 years old | 112 | 36.60 |
| | 40–49 years old | 105 | 34.31 |
| | ≥ 50 years old | 31 | 27.46 |
| degree of education | Junior college or below | 28 | 9.15 |
| | undergraduate | 59 | 19.28 |
| | master | 131 | 42.81 |
| | doctor | 88 | 28.75 |
| level | Ordinary team members | 255 | 83.33 |
| | Team leader | 51 | 16.67 |
| Industry | colleges and universities | 129 | 42.16 |
| | Automobile production | 24 | 7.84 |
| | Pharmaceutical production | 47 | 15.36 |
| | software development | 84 | 27.45 |
| | Traffic planning and design | 22 | 7.19 |
| Team size | ≤ 5 persons | 35 | 11.44 |
| | 6–10 persons | 94 | 30.72 |
| | 11–15 persons | 119 | 38.89 |
| | ≥ 15 persons | 58 | 18.95 |
| Team tenure | ≤ 3 years | 76 | 24.84 |
| | 4–6 years | 101 | 33.01 |
| | 7–9 years | 65 | 21.24 |
| | 10–12 years | 34 | 11.11 |
| | ≥ 13 years | 30 | 9.80 |

Table 2-1 shows that there are more males than females in innovation teams; the age of members is mostly between 30-39 and 40-49; the majority of them are masters and doctors, and those with junior college degrees or below are the least; most of the respondents are ordinary team members; the number of respondents of university innovation teams is the largest, followed by the software development industry; the team size of 11-15 people is the most common, and the number of ≤ 5 people is the rarest; in terms of team tenure, the number of respondents who have served for 4-6 years is the largest, while the number of respondents who have served for a long time (such as ≥ 13 years) is the smallest.

According to the descriptive statistics of the data (Table 2-2), members believe that the conflict level of their team is high (the average is 4.03), and the average value of B3 (is there a lot of tension between members of your team?) is 4.62, indicating that members believe that there are many tensions among members of their team. The absolute value of skewness is less than 3 and the absolute value of kurtosis is less than 10, indicating that the score of each item is subject to the data requirements of normal distribution, and subsequent analysis can be conducted.

**Table 2-2 Descriptive statistical results of the questionnaire on conflict types of innovation teams**

| entry | Minimum | maximum value | mean value | standard deviation | skewness | | kurtosis | |
|---|---|---|---|---|---|---|---|---|
| | | | | | statistic | Standard error | statistic | Standard error |
| B1 | 1 | 5 | 3.55 | 1.011 | -.354 | .139 | -.714 | .278 |
| B2 | 1 | 5 | 4.53 | .711 | -1.936 | .139 | 5.380 | .278 |
| B3 | 1 | 5 | 4.62 | .662 | -2.339 | .139 | 7.815 | .278 |
| B4 | 2 | 5 | 3.36 | .969 | -.142 | .139 | -1.123 | .278 |
| B5 | 2 | 5 | 4.60 | .631 | -1.571 | .139 | 2.293 | .278 |
| B6 | 2 | 5 | 3.43 | .980 | -.123 | .139 | -1.054 | .278 |
| B7 | 1 | 5 | 3.55 | .947 | -.326 | .139 | -.740 | .278 |
| B8 | 1 | 5 | 4.61 | .660 | -2.278 | .139 | 7.695 | .278 |
| total | 2.25 | 5 | 4.03 | .516 | -.618 | .139 | .285 | .278 |

Note: See Annex A for the specific meaning of B1-B8.

In order to know whether respondents with different background information had different perceptions of the type of innovation team conflict, this book uses one-way ANOVA to verify. SPSS analysis shows that there was no significant difference in perception of team conflict among members of different genders, ages, education levels, levels, sizes and tenures. Members of different industries had different perceptions concerning B2 (how often do members of your team lose their temper in public at work?). The homogeneity of the variance test is significant and combined with multiple LSD comparisons, it can be seen that members of innovation teams in colleges and universities have a significantly higher perception of B2 than team members in the software development and transportation planning and design industries. Team members in the automobile production industry also have a higher perception of B2 than team members in the software development industry, while team members in the pharmaceutical production, software development and transportation planning and design industries have no significant differences (see Table 2-3 and Table 2-4 for specific results). There is no significant difference in perception of other items among respondents in different industries.

**Table 2-3 Variance analysis results of measurement item B2 by industry**

| Measurement items | | Sum of squares | Df | mean square | F | Significance |
|---|---|---|---|---|---|---|
| B2 | Between groups | 5.736 | 4 | 1.434 | 2.781 | .031 |
| | Within group | 53.115 | 103 | .516 | | |
| | total | 58.852 | 107 | | | |

**Table 2-4 Multiple comparisons of LSD of measurement item B2 by industry**

| antecedent variable | (1) Industry | (J) Industry | Mean difference (I-J) | Standard error | Significance | 95% confidence interval lower limit | upper limit |
|---|---|---|---|---|---|---|---|
| B2 | colleges and universities | 2 | .198 | .221 | .374 | -.24 | .64 |
| | | 3 | -.125 | .401 | .756 | -.92 | .67 |
| | | 4 | .569* | .216 | .010 | .14 | 1.00 |
| | | 5 | .494* | .238 | .041 | .02 | .97 |
| | Automobile production | 1 | -.198 | .221 | .374 | -.64 | .24 |
| | | 3 | -.323 | .382 | .400 | -1.08 | .43 |
| | | 4 | .372* | .176 | .037 | .02 | .72 |
| | | 5 | .296 | .203 | .147 | -.11 | .70 |
| | Pharmaceutical production | 1 | .125 | .401 | .756 | -.67 | .92 |
| | | 2 | .323 | .382 | .400 | -.43 | 1.08 |
| | | 4 | .694 | .378 | .069 | -.06 | 1.45 |
| | | 5 | .619 | .392 | .117 | -.16 | 1.40 |
| | software development | 1 | -.569* | .216 | .010 | -1.00 | -.14 |
| | | 2 | -.372* | .176 | .037 | -.72 | -.02 |
| | | 3 | -.694 | .378 | .069 | -1.45 | .06 |
| | | 5 | -.075 | .197 | .703 | -.47 | .32 |
| | Traffic planning and design | 1 | -.494* | .238 | .041 | -.97 | -.02 |
| | | 2 | -.296 | .203 | .147 | -.70 | .11 |
| | | 3 | -.619 | .392 | .117 | -1.40 | .16 |
| | | 4 | .075 | .197 | .703 | -.32 | .47 |

*. The significance level of mean difference was 0.05.

## (3) Analysis of Data

Statistical software SPSS and AMOS were used for the exploratory and confirmatory analysis of the survey data.

1) Exploratory analysis

Before factor analysis, KMO sample measure and Bartlett sphere are generally used to test whether samples are suitable for exploratory factor analysis (Table 2-5). The KMO of this survey is 0.811, which indicates that the degree of information overlap among variables may be high, and it is worth doing factor analysis; the significance probability of Bartlett's spherical test is 0.000, indicating that there is a strong correlation between variables, and the assumption that each variable is independent is surely rejected.

**Table 2-5 KMO and Bartlett sphere test results of innovation team conflict type questionnaire**

| Kaiser Meyer Olkin measurement of sampling adequacy. | | .811 |
|---|---|---|
| | Approximate chi square | 2009.419 |
| Bartlett's Sphericity Test | Df | 28 |
| | Sig. | .000 |

The principal component analysis method is used to extract factors, and the selection of items refers to the criteria proposed by Hair et al., that is, if the number of factor loads exceeds 0.5, it means the item is very important[100]. In this book, 0.5 is taken as the critical point of factor load coefficient, and the number of factor loads of each item is shown in Table 2-6.

**Table 2-6 Factor loading coefficients of the questionnaire on the conflict types of innovation teams**

| entry | initial | extract |
|---|---|---|
| B2 | 1.000 | .917 |
| B3 | 1.000 | .915 |
| B5 | 1.000 | .900 |
| B8 | 1.000 | .886 |
| B1 | 1.000 | .594 |
| B4 | 1.000 | .714 |
| B6 | 1.000 | .769 |
| B7 | 1.000 | .532 |

It can be seen from Table 2-6 that the factor load coefficients of the eight items are greater than 0.5, fitting the conditions, so the next analysis can be carried out.

By looking at the correlation coefficient matrix (Table 2-7), it is found that there is a certain degree of correlation between variables.

**Table 2-7 Correlation coefficient matrix of the questionnaire on the conflict types of innovation teams**

| entry | B2 | B3 | B5 | B8 | B1 | B4 | B6 | B7 |
|---|---|---|---|---|---|---|---|---|
| B2 | 1.000 | .881 | .878 | .885 | .105 | -.004 | .010 | .015 |
| B3 | .881 | 1.000 | .896 | .865 | .071 | -.019 | .006 | .008 |
| B5 | .878 | .896 | 1.000 | .832 | .125 | -.011 | .001 | .008 |
| B8 | .885 | .865 | .832 | 1.000 | .126 | .045 | .025 | .025 |
| B1 | .105 | .071 | .125 | .126 | 1.000 | .627 | .509 | .341 |
| B4 | -.004 | -.019 | -.011 | .045 | .627 | 1.000 | .649 | .412 |
| B6 | .010 | .006 | .001 | .025 | .509 | .649 | 1.000 | .635 |
| B7 | .015 | .008 | .008 | .025 | .341 | .412 | .635 | 1.000 |

The principal component analysis was used to extract the factors and select the characteristic root greater than 1. Generally, the cumulative contribution rate of each factor variance reached more than 60%, indicating that the questionnaire had good structural validity. It can be seen from Table 2-8 that the cumulative contribution rate of variance of the two factors extracted from this book is 77.837%, and the structural validity of the questionnaire is satisfying.

**Table 2-8 Cumulative contribution rate of variance in the questionnaire of conflict types of innovation teams**

| Composition | Initial characteristic value | | | Extract Square Sum Load | | | Rotation sum of squares loading | | |
|---|---|---|---|---|---|---|---|---|---|
| | total | % of variance | Cumulative% | total | % of variance | Cumulative% | total | % of variance | Cumulative% |
| 1 | 3.644 | 45.548 | 45.548 | 3.644 | 45.548 | 45.548 | 3.627 | 45.343 | 45.343 |
| 2 | 2.583 | 32.289 | 77.837 | 2.583 | 32.289 | 77.837 | 2.600 | 32.494 | 77.837 |

From the rotating component matrix (Table 2-9), we can see that the 8 items are well aggregated into two factors.

**Table 2-9 Rotational component matrix of the questionnaire on the conflict types of innovation teams**

| entry | Composition | |
|-------|------|------|
|       | 1    | 2    |
| B2    | .958 | .018 |
| B3    | .957 | .000 |
| B5    | .948 | .016 |
| B8    | .940 | .050 |
| B6    | -.013 | .877 |
| B4    | -.017 | .845 |
| B1    | .109 | .763 |
| B7    | -.008 | .730 |

Reliability reflects the degree of systematic variation reflected in the measurement results. Cronbach's Alpha is generally used to evaluate reliability. It can be seen from the analysis that the reliability statistical result (Table 2-10) is 0.799, indicating that the internal consistency of the questionnaire is high, the overall reliability is good, and the measurement results are reliable.

**Table 2-10 Reliability statistical results of the questionnaire on the conflict types of innovation teams**

| factor | Cronbach's Alpha | Number of items |
|--------|------------------|-----------------|
| 1      | .748             | 4               |
| 2      | .786             | 4               |
| total  | .799             | 8               |

The specific items included in the two factors can be determined by combining the rotation component matrix (Table 2-11).

**Table 2-11 Analysis of the constructs belonging to each factor**

| factor | Include entries | Actual meaning of variables | Measurement index |
|---|---|---|---|
| 1 | B2 | The members of the team are angry in public at work | Relationship conflict |
| | B3 | Tensions between members of the team | |
| | B5 | Interpersonal conflict in the team | |
| | B8 | Jealousy and hostility among members of the team | |
| 2 | B6 | The extent to which members of the team argue about the team's tasks | Task conflict |
| | B4 | The extent to which members of the team have different opinions on how to complete the work | |
| | B1 | The degree of differences in the views of members of the team | |
| | B7 | The degree of dispute among members of the team about how to complete the work steps or procedures | |

It can be seen from the above table that the innovation team conflict is composed of two factors. Factor 1 is named as relationship conflict, and factor 2 is named as task conflict.

2) Confirmatory analysis

Based on exploratory factor analysis, confirmatory factor analysis is conducted to investigate the suitability of the constructed model. Structural equation model (SEM) is used in this book. For the analysis and application of SEM, the recommended minimum number of samples is 300. This book uses all 306 scales and uses maximum likelihood (ML) to estimate parameters.

First, a confirmatory factor analysis of factor 1 (relationship conflict) is conducted. The measurement model of relationship conflict built in this book is shown in Figure 2-5. It can be seen from the path map that the factor load standardization coefficients of the four observation variables of factor 1 are greater than 0.5 (the figures on the arrows in the figure are the standardized load coefficients). In view of the large and significant factor loads of observation variables on the specified factors, it is believed that the scale of factor 1 has good convergence validity.

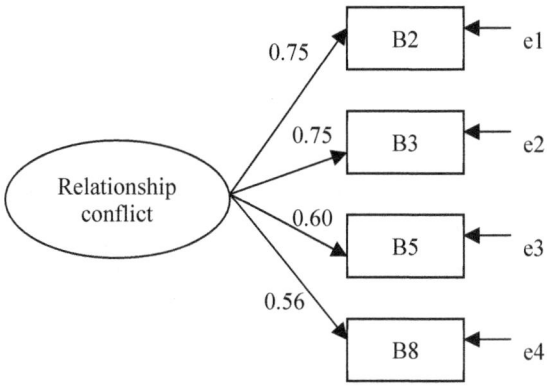

**Figure 2-5 Confirmatory analysis of relationship conflict**

According to the fitting results (Table 2-12), the chi-square DOF ratio is 2.297, ranging from 1-3; The value of *RMSEA* is 0.065, ranging between 0.05 and 0.08; The values of *NFI*, *CFI*, *IFI* and *TLI* are all greater than 0.9 and close to 1, indicating that the consistency between the hypothetical model and the sample data is acceptable.

**Table 2-12 Fitting results of relationship conflict measurement model**

| measurement model | $x^2/df$ | NFI | CFI | IFI | TLI | RMSEA |
|---|---|---|---|---|---|---|
| Measurement model of relationship conflict | 2.297 | 0.993 | 0.996 | 0.996 | 0.976 | 0.065 |

Secondly, a confirmatory factor analysis of factor 2 (task conflict) was conducted. The measurement model of task conflict in this book is shown in Figure 2-6. It can be seen from the path map that the factor load standardization coefficients of the four observation variables of factor 2 are greater than 0.5. In view of the large and significant factor load of observation variables on the specified factors, it is reasonable to think that the scale of factor 2 has good convergence validity.

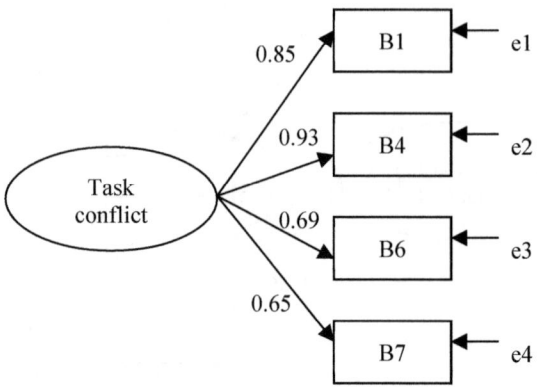

**Figure 2-6 Confirmatory analysis of task conflict**

The fitting results (Table 2-13) show that the data and task conflict measurement model are well fitted.

**Table 2-13 Fitting results of task conflict measurement model**

| measurement model | $\chi^2/df$ | NFI | CFI | IFI | TLI | RMSEA |
|---|---|---|---|---|---|---|
| Measurement model of task conflict | 2.462 | 0.996 | 0.998 | 0.998 | 0.987 | 0.069 |

Third, build a measurement model of innovation team conflict (Figure 2-7). The factor load standardization coefficients of the observed variables of the two factors are both greater than 0.5, and the correlation coefficient between factor 1 and factor 2 is 0.42.

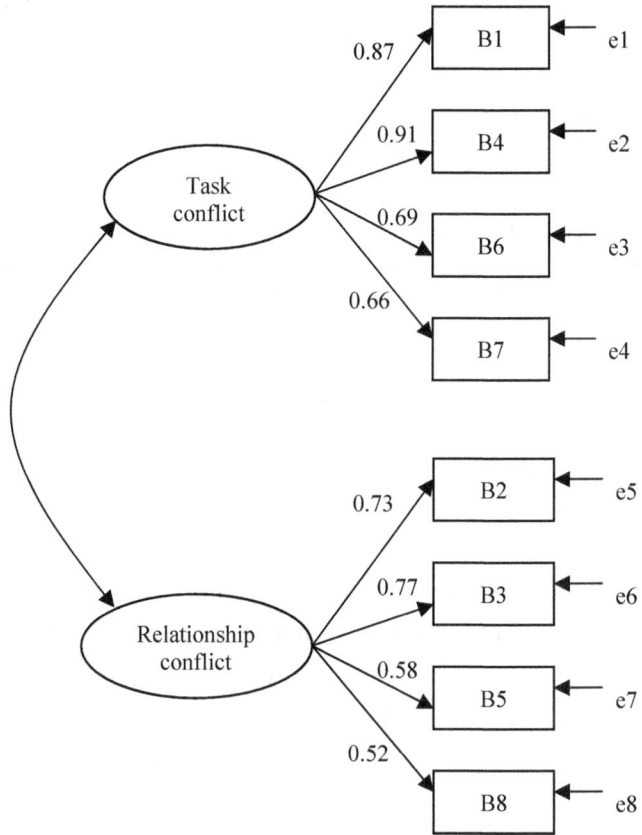

**Figure 2-7 Confirmatory analysis of innovation team conflict**

It can be seen from the fitting results of the two-factor measurement model (Table 2-14) that the data are well matched with the measurement model.

**Table 2-14 Fitting results of innovation team conflict measurement model**

| measurement model | $\chi^2/df$ | NFI | CFI | IFI | TLI | RMSEA |
|---|---|---|---|---|---|---|
| Two factor model | 2.609 | 0.964 | 0.977 | 0.978 | 0.958 | 0.073 |

Continue to build a single dimension model of innovation team conflict. By comparing the fitting results of the two models (Table 2-15), we can see that the two-dimensional model of innovation team conflict is better, and the fitting results are better.

**Table 2-15 Fitting results of the innovation team conflict comparison model**

| measurement model | $\chi^2/df$ | NFI | CFI | IFI | TLI | RMSEA |
|---|---|---|---|---|---|---|
| Model 1: Two-dimensional model | 2.609 | 0.964 | 0.977 | 0.978 | 0.958 | 0.073 |
| Model 2: Single dimensional model | 6.813 | 0.894 | 0.907 | 0.908 | 0.847 | 0.138 |

Note: The single dimension model is relationship conflict + task conflict.

By using the scale developed by Jehn and selecting 17 innovation teams to conduct a questionnaire survey, the results show that innovation team members can clearly distinguish two different types of team conflict (task conflict and relationship conflict) in the Chinese context, which lays a foundation for the study of antecedents.

## 2.2.2 Collection of Antecedent Variables

Based on the conflict brittleness model, the brittleness factor of innovation teams, and the research results of existing literature, this book systematically and comprehensively analyzes the antecedents of task conflict and relationship conflict of innovation teams through qualitative and quantitative methods. The brittleness theory of complex system defines brittleness factor as the internal or external fundamental inducement that excites brittleness. It is mainly differentiated according to the internal and external environment of the system, and can be divided into key brittleness factor and secondary brittleness factor. This book follows this basic point of view, trying to find the antecedents of conflict and determine the main antecedents from both inside and outside the innovation team. Because the causes of task conflict and relationship conflict are different, even if an antecedent variable can cause task conflict and relationship conflict at the same time, the impact of this variable on different types of conflict may be different, so it is necessary to study the antecedent variables of task conflict and relationship conflict separately.

In order to collect the antecedents of conflict in a comprehensive and detailed way, this book searches domestic and foreign databases. First of all, search foreign commonly used databases such as Sage Publications, ProQuest, Science Direct, Taylor & Francis, Emerald, and JSTOR. The research fields are humanities, social sciences, economic and management sciences, and the keywords are "group conflict," "task conflict," "cognitive conflict," "relationship conflict," "emotion conflict," and "affective conflict."[1] The *International Journal of Conflict Management*, a foreign specialized magazine, conducts research on team conflict. This book searches 25 issues of the magazine, and counts all the literature related to the antecedents of conflict. After a fuzzy search, 703 papers were extracted. Through reading the title, keywords and abstract, the literature that did not involve antecedent variable research was deleted, leaving 211 papers. Secondly, the CNKI database was selected to collect the research results of domestic teams on antecedent variables. In order to eliminate the interference of irrelevant literature, two requirements were deployed when searching: first, the keywords must be "team conflict," "task conflict," "cognitive conflict," "relationship conflict," "emotional conflict" and "emotional conflict"; second, only the journals with a strong academic performance in the database are selected; the research fields are humanities, social sciences, economic and management sciences. Through a fuzzy search, 679 documents were extracted, 214 duplicate documents were deleted, and then the title, keywords, and abstract of each document were read. The documents without an antecedent variable of the conflict were deleted, leaving 196 worth analyzing.

In the process of extracting the antecedent variable of team conflict, if the literature did not clearly indicate whether the antecedent variable is for task conflict or relationship conflict, the book defaults that the antecedent variable can cause two types of conflicts; if a antecedent variable is for process conflict, since both task conflict and process conflict are task-oriented, this book classifies the antecedent variables as task conflict.

---

[1] The reason for this is that "task conflict" can also be translated as "cognitive conflict" and "relationship conflict," and can also be translated as "emotional conflict" or "affective conflict."

Based on the reading of domestic and foreign literature, this book forms a list of antecedent variables of task conflict and relationship conflict (Table 2-16 and Table 2-17).

**Table 2-16 List of antecedent variables of task conflict**

| Level | concrete content | |
|---|---|---|
| individual | Individual trait | Personality (1) |
| | | Values (2) |
| | Attribution mode | Internal attribution (3) |
| | | External attribution (4) |
| | Interest Claim (5) | |
| | Cognition (6) | |
| | Vision (7) | |
| | Motivation (8) | |
| | Emotion (9) | |
| | Preferences (10) | |
| | Demand (11) | |
| | Skills (12) | |
| | Thinking Mode (13) | |
| | Ideology (14) | |
| | Behavior (15) | |
| | Roles (16) | |
| | Social Experience (17) | |
| | Status (18) | |
| | Working pressure (19) | |
| | Investment in organizational objectives (20) | |
| | Previous Interaction Behavior (21) | |
| | Perception of performance (22) | |
| | Target similarity (23) | |
| | Recognition (24) | |
| task | type | Routine (25) |
| | | Irregularities (26) |
| | Uncertainty degree (27) | |
| | Degree of interdependence (28) | |
| | Degree of difficulty (29) | |
| | Feedback clarity (30) | |
| | Allocation of responsibilities (31) | |
| team | Scale (32) | |
| | Objective (33) | |
| | Resources (34) | |
| | Previous Performance (35) | |

| | | |
|---|---|---|
| | Organizational Structure Characteristics (36) | |
| | Power Politics (37) | |
| | Management mechanism (38) | |
| | Communication skill level (39) | |
| | Information diversification (40) | |
| | Degree of information asymmetry (41) | |
| | Salary structure (42) | |
| | Common Vision (43) | |
| | Team pressure (44) | |
| | Distribution characteristics (45) | |
| | Interaction mode (46) | |
| | Level of Synergy (47) | |
| | Cohesion level (48) | |
| | Emotional Intelligence (49) | |
| | Team fault zone (50) | |
| | Development cycle | Previous period (51) |
| | | Later stage (52) |
| | Atmosphere level | Innovation atmosphere (53) |
| | | Fair atmosphere (54) |
| | | Support atmosphere (55) |
| | | Interpersonal atmosphere (56) |
| | | Membership identity atmosphere (57) |
| | Conflict management mode | Struggle (58) |
| | | Cooperation (59) |
| | | Avoidance (60) |
| | | Accommodation (61) |
| | | Compromise (62) |
| | Behavior integration level | Joint Decision Making (63) |
| | | Open communication (64) |
| | | Teamwork (65) |
| | Conflict specification mode | Open Conflict Specification (66) |
| | | Conflict Avoidance Specification (67) |
| | Power distribution model | Centralization (68) |
| | | Decentralization (69) |
| | Level of trust | Cognitive Trust (70) |
| | | Emotional Trust (71) |
| | Social capital level | Internal social capital (72) |
| | | External social capital (73) |

| | Leadership factors | Leadership Characteristics (74) |
|---|---|---|
| | | Leadership style (75) |
| | Heterogeneity | Surface heterogeneity (76) |
| | | Deep heterogeneity (77) |
| | | Team time focuses on heterogeneity (78) |
| External environment of the team | Cultural Context (79) | |
| | Environmental change (80) | |
| | External Support (81) | |
| | External Threats (82) | |
| | Environmental Complexity (83) | |

Note: The author obtained it through literature reading; the number in the bracket is the serial number of each antecedent variable.

## Table 2-17 List of antecedent variables of relationship conflict

| Level | Concrete Content | |
|---|---|---|
| | Individual trait | Character (1) |
| | | Values (2) |
| | Attribution mode | Internal attribution (3) |
| | | External attribution (4) |
| | Interest Claim (5) | |
| | Awareness (6) | |
| | Cognition (7) | |
| | Vision (8) | |
| | Motivation (9) | |
| | Emotion (10) | |
| | Preferences (11) | |
| | Demand (12) | |
| individual | Skills (13) | |
| | Fear (14) | |
| | Emotions (15) | |
| | Misunderstandings (16) | |
| | Enemy (17) | |
| | Competition (18) | |
| | Attitude (19) | |
| | Recognition (20) | |
| | Thinking Mode (21) | |
| | Behavior (22) | |
| | Ideology (23) | |
| | Roles (24) | |
| | Social Experience (25) | |

| | | |
|---|---|---|
| | Status (26) | |
| | Interpersonal Relations (27) | |
| | Mutual Suspicion (28) | |
| | Perception of fairness (29) | |
| | Perception of performance (30) | |
| | Target Similarity (31) | |
| | Investment in organizational goals (32) | |
| task | type | Routine (33) |
| | | Irregularities (34) |
| | Degree of difficulty (35) | |
| | Uncertainty degree (36) | |
| | Degree of interdependence (37) | |
| | Clarity of task feedback (38) | |
| team | Scale (39) | |
| | Time of establishment (40) | |
| | Resources (41) | |
| | Previous Performance (42) | |
| | Organizational Structure (43) | |
| | Power Politics (44) | |
| | Management mechanism (45) | |
| | Communication Technology (46) | |
| | Degree of information asymmetry (47) | |
| | Salary characteristics (48) | |
| | Common Vision (49) | |
| | Team pressure (50) | |
| | Distribution characteristics (51) | |
| | Interaction mode (52) | |
| | Level of Synergy (53) | |
| | Emotional Intelligence (54) | |
| | Cohesion level (55) | |
| | Social network group centrality (56) | |
| | Leader member exchange differences (57) | |
| | Task Conflict Level (58) | |
| | Emotional trust (59) | |
| | Team fault zone (60) | |
| | Shared Values (61) | |
| | Development cycle | Early stage (62) |
| | | Later stage (63) |
| | Atmosphere level | Innovation atmosphere (64) |

| | | Fair atmosphere (65) |
| | | Support atmosphere (66) |
| | | Interpersonal atmosphere (67) |
| | | Membership identity atmosphere (68) |
| | Behavior integration level | Joint Decision Making (69) |
| | | Open Communication (70) |
| | | Teamwork (71) |
| | Conflict specification mode | Open Conflict Specification (72) |
| | | Conflict Avoidance Specification (73) |
| | Power distribution model | Centralization (74) |
| | | Decentralization (75) |
| | Conflict management mode | Struggle (76) |
| | | Cooperation (77) |
| | | Avoidance (78) |
| | | Accommodation (79) |
| | | Compromise (80) |
| | Heterogeneity | Surface heterogeneity (81) |
| | | Deep heterogeneity (82) |
| | | Time Focus Heterogeneity (83) |
| | Social capital level | Internal social capital (84) |
| | | External social capital (85) |
| | Leadership factors | Leadership Characteristics (86) |
| | | Leadership Style (87) |
| | | Abuse management (88) |
| External environment of the team | Cultural Context (89) | |
| | Organizational support (90) | |
| | External Threats (91) | |
| | Environmental Complexity (92) | |

Note: The author obtained it through literature reading; the number in parentheses is the serial number of the antecedent variable.

It can be seen from Table 2-16 and Table 2-17 that the classification of antecedent variables of task conflict and relationship conflict at home and abroad can be divided into four levels: individual factors, task factors, team factors and external environmental factors. Among them, individual factors, task factors and team factors are internal factors of the team, and external environmental factors are external factors of the team. It is more comprehensive and systematic to study the antecedents of conflict from both internal and external environments, and it is also more consistent with the search conditions for brittleness factors of complex systems. In these four levels of factors, some can lead to task conflict and relationship conflict at the same time, such as individual cognitive and attribution style, task type, team size and development cycle, but the antecedents of different types of conflict are still quite different. Based on Table 2-16 and Table 2-17, this book screens these antecedents through large-scale questionnaires and data analysis to find out the main antecedents of task conflict and relationship conflict.

## 2.3 Main Antecedents of Task Conflict in Innovation Teams

### 2.3.1 Investigation Process and Preliminary Analysis

#### (1) Formation of the Questionnaire

Based on literature analysis, the book extracts the antecedents of task conflict (Table 2-16), but the number of factors involved is up to 83, which is too many and varied in importance. In order to further clarify the main antecedents of task conflict, these antecedents were screened and analyzed through questionnaires and mathematical statistics.

The questionnaire was formed according to the principles of questionnaire preparation. There are two types of questions: closed type and open type. The former examines respondents' feelings about the degree of influence, and designs five options ("no influence," "small influence," "medium influence," "large influence," "great influence"); the latter collects the respondents' further views and ideas on this issue, and mainly asks the respondents to explain the basis and relevant opinions for judging the influence degree of the antecedents in his/her opinion based on their own cognition and experience. At the same time, design personal background information, including gender, age, education level, level, industry, team size, team tenure and other contents, are collected, in order to understand the basic situation of the respondents and screen the survey questionnaire. As the antecedent variables involve management terminology, this book attaches some definitions of the antecedent variables at the back of the questionnaire to facilitate the respondents' understanding and judgment. The Questionnaire on the Causes of Task Conflict of Innovation Teams designed in this book is shown in Annex B.

**(2) Specific Investigation**

To ensure the relevance, recovery and effectiveness of samples, the following control measures are taken:

1) Control of research objects. The subjects of this survey are innovation team members of different gender, age, education level, level, industry, team size and team tenure in Nanjing.

2) Control of the questionnaire quality. Before the large-scale distribution of the questionnaire, a round of small-scale survey was conducted to allow 12 leaders and members of the innovation team from enterprises and universities to fill in the questionnaire and modify the language and content in a timely manner. At the same time, the first part required respondents to fill in background information to improve the reliability of the survey.

3) Control of the investigation process. The survey was handed out on the spot because the questionnaire involved many management terms and was difficult to fill in. Before the form was completed, the author first contacted the staff of the HR Department of the organization, who provided a name list of the innovation team of the organization, and then entrusted the staff of the HR Department to convene the team leaders and members to the conference room. Before filling in the questionnaire, the author explained some antecedent variables to minimize the respondents' misunderstanding of the indicators and facilitate their understanding and answering. If there was any doubt in the process of filling in the answer, the respondent could view the explanation of the antecedent variable at the end of the questionnaire.

4) Screening of effective questionnaires. The data collected this time was entered and checked by two master students. If there was any inconsistency, the original data was checked and corrected. More than 10% of the unanswered questionnaires were considered invalid. A total of 194 valid questionnaires were collected from 15 innovation teams in this survey.

**(3) Preliminary Analysis of Data**

1) Sample information. The sample collection information is shown in Table 2-18.

**Table 2-18 Sample information of antecedent variables investigation of task conflict**

| Investigation items | category | Number of people/persons | Proportion/% |
|---|---|---|---|
| Gender | Male | 134 | 69.07 |
| | Female | 60 | 30.93 |
| Age | 20–29 | 54 | 27.84 |
| | 30–39 years old | 96 | 49.48 |
| | 40–49 years old | 29 | 14.95 |
| | ≥ 50 years old | 15 | 7.73 |
| degree of education | Junior college or below | 8 | 4.12 |
| | undergraduate | 64 | 32.99 |
| | master | 75 | 38.66 |
| | doctor | 47 | 24.23 |
| level | Ordinary team members | 172 | 88.66 |
| | Team leader | 22 | 11.34 |
| Industry | colleges and universities | 63 | 32.47 |
| | software development | 69 | 35.57 |
| | Pharmaceutical development and production | 33 | 17.01 |
| | Development and production of household appliances | 29 | 14.95 |
| Team size | ≤ 5 persons | 12 | 6.19 |
| | 6–10 persons | 50 | 25.77 |
| | 11–15 persons | 73 | 37.63 |
| | ≥ 15 persons | 59 | 30.41 |
| Team tenure | ≤ 3 years | 19 | 9.79 |
| | 4–6 years | 62 | 31.96 |
| | 7–9 years | 69 | 35.57 |
| | 10–12 years | 37 | 19.07 |
| | ≥ 13 years | 7 | 3.61 |

It can be seen from the above table that about 70% of the respondents are male, and few are female; the number of people aged 20–29 and 30–39 is the largest, accounting for 77% of the total; most of the respondents have bachelor's degree or above; there are many ordinary team members, and only 11% of respondents are team leaders; the number of people in universities and software development industry is relatively large, accounting for about 30% each, while the number of people in pharmaceutical development and production, household appliance development and production industries is relatively small; the number of respondents in the team size of 11–15 is the largest, and the number of respondents in the team size ≤ 5 is the smallest, accounting for only about 6%; The number of team members whose tenure is 7-9 years is the largest, and the number of team members whose tenure is ≤ 3 years and ≥ 13 years is the smallest.

2) Reliability and validity. This book uses the internal consistency coefficient to evaluate the reliability of the questionnaire (Table 2-19). The value of Cronbach' α is 0.899, indicating good reliability.

**Table 2-19 Reliability statistical results of the questionnaire on antecedent variables of task conflict**

| Cronbach's Alpha | Number of items |
| --- | --- |
| .899 | 83 |

Content validity is generally used to estimate the validity of the questionnaire. This book ensures the research validity through two aspects: first, through the study of domestic and foreign literature, we collect the antecedent variable of task conflict as much as possible; second, we conduct a small-scale survey before large-scale distribution of the questionnaire, so that leaders and members of the innovation team can make comments and suggestions, and modify the content and expression of the questionnaire.

3) Positive coefficient of respondents. The positive coefficient $C$ is generally expressed by the survey recovery rate, and the calculation formula is:

$$C = M_j \big/ M \quad \text{Equation (2.1)}$$

wherein, $C$ is the enthusiasm coefficient, $M_j$ is the number of responses, and $M$ is the total number of respondents. It is generally believed that 50% recovery is the minimum requirement, 60% recovery is good, and 80% recovery indicates a very good positive coefficient. A total of 259 questionnaires were collected from

15 innovation teams in this survey, and 194 valid questionnaires were left after deducting invalid questionnaires. The effective recovery rate was 74.9%, and the enthusiasm coefficient of this survey was 74.9%.

4) Authoritative analysis of respondents. Authority Q is determined by three factors: the respondents' own academic attainments, the main basis for making judgments on issues and their familiarity with issues.

Q1: Academic level. The educational level of respondents is used to represent their academic level. It is generally believed that the higher their educational level is, the greater the value of their opinions will be. Therefore, a weight table for academic level is designed (Table 2-20):

**Table 2-20 Weight of respondents' education level**

| degree of education | doctor | master | undergraduate | Junior college or below |
|---|---|---|---|---|
| weight | 1 | 0.7 | 0.5 | 0.3 |

According to the sample information table, among the 194 respondents, there are 8 people with college or below degrees, 64 people with bachelor's degrees, 75 people with master's degrees, and 47 people with doctor's degrees. Therefore, $Q1 = (47 \times 1 + 75 \times 0.7 + 64 \times 0.5 + 8 \times 0) / 194 = 0.68$.

Q2: The judgment basis weight table is also set for the judgment basis of the problem (Table 2-21):

**Table 2-21 The basis of respondents' judgment on the problem**

| Type of judgment basis | Self-evaluation of experts | | |
|---|---|---|---|
| | Weight (large) | Weight (medium) | Weight (small) |
| theoretical analysis | 0.3 | 0.2 | 0.1 |
| practical experience | 0.45 | 0.35 | 0.25 |
| Reference to foreign materials | 0.1 | 0.075 | 0.05 |
| Reference to domestic data | 0.1 | 0.075 | 0.05 |
| subjective judgment | 0.05 | 0.05 | 0.05 |
| total | 1 | 0.75 | 0.5 |

According to the above table, the basis of the respondents' judgment can be divided into five categories: theoretical analysis, practical experience, reference to domestic data, reference to foreign data, and subjective judgment. The respondents had a good educational background, and 103 said that the weight value of their judgment basis was 0.95 (theoretical analysis weight was 0.3, practical experience weight was 0.45, reference to foreign and domestic data was 0.075 each, and subjective judgment weight was 0.05); 31 persons indicated that the weight value of their judgment basis was 0.85 (the weight of theoretical analysis was 0.2, the weight of practical experience was 0.45, the reference to foreign and domestic data was 0.075 each, and the weight of subjective judgment was 0.05); 27 persons indicated that the weight value of their judgment basis was 0.7 (the weight of theoretical analysis was 0.2, the weight of practical experience was 0.35, the reference to foreign and domestic data was 0.05 each, and the weight of subjective judgment was 0.05); The remaining 33 figures indicate that the weight value of their judgment basis is 0.55 (the weight of theoretical analysis was 0.2, the weight of practical experience was 0.25, the reference to foreign data and domestic data was 0.05 each, and the weight of subjective judgment was 0.05). Therefore, 194 respondents judged the problem on the basis of

$$Q2 = \frac{(103 \times 0.95 + 31 \times 0.85 + 27 \times 0.7 + 33 \times 0.55)}{194} = 0.83 .$$

Q3: familiarity. The degree of familiarity of respondents with each question is different, and specific calibration should be carried out according to the question. The former antecedent variables 1 (personality) and 3 (internal attribution) were taken as examples to show that the respondents were familiar with "personality" and had less judgment bias; as for "internal attribution," although the author explained this variable in detail before the survey, some respondents still had an incomplete understanding of it and had a large deviation in judgment (Table 2-22).

**Table 2-22 The familiarity of respondents with each question**

| Antecedent variable | Familiarity | | | | |
| --- | --- | --- | --- | --- | --- |
| | be familiar with (1.0) | Familiar (0.8) | commonly (0.5) | be unfamiliar with (0.2) | Not at all (0) |
| personality (Antecedent variable 1) | 104 | 90 | 0 | 0 | 0 |
| Internal attribution (Antecedent variable 3) | 23 | 92 | 79 | 0 | 0 |

Note: This table takes "character" and "internal attribution" as examples for explanation.

By analogy, the familiarity of respondents with the remaining 81 antecedents was investigated. Statistics show that, based on the explanations in the early stage of the survey, most respondents have a certain degree of understanding of the antecedents of task conflict, and there is no unfamiliar or completely unknown situations. Through calculation, the overall familiarity of the respondents with the antecedents is 0.87.

According to the respective calculation results, the authority $Q$ of the respondents can be summarized as:

$$Q = (Q1+Q2+Q3)\Big/3 = (0.68+0.83+0.87)\Big/3 = 0.79.$$

It is generally believed that $Q > 0.70$ is acceptable, indicating that the respondents' assessment content and the authority of the problem judgment are high, and the results are reliable.

## 2.3.2 Research on Main Antecedent Variables

### (1) The Steps of Ridit Analysis

The Ridit analysis method is used to process the data to determine the main antecedents of task conflict. Ridit analysis can not only point out the different components of each group, but also compare the results of each group. As the survey data belongs to hierarchical data, it is better to use this method to compare multiple groups of hierarchical data.

First, select a reference group. Since there is no obvious difference in the number of cases of 83 antecedent variables and there is no traditional reference, the number of cases corresponding to the level of antecedent variables is selected to total to form a standard group.

Second, convert the frequency distribution of the standard group into a specific R distribution, which is traditionally arranged from weak to strong. The Ridit value of each grade of the standard group can be obtained by calculation (Table 2-23).

**Table 2-23 Ridit values for each level of the standard group of antecedent variables of task conflict**

| Levels | Number of merged cases | R value |
|---|---|---|
| 1 | 2078 | 0.0645 |
| 2 | 2285 | 0.2000 |
| 3 | 2928 | 0.3619 |
| 4 | 3319 | 0.5559 |
| 5 | 5492 | 0.8295 |

Third, calculate the number of cases of 83 antecedent variables and the R value of each triggering degree.

Fourth, calculate the average Ridit value of 83 antecedent variables (Table 2-24).

**Table 2-24 The average Ridit value of 83 antecedent variables**

| Initial factors | Average Ridit value | Initial factors | Average Ridit value |
|---|---|---|---|
| Factor 1 | .333069 | Factor 43 | .331715 |
| Factor 2 | .332192 | Factor 44 | .520826 |
| Factor 3 | .368820 | Factor 45 | .342077 |
| Factor 4 | .688075 | Factor 46 | .606982 |
| Factor 5 | .352179 | Factor 47 | .499242 |
| Factor 6 | .591261 | Factor 48 | .742469 |
| Factor 7 | .318133 | Factor 49 | .517693 |
| Factor 8 | .360447 | Factor 50 | .346202 |
| Factor 9 | .407408 | Factor 51 | .488114 |
| Factor 10 | .428609 | Factor 52 | .308489 |
| Factor 11 | .406780 | Factor 53 | .787535 |
| Factor 12 | .514423 | Factor 54 | .565169 |
| Factor 13 | .509389 | Factor 55 | .812503 |

| Initial factors | Average Ridit value | Initial factors | Average Ridit value |
| --- | --- | --- | --- |
| Factor 14 | .391733 | Factors 56 | .562572 |
| Factor 15 | .458850 | Factors 57 | .637614 |
| Factor 16 | .521704 | Factor 58 | .709007 |
| Factor 17 | .399749 | Factor 59 | .379292 |
| Factor 18 | .400531 | Factor 60 | .470004 |
| Factor 19 | .547700 | Factor 61 | .308650 |
| Factor 20 | .293675 | Factor 62 | .467097 |
| Factor 21 | .516871 | Factor 63 | .553097 |
| Factor 22 | .444243 | Factor 64 | .696386 |
| Factor 23 | .422428 | Factor 65 | .567887 |
| Factor 24 | .483419 | Factor 66 | .506172 |
| Factor 25 | .317343 | Factor 67 | .310497 |
| Factor 26 | .668405 | Factor 68 | .302186 |
| Factor 27 | .647188 | Factor 69 | .643627 |
| Factor 28 | .759149 | Factor 70 | .629563 |
| Factor 29 | .720742 | Factor 71 | .406056 |
| Factor 30 | .758924 | Factor 72 | .376284 |
| Factor 31 | .305608 | Factor 73 | .384933 |
| Factor 32 | .359394 | Factor 74 | .624797 |
| Factor 33 | .433576 | Factor 75 | .540456 |
| Factor 34 | .745930 | Factor 76 | .327709 |
| Factor 35 | .773088 | Factor 77 | .543678 |
| Factor 36 | .302984 | Factor 78 | .425744 |
| Factor 37 | .666918 | Factor 79 | .707012 |
| Factor 38 | .503667 | Factor 80 | .491959 |
| Factor 39 | .664568 | Factor 81 | .393364 |
| Factor 40 | .703050 | Factor 82 | .604421 |
| Factor 41 | .371209 | Factor 83 | .540616 |
| Factor 42 | .326873 | Standard group | .500000 |

The book places the highest level of "5" at the back of the statistics. It shows that the higher the degree of task conflict caused by the antecedent variable, the greater the average Ridit value of the factor. When using the Ridit analysis method to calculate, the average Ridit value of the standard group is always 0.5. When the average Ridit value of an antecedent variable exceeds 0.5, the more it can cause task conflict, and vice versa. It can be seen from Table 2-24 that the average Ridit value of 40 factors, such as antecedent variables 4 and 6, is greater than 5, but it does not mean that these factors are the main antecedent variables of task conflict and should continue to be tested.

Fifthly, U test the average Ridit value of the antecedent variable. According to Table 2-24, it cannot be determined that the average Ridit value of each factor is the degree of task conflict, and the average Ridit value should also be statistically tested. The calculation formula of U value is:

$$U = \frac{\left| \bar{R_i} - 0.5 \right|}{\sqrt{S_{\bar{R}}^2 \left( \frac{1}{n_i} + \frac{1}{n_c} \right)}} \quad \text{Equation (2.2)}$$

$n_c$ is the number of cases in the standard group, $n_i$ is the number of cases in a antecedent variable, 0.5 is the average Ridit value of the standard group, $\bar{R_i}$ is the average Ridit value of a antecedent variable, and $S_{\bar{R}}^2$ is the total variance (its approximate value is $\frac{1}{12}$).

Table 2-23 shows that the total number of cases in the standard group is 16102, and the number of cases in each antecedent variable is 194, so equation (2.2) can be simplified as:

$$U = \frac{\left| \bar{R_i} - 0.5 \right|}{\sqrt{\frac{1}{12} \left( \frac{1}{16102} + \frac{1}{194} \right)}} = \frac{\left| \bar{R_i} - 0.5 \right|}{0.02085} \quad \text{Equation (2.3)}$$

The formula for calculating the 95% confidence interval for the average Ridit value of the antecedent variable is:

$$\bar{R_i} \pm \frac{1}{\sqrt{3n}} \quad \text{Equation (2.4)}$$

Since the number of antecedent variables is 194, equation (2.4) can be simplified as:

$$\bar{R_i} \pm \frac{1}{\sqrt{3n}} = \bar{R_i} \pm \frac{1}{\sqrt{3 \times 194}} = \bar{R_i} \pm 0.0415 \quad \text{Equation (2.5)}$$

If the 95% confidence interval of the average Ridit value of a antecedent variable does not include 0.5, then $P < 0.05$, the difference is statistically significant. Substitute the average Ridit value of each antecedent variable into Equation (2.3) and Equation (2.5) to calculate, and the U statistic and 95% confidence interval of the average Ridit value of each antecedent variable can be obtained (Table 2-25).

**Table 2-25 U test of the average Ridit value of 83 antecedent variables**

| Index factor | Average Ridit value | U statistics | 95% confidence interval | | Reject zero assumption |
|---|---|---|---|---|---|
| | | | upper limit | lower limit | |
| Factor 1 | .333069 | 8.0063 | 0.3746 | 0.2916 | √ |
| Factor 2 | .332192 | 8.0483 | 0.3737 | 0.2907 | √ |
| Factor 3 | .368820 | 6.2916 | 0.4103 | 0.3273 | √ |
| Factor 4 | .688075 | 9.0204 | 0.7296 | 0.6466 | √ |
| Factor 5 | .352179 | 7.0897 | 0.3937 | 0.3107 | √ |
| Factor 6 | .591261 | 4.3770 | 0.6328 | 0.5498 | √ |
| Factor 7 | .318133 | 8.7226 | 0.3596 | 0.2766 | √ |
| Factor 8 | .360447 | 6.6932 | 0.4019 | 0.3189 | √ |
| Factor 9 | .407408 | 4.4409 | 0.4489 | 0.3659 | √ |
| Factor 10 | .428609 | 3.4240 | 0.4701 | 0.3871 | √ |
| Factor 11 | .406780 | 4.4710 | 0.4483 | 0.3653 | √ |
| Factor 12 | .514423 | 0.6918 | 0.5559 | 0.4729 | × |
| Factor 13 | .509389 | 0.4503 | 0.5509 | 0.4679 | × |
| Factor 14 | .391733 | 5.1927 | 0.4332 | 0.3502 | √ |
| Factor 15 | .458850 | 1.9736 | 0.5004 | 0.4174 | × |
| Factor 16 | .521704 | 1.0410 | 0.5632 | 0.4802 | × |
| Factor 17 | .399749 | 4.8082 | 0.4412 | 0.3582 | √ |
| Factor 18 | .400531 | 4.7707 | 0.4420 | 0.3590 | √ |
| Factor 19 | .547700 | 2.2878 | 0.5892 | 0.5062 | √ |
| Factor 20 | .293675 | 9.8957 | 0.3352 | 0.2522 | √ |
| Factor 21 | .516871 | 0.8092 | 0.5584 | 0.4754 | × |
| Factor 22 | .444243 | 2.6742 | 0.4857 | 0.4027 | √ |
| Factor 23 | .422428 | 3.7205 | 0.4639 | 0.3809 | √ |
| Factor 24 | .483419 | 0.7953 | 0.5249 | 0.4419 | × |
| Factor 25 | .317343 | 8.7605 | 0.3588 | 0.2758 | √ |
| Factor 26 | .668405 | 8.0770 | 0.7099 | 0.6269 | √ |
| Factor 27 | .647188 | 7.0594 | 0.6887 | 0.6057 | √ |
| Factor 28 | .759149 | 12.4292 | 0.8006 | 0.7176 | √ |
| Factor 29 | .720742 | 10.5871 | 0.7622 | 0.6792 | √ |
| Factor 30 | .758924 | 12.4184 | 0.8004 | 0.7174 | √ |
| Factor 31 | .305608 | 9.3234 | 0.3471 | 0.2641 | √ |
| Factor 32 | .359394 | 6.7437 | 0.4009 | 0.3179 | √ |
| Factor 33 | .433576 | 3.1858 | 0.4751 | 0.3921 | √ |
| Factor 34 | .624797 | 5.9855 | 0.6663 | 0.5833 | √ |
| Factor 35 | .773088 | 13.0977 | 0.8146 | 0.7316 | √ |
| Factor 36 | .302984 | 9.4492 | 0.3445 | 0.2615 | √ |
| Factor 37 | .666918 | 8.0057 | 0.7084 | 0.6254 | √ |
| Factor 38 | .503667 | 0.1759 | 0.5452 | 0.4622 | × |
| Factor 39 | .664568 | 7.8929 | 0.7061 | 0.6231 | √ |
| Factor 40 | .703050 | 9.7386 | 0.7446 | 0.6616 | √ |

| Index factor | Average Ridit value | U statistics | 95% confidence interval | | Reject zero assumption |
|---|---|---|---|---|---|
| | | | upper limit | lower limit | |
| Factor 41 | .371209 | 6.1770 | 0.4127 | 0.3297 | √ |
| Factor 42 | .326873 | 8.3035 | 0.3684 | 0.2854 | √ |
| Factor 43 | .331715 | 8.0712 | 0.3732 | 0.2902 | √ |
| Factor 44 | .520826 | 0.9988 | 0.5623 | 0.4793 | × |
| Factor 45 | .342077 | 7.5742 | 0.3836 | 0.3006 | √ |
| Factor 46 | .606982 | 5.1310 | 0.6485 | 0.5655 | √ |
| Factor 47 | .499242 | 0.0364 | 0.5407 | 0.4577 | × |
| Factor 48 | .742469 | 11.6292 | 0.7840 | 0.7010 | √ |
| Factor 49 | .517693 | 0.8486 | 0.5592 | 0.4762 | × |
| Factor 50 | .346202 | 7.3764 | 0.3877 | 0.3047 | √ |
| Factor 51 | .488114 | 0.5701 | 0.5296 | 0.4466 | × |
| Factor 52 | .308489 | 9.1852 | 0.3500 | 0.2670 | √ |
| Factor 53 | .787535 | 13.7906 | 0.8290 | 0.7460 | √ |
| Factor 54 | .565169 | 3.1256 | 0.6067 | 0.5237 | √ |
| Factor 55 | .812503 | 14.9882 | 0.8540 | 0.7710 | √ |
| Factors 56 | .562572 | 3.0011 | 0.6041 | 0.5211 | √ |
| Factors 57 | .637614 | 6.6002 | 0.6791 | 0.5961 | √ |
| Factor 58 | .709007 | 10.0243 | 0.7505 | 0.6675 | √ |
| Factor 59 | .379292 | 5.7894 | 0.4208 | 0.3378 | √ |
| Factor 60 | .470004 | 1.4387 | 0.5115 | 0.4285 | × |
| Factor 61 | .308650 | 9.1775 | 0.3502 | 0.2672 | × |
| Factor 62 | .467097 | 1.5781 | 0.5086 | 0.4256 | × |
| Factor 63 | .553097 | 2.5466 | 0.5946 | 0.5116 | √ |
| Factor 64 | .696386 | 9.4190 | 0.7379 | 0.6549 | √ |
| Factor 65 | .567887 | 3.2560 | 0.6094 | 0.5264 | √ |
| Factor 66 | .506172 | 0.2960 | 0.5477 | 0.4647 | × |
| Factor 67 | .310497 | 9.0889 | 0.3520 | 0.2690 | √ |
| Factor 68 | .302186 | 9.4875 | 0.3437 | 0.2607 | √ |
| Factor 69 | .643627 | 6.8886 | 0.6851 | 0.6021 | √ |
| Factor 70 | .629563 | 6.2141 | 0.6711 | 0.5881 | √ |
| Factor 71 | .406056 | 4.5057 | 0.4476 | 0.3646 | √ |
| Factor 72 | .376284 | 5.9336 | 0.4178 | 0.3348 | √ |
| Factor 73 | .384933 | 5.5188 | 0.4264 | 0.3434 | √ |
| Factor 74 | .745930 | 11.7952 | 0.7874 | 0.7044 | √ |
| Factor 75 | .540456 | 1.9403 | 0.5820 | 0.4990 | × |
| Factor 76 | .327709 | 8.2634 | 0.3692 | 0.2862 | √ |
| Factor 77 | .543678 | 2.0949 | 0.5852 | 0.5022 | √ |
| Factor 78 | .425744 | 3.5614 | 0.4672 | 0.3842 | √ |
| Factor 79 | .707012 | 9.9286 | 0.7485 | 0.6655 | √ |
| Factor 80 | .491959 | 0.3857 | 0.5335 | 0.4505 | × |
| Factor 81 | .393364 | 5.1144 | 0.4349 | 0.3519 | √ |

| Index factor | Average Ridit value | U statistics | 95% confidence interval | | Reject zero assumption |
|---|---|---|---|---|---|
| | | | upper limit | lower limit | |
| Factor 82 | .604421 | 5.0082 | 0.6459 | 0.5629 | √ |
| Factor 83 | .540616 | 1.9480 | 0.5821 | 0.4991 | × |

It can be seen from Table 2-25 that, although the average Ridit value of 40 antecedent variables, such as factor 4 and 6, is greater than 0.5, 10 of them, including 12, 13, 16, 21, 38, 44, 49, 66, 75 and 83, have not passed the significance test, and they are not the main antecedent variables of task conflict. The average Ridit value of the remaining 43 antecedent variables, such as 1, 2, and 3, is less than 0.5. Although some of these factors passed the significance test, due to prudence, this book does not regard the factors whose average Ridit value is less than 0.5 but passed the significance test as the main antecedent variables of task conflict.

## (2) Determination of Main Antecedent Variables

So far, through the questionnaire survey of 194 respondents and Ridit analysis, this book has extracted 30 main antecedents of task conflict of innovation teams from 83 antecedents (Table 2-26).

**Table 2-26 The main antecedent variables of task conflict**

| Serial No | Main antecedent variables | Meaning | Level |
|---|---|---|---|
| 1 | Factor 4 | Individual external attribution | Individual factors |
| 2 | Factor 6 | Individual cognitive level | |
| 3 | Factor 19 | Individual work pressure | |
| 4 | Factor 26 | Non routine task type | Task factors |
| 5 | Factor 27 | Task uncertainty | |
| 6 | Factor 28 | Task interdependence | |
| 7 | Factor 29 | Task difficulty | |
| 8 | Factor 30 | Clarity of task feedback | |
| 9 | Factor 34 | Team resources | Team factors |
| 10 | Factor 35 | Previous performance of the team | |
| 11 | Factor 37 | Power politics of the team | |
| 12 | Factor 39 | Communication techniques used by the team | |
| 13 | Factor 40 | Diversity of team information | |
| 14 | Factor 46 | Team interaction mode | |

| Serial No | Main antecedent variables | Meaning | Level |
|---|---|---|---|
| 15 | Factor 48 | Team cohesion level | |
| 16 | Factor 53 | Team innovation atmosphere level | |
| 17 | Factor 54 | Level of team fair atmosphere | |
| 18 | Factor 55 | Level of team support atmosphere | |
| 19 | Factors 56 | Team interpersonal atmosphere level | |
| 20 | Factors 57 | Level of team identity atmosphere | |
| 21 | Factor 58 | The team adopts a fighting conflict handling method | |
| 22 | Factor 63 | Joint Decision Level in Team Behavior Integration | |
| 23 | Factor 64 | Open communication level in team behavior integration | |
| 24 | Factor 65 | Team cooperation level in team behavior integration | |
| 25 | Factor 69 | Team decentralization | |
| 26 | Factor 70 | Team cognitive trust level | |
| 27 | Factor 74 | Team Leadership Traits | |
| 28 | Factor 77 | Level of team deep heterogeneity | |
| 29 | Factor 79 | External cultural context of the team | External factors of the team |
| 30 | Factor 82 | External threats to the team | |

It can be seen from Table 2-26 that the 30 main antecedents of task conflict can be summarized into four levels: individual, task, team and external factors. Among them, the team level involves the most factors, while the individual factors and team external factors are less. According to the average value of Ridit, the book lists the top five antecedent variables that cause the greatest degree of task conflict: team support atmosphere level, team innovation atmosphere level, team previous performance level, task interdependence and task feedback clarity.

According to the types of team conflict brittleness factors (Figure 2-4), the team support atmosphere level and team innovation atmosphere level are enhanced and expanded brittleness factors. Their influence on task conflict are ranging from small to large, from weak to strong. Team atmosphere is the team environment perceived by members and is the implicit dynamic mechanism of the team. Therefore, if the team's support atmosphere and innovation atmosphere are good, all institutional arrangements in the team will treat members equally, encourage members to try new technologies and methods, allow a high degree of mistakes and mistakes within the team, and the team regards task conflict as a normal state, so that members can discuss issues and express opinions more openly, and the level of task conflict will continue to improve. The previous performance level of the team is a declining brittleness factor, which can cause task conflict at first, but its impact on task conflict will gradually weaken over time. The degree of task interdependence and the clarity of task feedback are step type, which have a great impact on task conflict and can last for a long time.

## 2.4 Main Antecedents of Innovation Team Relationship Conflict

### 2.4.1 Investigation Process and Preliminary Analysis

#### (1) Formation of the Questionnaire

This book still uses a questionnaire and Ridit analysis to screen and analyze the antecedent variable of the relationship conflict. There are two types of topics designed: closed type and open type. The former examines the respondents' feelings about the degree of influence, and designs five options; the latter collects the respondents' views and ideas on this issue, and at the same time, designs personal background information, including gender, age, education level, level, industry, team size and team tenure. Because the antecedent variable of the relationship conflict is not completely consistent with that of the task conflict, an explanation of the antecedent variable of the relationship conflict is attached to this book to facilitate the respondents' understanding and filling in. See Annex C for the designed Questionnaire on the Causes of Conflict in Innovation Team Relationships.

#### (2) Specific Process

After the respondents completed the Questionnaire on the Causes of Innovation Team Task Conflict, the author immediately explained and explained the antecedents of the relationship conflict, and then issued the Questionnaire on the Causes of Innovation Team Relationship Conflict for the respondents to fill in.

The recovered data shall be entered and checked by two master students. If there is any inconsistency, the original data shall be checked and corrected. More than 10% of the unanswered questionnaires are considered invalid. A total of 203 valid questionnaires were collected from 15 innovation teams.

### (3) Preliminary Analysis of Data

1) Sample information. See Table 2-27 for specific sample information.

**Table 2-27 Sample information for the survey of antecedent variables of relationship conflict**

| Investigation items | category | Number of people | Proportion |
|---|---|---|---|
| Gender | Male | 136 | 67.00% |
| | Female | 67 | 33.00% |
| Age | 20–29 | 54 | 26.60% |
| | 30–39 years old | 96 | 47.29% |
| | 40–49 years old | 36 | 17.73% |
| | ≥ 50 years old | 17 | 8.38% |
| degree of education | Junior college or below | 9 | 4.43% |
| | undergraduate | 66 | 32.51% |
| | master | 81 | 39.90% |
| | doctor | 47 | 23.16% |
| level | Ordinary team members | 180 | 88.67% |
| | Team leader | 23 | 11.33% |
| Industry | colleges and universities | 63 | 31.03% |
| | software development | 75 | 36.95% |
| | Pharmaceutical development and production | 34 | 16.75% |
| | Development and production of household appliances | 31 | 15.27% |
| Team size | ≤ 5 persons | 14 | 6.90% |
| | 6–10 persons | 51 | 25.12% |
| | 11–15 persons | 78 | 38.42% |
| | ≥ 15 persons | 60 | 29.56% |
| Team tenure | ≤ 3 years | 23 | 11.33% |
| | 4–6 years | 63 | 31.03% |
| | 7–9 years | 71 | 34.98% |
| | 10–12 years | 39 | 19.21% |
| | ≥ 13 years | 7 | 3.45% |

It can be seen from Table 2-27 that men account for the majority; the number of people aged 20–29 and 30–39 is the largest, accounting for 73% of the total; most of the respondents have a bachelor's degree or above; there are more ordinary team members; the number of people in universities and software development industry is relatively large, accounting for about 30% respectively. The number of respondents in pharmaceutical development and production, household appliance development and production industries is relatively small; the number of respondents in teams with 11–15 people is the largest, and the number of respondents with ≤ 5 people is the smallest, accounting for only about 7%; the number of team members with tenure of 7–9 years is the largest, and the number of team members with tenure of ≤ 3 years and ≥ 13 years is the smallest.

2) Reliability and validity. According to statistics, the value of Cronbach's α is 0.869, indicating that the reliability of the questionnaire is good (Table 2-28).

**Table 2-28 Reliability statistical results of the questionnaire on the antecedent variables of relationship conflict**

| Cronbach's Alpha | Number of items |
|---|---|
| .869 | 92 |

Consistent with the validity test of the antecedent questionnaire of task conflict, this book ensures the validity of the antecedent questionnaire of relationship conflict through two aspects: first, find out the antecedent variables of relationship conflict as much as possible through the study of domestic and foreign literature; second, conduct a small survey before large-scale distribution of the questionnaire, and modify the content and expression of the questionnaire in a timely manner.

3) Positive coefficient of respondents. Generally, the positive coefficient is expressed by the survey recovery rate. In this study, 259 questionnaires were distributed and collected on site, and 203 questionnaires remained after deducting invalid questionnaires. The effective recovery rate is 78.4%, that is, the enthusiasm coefficient of this survey is 78.4%.

4) Authoritative analysis of respondents.

Q1: Academic level. This is calculated according to the education level weight of the antecedent variable of the task conflict (Table 2-20). According to the sample information table, among the 203 respondents, 9 have college or below degrees, 66 have bachelor's degrees, 81 have master's degrees, and 47 have doctor's degrees, so it can be calculated that

$$Q1 = {(47 \times 1 + 81 \times 0.7 + 66 \times 0.5 + 9 \times 0)}\big/{203} = 0.67 \,.$$

Q2: Judgment basis for the problem. This study calculates this according to the expert's judgment basis (Table 2-21). Compared with task conflict, the respondents have a clearer understanding of relationship conflict. 114 respondents said that the weight of their judgment basis was 0.95 (the weight of theoretical analysis was 0.3, the weight of practical experience was 0.45, the weight of reference to foreign and domestic data was 0.075, and the weight of subjective judgment was 0.05); 32 respondents indicate that the weight of their judgment basis is 0.85 (the weight of theoretical analysis is 0.2, the weight of practical experience is 0.45, the weight of reference to foreign and domestic data is 0.075, and the weight of subjective judgment is 0.05); 35 respondents indicated that the weight of their judgment basis was 0.8 (the weight of theoretical analysis was 0.2, the weight of practical experience was 0.45, the weight of reference foreign data and domestic data was 0.05, and the weight of subjective judgment was 0.05); the remaining 22 respondents indicate that the weight of their judgment basis is 0.55 (the weight of theoretical analysis is 0.2, the weight of practical experience is 0.25, the weight of reference foreign data and domestic data is 0.05, and the weight of subjective judgment is 0.05). Therefore, the 203 respondents judged the question based on

$$Q2 = {(114 \times 0.95 + 32 \times 0.85 + 35 \times 0.8 + 22 \times 0.55)}\big/{203} = 0.86 \,.$$

Q3: familiarity. The degree of familiarity of respondents with each question is different, and specific calibration should be carried out according to each question. According to the statistics, based on the explanations before the survey, most of the respondents have a certain degree of understanding of the antecedent variables of the relationship conflict, and there is no unfamiliar or completely unfamiliar situation. The overall familiarity of 203 respondents with 92 antecedent variables is 0.89.

According to the respective calculation results, the authority of the respondents is $Q = (Q1 + Q2 + Q3) / 3 = \dfrac{(0.67 + 0.86 + 0.89)}{3} = 0.81$ , which indicates that the assessment content and judgment of the respondents are highly authoritative and the results are reliable.

## 2.4.2 Research on the Main Antecedent Variables

### (1) The Steps of Ridit Analysis

This book uses Ridit analysis to screen 92 factors to extract the main antecedents of relationship conflict.

First, select a reference group. Since there is no obvious difference in the number of cases of each antecedent variable and there is no traditional reference, the number of cases of 92 antecedent variables corresponding to the level is selected to form a reference group.

Second, convert the frequency distribution of the standard group into a specific R distribution, which is traditionally arranged from weak to strong. The Ridit value of each grade of the standard group can be obtained by calculation (Table 2-29).

Table 2-29 The Ridit value of each level of the antecedent variable standard group of the relationship conflict

| Levels | Number of merged cases | R value |
|--------|------------------------|---------|
| 1 | 3004 | 0.0804 |
| 2 | 3431 | 0.4202 |
| 3 | 3482 | 0.6053 |
| 4 | 3129 | 0.2446 |
| 5 | 5630 | 0.8493 |

Third, calculate the number of cases of 92 antecedent variables and the R value of each triggering degree. The R value of each triggering degree of the antecedent variable can be obtained through calculation.

Fourth, calculate the average Ridit value of 92 antecedent variables (Table 2-30).

## Table 2-30 Average Ridit value of 92 antecedent variables

| Initial factors | Average Ridit value | Initial factors | Average Ridit value |
|---|---|---|---|
| Factor 1 | .495946 | Factor 47 | .589424 |
| Factor 2 | .542599 | Factor 48 | .281019 |
| Factor 3 | .777586 | Factor 49 | .444629 |
| Factor 4 | .363426 | Factor 50 | .718745 |
| Factor 5 | .541582 | Factor 51 | .366445 |
| Factor 6 | .631985 | Factor 52 | .542644 |
| Factor 7 | .416371 | Factor 53 | .574160 |
| Factor 8 | .549812 | Factor 54 | .609542 |
| Factor 9 | .546003 | Factor 55 | .564395 |
| Factor 10 | .525247 | Factors 56 | .549217 |
| Factor 11 | .506331 | Factors 57 | .705203 |
| Factor 12 | .257417 | Factor 58 | .671309 |
| Factor 13 | .386440 | Factor 59 | .579008 |
| Factor 14 | .423743 | Factor 60 | .375236 |
| Factor 15 | .574883 | Factor 61 | .390340 |
| Factor 16 | .617655 | Factor 62 | .396796 |
| Factor 17 | .603932 | Factor 63 | .450001 |
| Factor 18 | .665021 | Factor 64 | .388118 |
| Factor 19 | .602493 | Factor 65 | .650668 |
| Factor 20 | .431888 | Factor 66 | .458901 |
| Factor 21 | .347507 | Factor 67 | .635259 |
| Factor 22 | .542738 | Factor 68 | .422994 |
| Factor 23 | .353716 | Factor 69 | .373898 |
| Factor 24 | .462906 | Factor 70 | .518752 |
| Factor 25 | .469844 | Factor 71 | .432898 |
| Factor 26 | .405798 | Factor 72 | .312453 |
| Factor 27 | .604162 | Factor 73 | .536477 |
| Factor 28 | .753307 | Factor 74 | .359883 |
| Factor 29 | .649243 | Factor 75 | .411981 |
| Factor 30 | .397583 | Factor 76 | .602069 |
| Factor 31 | .418228 | Factor 77 | .474179 |
| Factor 32 | .463485 | Factor 78 | .473053 |
| Factor 33 | .367402 | Factor 79 | .337192 |
| Factor 34 | .387656 | Factor 80 | .331222 |
| Factor 35 | .283877 | Factor 81 | .556942 |
| Factor 36 | .440125 | Factor 82 | .661270 |
| Factor 37 | .369101 | Factor 83 | .375136 |
| Factor 38 | .416709 | Factor 84 | .413481 |
| Factor 39 | .669679 | Factor 85 | .414653 |
| Factor 40 | .433766 | Factor 86 | .410759 |
| Factor 41 | .690768 | Factor 87 | .563876 |

| Initial factors | Average Ridit value | Initial factors | Average Ridit value |
|---|---|---|---|
| Factor 42 | .549217 | Factor 88 | .743442 |
| Factor 43 | .370893 | Factor 89 | .658804 |
| Factor 44 | .610202 | Factor 90 | .360814 |
| Factor 45 | .572841 | Factor 91 | .468108 |
| Factor 46 | .654205 | Factor 92 | .699286 |
| Standard group | .500000 | ...... | ...... |

The highest level of "5" is placed at the end, indicating that the higher the degree of relationship conflict caused by the antecedent variable, the greater the average Ridit value of the factor; The Ridit value of the standard group is always 0.5. When the average Ridit value of an antecedent variable exceeds 0.5, it indicates that the higher the degree of relationship conflict it can cause, and vice versa. It can be seen from Table 2-30 that the average Ridit value of 44 factors, such as antecedent variables 2 and 3, is greater than 0.5. But it does not indicate that these factors are the main antecedent variables of relationship conflict and should continue to be tested.

Fifthly, U test the average Ridit value of each antecedent variable. According to Table 2-29, the total number of cases in the standard group is 18676, and the number of cases in 92 antecedent variables is 203. Therefore, the formula for calculating the U value of the average Ridit value (Formula (2.2)) can be simplified as follows:

$$U = \frac{\left| \bar{R}_i - 0.5 \right|}{\sqrt{\frac{1}{12}(\frac{1}{18676} + \frac{1}{203})}} = \frac{\left| \bar{R}_i - 0.5 \right|}{0.020371} \quad \text{Equation (2.6)}$$

The 95% confidence interval formula for calculating the average Ridit value of 92 antecedent variables is Formula (2.4). Since the number of antecedent variables is 203, the formula is simplified as:

$$\bar{R}_i \pm \frac{1}{\sqrt{3n}} = \bar{R}_i \pm \frac{1}{\sqrt{3 \times 203}} = \bar{R}_i \pm 0.0405 \quad \text{Equation (2.7)}$$

Substitute the average Ridit value of 92 antecedent variables into Equation (2.6) and Equation (2.7) to obtain the U statistic and 95% confidence interval of the average Ridit value of each antecedent variable (Table 2-31).

**Table 2-31 U test of the average Ridit value of 92 antecedent variables**

| Index factor | Average Ridit value | U statistics | 95% confidence interval upper limit | lower limit | Reject zero assumption |
|---|---|---|---|---|---|
| Factor 1 | .495946 | 0.1990 | 0.5364 | 0.4554 | × |
| Factor 2 | .542599 | 2.0912 | 0.5831 | 0.5021 | √ |
| Factor 3 | .777586 | 13.6265 | 0.8181 | 0.7371 | √ |
| Factor 4 | .363426 | 6.7043 | 0.4039 | 0.3229 | √ |
| Factor 5 | .541582 | 2.0412 | 0.5821 | 0.5011 | √ |
| Factor 6 | .631985 | 6.4791 | 0.6725 | 0.5915 | √ |
| Factor 7 | .416371 | 4.1053 | 0.4569 | 0.3759 | √ |
| Factor 8 | .549812 | 2.4452 | 0.5903 | 0.5093 | √ |
| Factor 9 | .546003 | 2.2583 | 0.5865 | 0.5055 | √ |
| Factor 10 | .525247 | 1.2394 | 0.5657 | 0.4847 | × |
| Factor 11 | .506331 | 0.3108 | 0.5468 | 0.4658 | × |
| Factor 12 | .257417 | 11.9083 | 0.2979 | 0.2169 | √ |
| Factor 13 | .386440 | 5.5746 | 0.4269 | 0.3459 | √ |
| Factor 14 | .423743 | 3.7434 | 0.4642 | 0.3832 | √ |
| Factor 15 | .574883 | 3.6760 | 0.6154 | 0.5344 | √ |
| Factor 16 | .617655 | 5.7756 | 0.6582 | 0.5772 | √ |
| Factor 17 | .603932 | 5.1020 | 0.6444 | 0.5634 | √ |
| Factor 18 | .665021 | 8.1008 | 0.7055 | 0.6245 | √ |
| Factor 19 | .602493 | 5.0313 | 0.6430 | 0.5620 | √ |
| Factor 20 | .431888 | 3.3436 | 0.4724 | 0.3914 | √ |
| Factor 21 | .347507 | 7.4858 | 0.3880 | 0.3070 | √ |
| Factor 22 | .542738 | 2.0980 | 0.5832 | 0.5022 | √ |
| Factor 23 | .353716 | 7.1810 | 0.3942 | 0.3132 | √ |
| Factor 24 | .462906 | 1.8209 | 0.5034 | 0.4224 | × |
| Factor 25 | .469844 | 1.4803 | 0.5103 | 0.4293 | × |
| Factor 26 | .405798 | 4.6243 | 0.4463 | 0.3653 | √ |
| Factor 27 | .604162 | 5.1132 | 0.6447 | 0.5637 | √ |
| Factor 28 | .753307 | 12.4347 | 0.7938 | 0.7128 | √ |
| Factor 29 | .649243 | 7.3262 | 0.6897 | 0.6087 | √ |
| Factor 30 | .397583 | 5.0276 | 0.4381 | 0.3571 | √ |
| Factor 31 | .418228 | 4.0141 | 0.4587 | 0.3777 | √ |
| Factor 32 | .463485 | 1.7925 | 0.5040 | 0.4230 | × |
| Factor 33 | .367402 | 6.5092 | 0.4079 | 0.3269 | √ |
| Factor 34 | .387656 | 5.5149 | 0.4282 | 0.3472 | √ |
| Factor 35 | .283877 | 10.6093 | 0.3244 | 0.2434 | √ |
| Factor 36 | .440125 | 2.9392 | 0.4806 | 0.3996 | √ |
| Factor 37 | .369101 | 6.4258 | 0.4096 | 0.3286 | √ |
| Factor 38 | .416709 | 4.0887 | 0.4572 | 0.3762 | √ |
| Factor 39 | .669679 | 8.3294 | 0.7102 | 0.6292 | √ |
| Factor 40 | .433766 | 3.2514 | 0.4743 | 0.3933 | √ |

| Index factor | Average Ridit value | U statistics | 95% confidence interval | | Reject zero assumption |
| --- | --- | --- | --- | --- | --- |
| | | | upper limit | lower limit | |
| Factor 41 | .690768 | 9.3647 | 0.7313 | 0.6503 | √ |
| Factor 42 | .549217 | 2.4160 | 0.5897 | 0.5087 | √ |
| Factor 43 | .370893 | 6.3378 | 0.4114 | 0.3304 | √ |
| Factor 44 | .610202 | 5.4097 | 0.6507 | 0.5697 | √ |
| Factor 45 | .572841 | 3.5757 | 0.6133 | 0.5323 | √ |
| Factor 46 | .654205 | 7.5698 | 0.6947 | 0.6137 | √ |
| Factor 47 | .589424 | 4.3898 | 0.6299 | 0.5489 | √ |
| Factor 48 | .281019 | 10.7496 | 0.3215 | 0.2405 | √ |
| Factor 49 | .444629 | 2.7181 | 0.4851 | 0.4041 | √ |
| Factor 50 | .718745 | 10.7381 | 0.7592 | 0.6782 | √ |
| Factor 51 | .366445 | 6.5561 | 0.4069 | 0.3259 | √ |
| Factor 52 | .542644 | 2.0934 | 0.5831 | 0.5021 | √ |
| Factor 53 | .574160 | 3.6405 | 0.6147 | 0.5337 | √ |
| Factor 54 | .609542 | 5.3774 | 0.6500 | 0.5690 | √ |
| Factor 55 | .564395 | 3.1611 | 0.6049 | 0.5239 | √ |
| Factors 56 | .549217 | 2.4160 | 0.5897 | 0.5087 | √ |
| Factors 57 | .705203 | 10.0733 | 0.7457 | 0.6647 | √ |
| Factor 58 | .671309 | 8.4095 | 0.7118 | 0.6308 | √ |
| Factor 59 | .579008 | 3.8785 | 0.6195 | 0.5385 | √ |
| Factor 60 | .375236 | 6.1246 | 0.4157 | 0.3347 | √ |
| Factor 61 | .390340 | 5.3831 | 0.4308 | 0.3498 | √ |
| Factor 62 | .396796 | 5.0662 | 0.4373 | 0.3563 | √ |
| Factor 63 | .450001 | 2.4544 | 0.4905 | 0.4095 | √ |
| Factor 64 | .388118 | 5.4922 | 0.4286 | 0.3476 | √ |
| Factor 65 | .650668 | 7.3962 | 0.6912 | 0.6102 | √ |
| Factor 66 | .458901 | 2.0175 | 0.4994 | 0.4184 | √ |
| Factor 67 | .635259 | 6.6398 | 0.6758 | 0.5948 | √ |
| Factor 68 | .422994 | 3.7802 | 0.4635 | 0.3825 | √ |
| Factor 69 | .373898 | 6.1903 | 0.4144 | 0.3334 | √ |
| Factor 70 | .518752 | 0.9205 | 0.5593 | 0.4783 | × |
| Factor 71 | .432898 | 3.2940 | 0.4734 | 0.3924 | √ |
| Factor 72 | .312453 | 9.2066 | 0.3530 | 0.2720 | √ |
| Factor 73 | .536477 | 1.7906 | 0.5770 | 0.4960 | × |
| Factor 74 | .359883 | 6.8783 | 0.4004 | 0.3194 | √ |
| Factor 75 | .411981 | 4.3208 | 0.4525 | 0.3715 | √ |
| Factor 76 | .602069 | 5.0105 | 0.6426 | 0.5616 | √ |
| Factor 77 | .474179 | 1.2675 | 0.5147 | 0.4337 | × |
| Factor 78 | .473053 | 1.3228 | 0.5136 | 0.4326 | × |
| Factor 79 | .337192 | 7.9921 | 0.3777 | 0.2967 | √ |
| Factor 80 | .331222 | 8.2852 | 0.3717 | 0.2907 | √ |
| Factor 81 | .556942 | 2.7952 | 0.5974 | 0.5164 | √ |

| Index factor | Average Ridit value | U statistics | 95% confidence interval | | Reject zero assumption |
|---|---|---|---|---|---|
| | | | upper limit | lower limit | |
| Factor 82 | .661270 | 7.9166 | 0.7018 | 0.6208 | √ |
| Factor 83 | .375136 | 6.1295 | 0.4156 | 0.3346 | √ |
| Factor 84 | .413481 | 4.2472 | 0.4540 | 0.3730 | √ |
| Factor 85 | .414653 | 4.1896 | 0.4552 | 0.3742 | √ |
| Factor 86 | .410759 | 4.3808 | 0.4513 | 0.3703 | √ |
| Factor 87 | .563876 | 3.1356 | 0.6044 | 0.5234 | √ |
| Factor 88 | .743442 | 11.9504 | 0.7839 | 0.7029 | √ |
| Factor 89 | .658804 | 7.7956 | 0.6993 | 0.6183 | √ |
| Factor 90 | .360814 | 6.8326 | 0.4013 | 0.3203 | √ |
| Factor 91 | .468108 | 1.5656 | 0.5086 | 0.4276 | × |
| Factor 92 | .699286 | 9.7828 | 0.7398 | 0.6588 | √ |

It can be seen from Table 2-31 that, although the average Ridit value of 44 antecedent variables, such as factors 2 and 3, is greater than 0.5, the four factors 10, 11, 70 and 73 did not pass the significance test; therefore, they are not the main antecedent variables of relationship conflict. The average Ridit value of 48 other factors, such as 1 and 4, is less than 0.5. Although some factors pass the significance test, considering the principle of prudence, these factors are not considered as the main antecedents of relationship conflict in this book.

## (2) Determination of Main Antecedent Variables

Through the questionnaire survey and Ridit statistical analysis of 203 members of the innovation team, the book extracts 40 main antecedents of the relationship conflict of the innovation team from 92 antecedents (Table 2-32).

It can be seen from Table 2-32 that the 40 main antecedents of relationship conflict can be summarized into three levels: individual, team and team external environment. Different from task conflict, there are no factors involved in task level, which is consistent with their definitions. The main antecedents of relationship conflict involve many factors at the individual level, such as members' interest demands, values, emotions, hostility to others, etc. Compared with task conflict, it is found that some factors can trigger task conflict and relationship conflict at the same time, such as individual attribution, team resources and cultural context outside the team. However, in many cases, the main antecedents of different types of conflict are different.

### Table 2-32 The main antecedent variables of relationship conflict

| Serial No | Factor | Meaning | Level |
|---|---|---|---|
| 1 | Factor 2 | Members' values | Individual factors |
| 2 | Factor 3 | Internal attribution of members | |
| 3 | Factor 5 | Members' interest demands | |
| 4 | Factor 6 | Awareness of members | |
| 5 | Factor 8 | Member's Vision | |
| 6 | Factor 9 | Motivation of members | |
| 7 | Factor 15 | Members' own emotions | |
| 8 | Factor 16 | Members' misunderstanding of others | |
| 9 | Factor 17 | Hostility of members to others | |
| 10 | Factor 18 | Competition among members | |
| 11 | Factor 19 | Attitude of members | |
| 12 | Factor 22 | Behavior of members | |
| 13 | Factor 27 | Interpersonal relationship among members | |
| 14 | Factor 28 | Mutual suspicion among members | |
| 15 | Factor 29 | Members' perception of fairness | |
| 16 | Factor 39 | Team size | Team factors |
| 17 | Factor 41 | Resources of the team | |
| 18 | Factor 42 | Previous performance of the team | |
| 19 | Factor 44 | Power politics of the team | |
| 20 | Factor 45 | Management mechanism of the team | |
| 21 | Factor 46 | Team communication skills | |
| 22 | Factor 47 | Team information asymmetry | |
| 23 | Factor 50 | Team pressure | |
| 24 | Factor 52 | Team interaction | |
| 25 | Factor 53 | Level of teamwork | |
| 26 | Factor 54 | Team's emotional intelligence level | |
| 27 | Factor 55 | Team cohesion level | |
| 28 | Factor 56 | Group centrality of the team's social network | |
| 29 | Factor 57 | Team leader-member exchange differences | |
| 30 | Factor 58 | Level of team task conflict | |
| 31 | Factor 59 | Emotional trust level of the team | |
| 32 | Factor 65 | Level of the team's fair atmosphere | |
| 33 | Factor 67 | The team's interpersonal atmosphere level | |
| 34 | Factor 76 | The team adopts a conflict fighting approach | |
| 35 | Factor 81 | Team surface heterogeneity | |
| 36 | Factor 82 | Deep team heterogeneity | |

| Serial No | Factor | Meaning | Level |
|---|---|---|---|
| 37 | Factor 87 | Leadership style of team leader | |
| 38 | Factor 88 | Abusive supervision of team leaders | |
| 39 | Factor 89 | Cultural situation outside the team | External factors of the team |
| 40 | Factor 92 | Complexity of the team's external environment | |

From the average Ridit value of the 40 antecedents, the top five antecedents causing relationship conflict were: individual internal attribution, mutual suspicion among members, abusive supervision, team pressure and differences in leader-member exchange differences.

According to the types of team conflict brittleness factors (Figure 2-4), individual internal attribution and abusive supervision are of a step type, that is, these two types can continuously trigger relationship conflicts; members' mutual suspicions is a linear type and only has a temporary impact on the relationship conflict at Moment t; the team pressure is a decline type, which can quickly cause relationship conflicts at the beginning, but will slowly disappear after a period of time; the differences inleader-member exchange is an enhanced and expanded type, which may have little impact on relationship conflict at the beginning, but with the evolution of conflict, its negative impact on relationship conflict will be greatly enhanced.

## 2.5 Summary

This chapter aims to study the antecedents of innovation team conflict in the "input" stage of team operation. Firstly, based on the theory of complex system brittleness, this paper analyzes the brittleness of innovation team conflict, constructs the model of innovation team conflict brittleness and classifies the factors of conflict brittleness to guide the research on the antecedents of innovation team conflict. Secondly, this book verifies the applicability of the two-dimensional model of innovation team conflict (task conflict and relationship conflict) in China, and lays a foundation for the research on the antecedents of team conflict. Finally, the main antecedents of task conflict and relationship conflict of innovation teams were studied by literature analysis, questionnaire survey and Ridit analysis. The empirical results show that: (1) The 30 main antecedents that cause task conflicts can be summarized into four levels: individual, task, team and team external environment. The top five antecedents are team support atmosphere, team innovation atmosphere, team previous performance, task interdependence and task feedback clarity. (2) The 40 major antecedents that triggered relationship conflict can be summarized into three levels: individual, team and team external environment. The top five antecedents are individual internal attribution, mutual suspicion among members, abusive supervision, team pressure and differences in leader-member exchange. (3) Some factors can cause task conflict and relationship conflict at the same time, but in many cases, the main antecedents of different types of conflict are obviously different.

# Conflict Relationship between Innovation Team Members

In the existing literature, there is little research focusing on conflict relationship among team members, which is still a "black box." Since conflict is the product of the interaction between members, analyzing the conflict relationship between members is an unavoidable problem for the in-depth study of team conflict. Only by in-depth analysis of the conflict relationship between members can we fully grasp the development of conflict, so as to better monitor and manage team conflict. To achieve this goal, in the "process" stage of team operation, this book applies the complex system brittleness theory and social network theory to systematically study the conflict relationships among members of the innovation team from three levels: team, individual and team, and individual and individual. The first step is to build and analyze the conflict network formed within the team by using the social network analysis method from the perspective of the entire innovation team; the second step is to judge the influence of each member on the conflict network by combining the content of the brittleness source identification of the complex system; the third step is to use the cusp catastrophe model to reveal the conflict relationship between members based on the conflict correlation between members.

The research steps of the conflict relationship among innovation team members formed in this chapter are shown in Figure 3-1. As the conflict network formed within each innovation team and the specific conflict relationship between members are different, this book selects the financial service team under Jiangsu Hongtu High-Tech Co., Ltd. for specific research.[1]

---

[1] Founded in 1998, Jiangsu Hongtu High-Tech Co., Ltd. is a high-tech enterprise recognized

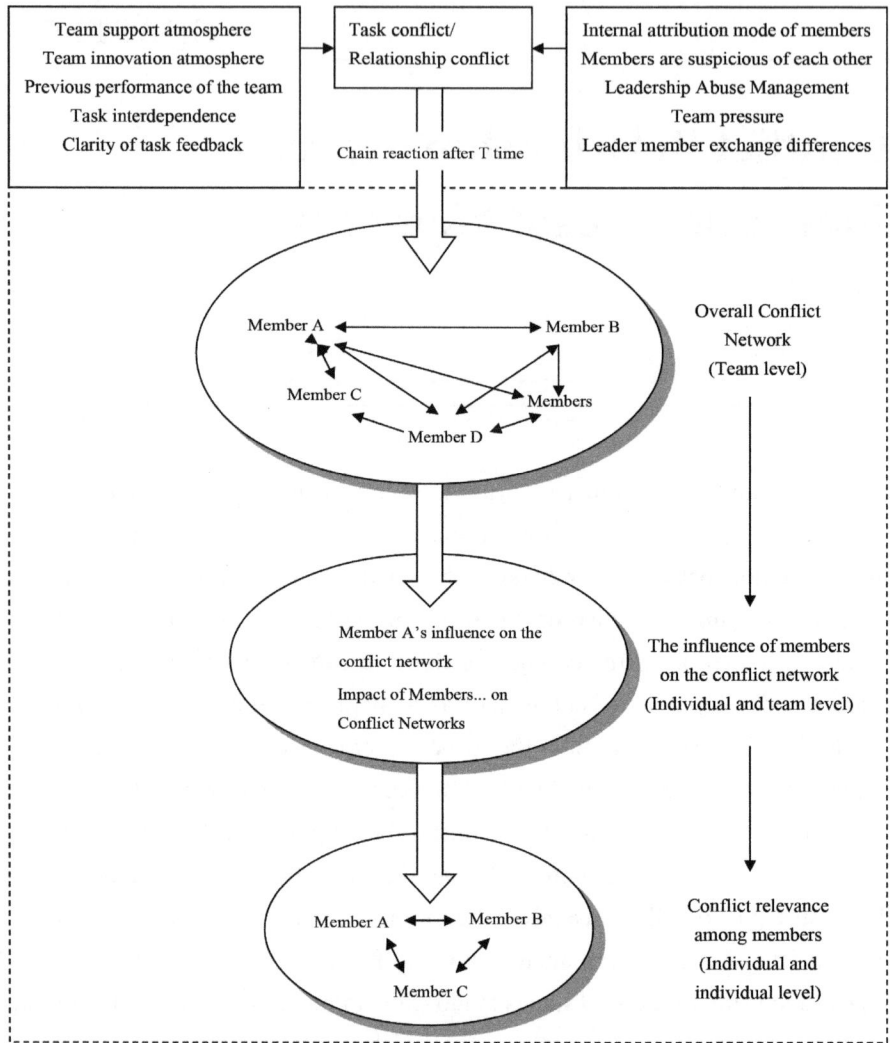

**Figure 3-1 Research steps of conflict relationship among innovation team members**

by the Jiangsu Provincial Science and Technology Department, with more than 2,500 employees. Committed to promoting the era of "big consumption and big finance" through innovation, the financial service team relies on professional research and development and strict risk control system to innovate and launch a comprehensive payment platform integrating diversified payment methods such as Internet, cell phone, telephone voice and offline terminal, which mainly provides in-depth customized payment solutions for Internet financial products. At present, the financial service team has realized real-time networking with UnionPay and major banks, telecom operators and upstream partners, and has established strategic partnerships with large government agencies such as China Public Procurement Network and Central Government Procurement Center.

## 3.1 Construction and Analysis of Innovation Team Conflict Network

### 3.1.1 Determination of Team Conflict Level

Before building a conflict network, this book first examines the level of conflict within the financial services team, because if the level of conflict perceived by members of the financial services team is very low, it indicates that the conflict within the team is not serious, and most members may not be involved in the conflict network.

### (1) Investigation Process

Following the scale developed by Jehn, the questionnaire for measuring the conflict level of financial service teams is detailed in Annex D, which is mainly used to let members evaluate the perceived level of task conflict and relationship conflict. The questionnaire adopts the Richter 5-point scale (1 indicates low level, 5 indicates high level), and adds 4 control variables including gender, age, education level and team tenure. There are 31 members in the team, including 3 general administrative assistants. Because their work nature does not involve innovation activities and does not meet the survey requirements, they are excluded from questionnaire. The remaining 28 members fill in the questionnaire on the spot.

### (2) Sample Information

The recovery rate of this survey is 100%. After preliminary screening, all the questionnaires are valid (the questionnaires with more than 10% unanswered and all the questions with the same score are considered invalid). The sample information of 28 members is shown in Table 3-1.

**Table 3-1 Information on sample collection of financial service conflict level survey**

| variable | category | Number of people/person | Proportion/% |
|---|---|---|---|
| Gender | male | 20 | 71.4 |
| | female | 8 | 28.6 |
| Age | 20–29 | 8 | 28.6 |
| | 30–39 years old | 10 | 35.7 |
| | 40–49 years old | 9 | 32.1 |
| | ≥ 50 years old | 1 | 3.6 |

|                      |                        |    |      |
|----------------------|------------------------|----|------|
|                      | Junior college or below | 2  | 7    |
| Degree of Education  | undergraduate          | 5  | 18   |
|                      | master                 | 14 | 50   |
|                      | doctor                 | 7  | 25   |
|                      | ≤ 3 years              | 6  | 21.4 |
|                      | 4–6 years              | 8  | 28.6 |
| Team tenure          | 7–9 years              | 5  | 17.9 |
|                      | 10–12 years            | 4  | 14.3 |
|                      | ≥ 13 years             | 5  | 17.9 |

## (3) Descriptive Statistics

From the descriptive statistics results (Table 3-2), we can see that there is a moderate level of task conflict and relationship conflict within the financial services team, and there may be a more complex conflict network within the team.

**Table 3-2 Descriptive statistics of financial services team conflict level**

| entry | Minimum | maximum value | mean value | standard deviation | skewness statistic | Standard error | kurtosis statistic | Standard error |
|-------|---------|---------------|------------|--------------------|--------------------|----------------|--------------------|----------------|
| TC1 | 2 | 5 | 3.36 | 0.989 | .429 | .441 | -.735 | .858 |
| TC2 | 2 | 5 | 2.89 | 0.832 | 1.042 | .441 | 1.291 | .858 |
| TC3 | 2 | 5 | 3.00 | 0.816 | .879 | .441 | 1.008 | .858 |
| TC4 | 1 | 5 | 3.11 | 1.133 | .105 | .441 | -.477 | .858 |
| RC1 | 1 | 4 | 2.57 | 0.742 | -.263 | .441 | .007 | .858 |
| RC2 | 2 | 5 | 3.32 | 0.905 | .579 | .441 | -.247 | .858 |
| RC3 | 1 | 5 | 3.50 | 1.036 | -.537 | .441 | -.126 | .858 |
| RC4 | 2 | 5 | 3.71 | 0.937 | .047 | .441 | -1.006 | .858 |
| TC | 2.25 | 5.00 | 3.09 | 0.727 | 1.290 | .441 | 1.817 | .858 |
| RC | 2.00 | 4.75 | 3.28 | 0.591 | .371 | .441 | .510 | .858 |

Note: TC refers to task conflict and RC refers to relationship conflict

## 3.1.2 Construction of Conflict Network

There are few articles on team conflict from the perspective of social networks. Most previous studies on social networks only focused on positive relationships, such as the positive impact of centrality and proximity to centrality of consulting networks on members' innovation behavior[101], and the positive impact of relationship embeddedness strength on enterprises' technological innovation performance[102]. However, Labianca et al. proposed that some negative relationships (such as conflicts) in social networks are more important than positive relationships in understanding members' attitudes and behaviors, because negative relationships are more prominent[103]. At the same time, as early as 1995, Jehn pointed out that since conflict is the product of team members' interaction, scholars must fill the gap between conflict theory and social network theory. To sum up, this book uses the social network theory to analyze the conflict relationship within the innovation team from a macro perspective.

## (1) Formation of Questionnaire

Based on the social network theory, this book defines "team conflict network" as "the conflict structure formed in the team by the degree of incompatibility perceived by members with other members." According to the two-dimensional model of team conflict, "conflict network" can be divided into "task conflict network" and "relationship conflict network." For the measurement of this variable, scholars generally use the survey method of social network, that is, ask respondents to list the names of their team members. Translation and back translation of the English version of the scale was used to form a Chinese version, and we invited five members of the financial services team to propose amendments to the questionnaire, so that the meaning of each question is expressed more clearly, the wording is more accurate, and does not involve sensitive issues. In the questionnaire, there are three questions about the task conflict network, such as "Who do you often have to discuss with to complete the task?"; the relationship conflict network section also contains three questions, such as "Who are you often angry or dissatisfied with in the team?"

The Conflict Network Questionnaire of Financial Service Innovation Teams formed in this book is shown in Appendix E.

Holland et al. proposed that all members of the whole network should be included in the questionnaire when conducting social network survey, so as to obtain a more accurate network interaction mode. In order to reduce errors, this book lists the team members in the questionnaire according to the traditional measurement method of social network, so that members can fill in the questionnaire easily.

## (2) Data Collection

According to different research purposes, different collection methods can be used for social network analysis, and the overall network analysis generally needs to consider the entire social network group in the sample. With the support of the team leader, the book first conducts a two-week direct observation of the entire innovation team. Through participating in four regular meetings, recording the communication content of members at work and their personal communication activities at break, the book generally understands the daily operation of the team, the division of work and cooperation of members, personal relations and other preliminary conditions. Two weeks later, 28 team members were summoned to the conference room and they were given the Conflict Network Questionnaire for Financial Service Innovation Teams on the spot. In order to dispel the concerns of members, it was stated that each questionnaire would only be collected by researchers and the final research results would be anonymous. A total of 28 questionnaires were completed and collected on the spot.

## (3) Analysis of Reliability and Validity

The social network questionnaire is generally semi-open. This book guarantees the reliability and validity of the survey through the following ways: on the one hand, the survey uses the scale widely used by predecessors and combines the current standardized social network survey method to ensure the reliability of the questionnaire; on the other hand, regarding the validity of the questionnaire, this book invited engineer Zhang to conduct visual inspection and preliminary screening. Zhang has been working in financial services for a long time and has moved to another department for personal reasons, but he is familiar with most of his colleagues and their formal working relationships and informal personal relationships. Through screening, it was found that the quality of 28 questionnaires was high and no important person was omitted.

## (4) Construction of Task Conflict Network

This book uses UCINET software to build a financial services task conflict network, which can intuitively describe the structure of the team's internal task conflict network.

1) Task conflict matrix. It can be seen from Table 3-3 that the financial services task conflict matrix is a square matrix, and the rows and columns are all from the "actors" of a set of actors, which is a 1-module network; the number represents the "relationship" between various actors. For example, $a_{\text{Member 1,Member 2}} = 1$ indicates that Member 1 and Member 2 will have task conflicts, where Member 1 is active and Member 2 is passive. In the community diagram, it indicates that a directional arrow starting from Member 1 points to Member 2; $a_{\text{Member 2,Member 22}} = 0$ means that member 2 and member 22 will not have task conflicts, and there is no connection between these two nodes in the community graph.

2) Task conflict community diagram. The community map is mainly composed of points and lines. Points represent actors, that is, 28 members of financial services; lines represent relationships between members. It can be seen from Figure 3-2 that the community graph of financial service task conflict is a "binary directed graph."

## (5) The Construction of a Relationship Conflict Network

1) Relationship conflict matrix. It can be seen from Table 3-4 that the financial service relationship conflict matrix is a square matrix, which is a 1-module network; the number represents the "relationship" between various actors. For example, $a_{\text{Member 1,Member 2}} = 0$ means that there is no relationship conflict between Member 1 and Member 2. In the community diagram, it means that there is no connection between these two nodes; $a_{\text{Member 1,Member 3}} = 1$ indicates that member 1 and member 3 have relationship conflicts and such relationship conflicts are perceived by member 1, that is, member 1 thinks that the relationship between member 1 and member 3 is tense and there is friction. In the community diagram, it indicates that a directional arrow starting from member 1 points to member 3.

2) Relationship conflict community diagram. The financial service relationship conflict community graph (Figure 3-3) is also a "binary directed graph." It can be seen from the community diagram of the two types of conflicts that in financial service innovation teams, task conflicts are more complex and involve more members than relationship conflicts.

## Table 3-3 Financial services task conflict matrix

| M | M 1 | M 2 | M 3 | M 4 | M 5 | M 6 | M 7 | M 8 | M 9 | M 10 | M 11 | M 12 | M 13 | M 14 | M 15 | M 16 | M 17 | M 18 | M 19 | M 20 | M 21 | M 22 | M 23 | M 24 | M 25 | M 26 | M 27 | M 28 |
|---|---|---|---|---|---|---|---|---|---|---|---|---|---|---|---|---|---|---|---|---|---|---|---|---|---|---|---|---|
| M 1 |   | 1 | 1 | 1 | 1 | 1 | 1 | 1 | 1 | 1 | 1 | 1 | 1 | 1 | 1 | 1 | 1 | 1 | 1 | 1 | 1 | 1 | 1 | 1 | 1 | 1 | 1 | 1 |
| M 2 | 1 |   | 1 | 1 | 1 | 1 | 1 | 1 | 1 | 1 | 1 | 1 | 1 | 1 | 1 | 1 | 1 | 1 | 1 | 1 | 1 | 0 | 0 | 0 | 0 | 0 | 0 | 0 |
| M 3 | 1 | 1 |   | 1 | 1 | 1 | 1 | 1 | 0 | 0 | 1 | 0 | 1 | 0 | 0 | 0 | 0 | 0 | 0 | 1 | 0 | 0 | 0 | 0 | 0 | 0 | 0 | 0 |
| M 4 | 1 | 1 | 1 |   | 1 | 1 | 1 | 0 | 0 | 1 | 1 | 1 | 1 | 1 | 1 | 1 | 0 | 1 | 0 | 1 | 0 | 0 | 1 | 1 | 0 | 0 | 0 | 0 |
| M 5 | 1 | 1 | 1 | 1 |   | 1 | 1 | 1 | 1 | 0 | 1 | 1 | 1 | 1 | 1 | 1 | 1 | 1 | 1 | 1 | 1 | 1 | 1 | 1 | 1 | 1 | 1 | 1 |
| M 6 | 1 | 1 | 1 | 1 | 1 |   | 1 | 1 | 0 | 1 | 1 | 1 | 1 | 1 | 1 | 1 | 1 | 1 | 1 | 1 | 1 | 1 | 1 | 1 | 1 | 1 | 0 | 0 |
| M 7 | 1 | 1 | 1 | 1 | 1 | 1 |   | 1 | 1 | 1 | 1 | 1 | 1 | 1 | 1 | 1 | 1 | 1 | 1 | 1 | 1 | 1 | 1 | 1 | 1 | 1 | 1 | 1 |
| M 8 | 1 | 1 | 1 | 1 | 1 | 1 | 1 |   | 1 | 1 | 1 | 1 | 1 | 1 | 0 | 0 | 0 | 0 | 0 | 1 | 0 | 0 | 1 | 0 | 0 | 0 | 0 | 0 |
| M 9 | 1 | 1 | 1 | 1 | 1 | 1 | 1 | 1 |   | 1 | 1 | 1 | 1 | 1 | 0 | 0 | 0 | 0 | 1 | 0 | 0 | 0 | 0 | 0 | 0 | 0 | 0 | 1 |
| M 10 | 1 | 1 | 1 | 1 | 1 | 1 | 1 | 1 | 1 |   | 1 | 1 | 1 | 1 | 0 | 1 | 0 | 1 | 0 | 0 | 1 | 0 | 1 | 0 | 0 | 0 | 0 | 0 |
| M 11 | 1 | 0 | 1 | 1 | 1 | 1 | 1 | 1 | 0 | 1 |   | 1 | 0 | 1 | 0 | 1 | 1 | 1 | 1 | 1 | 1 | 0 | 0 | 1 | 1 | 0 | 1 | 1 |
| M 12 | 1 | 0 | 0 | 1 | 1 | 0 | 1 | 0 | 1 | 0 | 1 |   | 1 | 1 | 1 | 1 | 0 | 1 | 1 | 1 | 1 | 0 | 1 | 0 | 0 | 0 | 0 | 0 |
| M 13 | 1 | 1 | 1 | 1 | 1 | 1 | 1 | 0 | 1 | 0 | 0 | 1 |   | 1 | 0 | 0 | 0 | 0 | 0 | 0 | 0 | 0 | 0 | 0 | 0 | 0 | 0 | 0 |
| M 14 | 1 | 1 | 1 | 1 | 1 | 1 | 1 | 0 | 1 | 1 | 1 | 1 | 1 |   | 0 | 0 | 0 | 0 | 0 | 0 | 0 | 0 | 0 | 0 | 0 | 0 | 0 | 0 |
| M 15 | 1 | 1 | 0 | 1 | 1 | 1 | 1 | 0 | 0 | 0 | 0 | 1 | 0 | 0 |   | 0 | 0 | 0 | 0 | 0 | 0 | 0 | 0 | 0 | 0 | 0 | 0 | 0 |
| M 16 | 1 | 1 | 0 | 1 | 1 | 1 | 1 | 1 | 0 | 1 | 1 | 1 | 0 | 0 | 0 |   | 0 | 1 | 0 | 0 | 0 | 0 | 0 | 0 | 0 | 0 | 0 | 0 |
| M 17 | 1 | 0 | 0 | 1 | 1 | 1 | 1 | 0 | 0 | 0 | 1 | 0 | 0 | 0 | 0 | 0 |   | 1 | 1 | 0 | 0 | 0 | 0 | 0 | 0 | 0 | 0 | 0 |
| M 18 | 1 | 0 | 0 | 1 | 1 | 1 | 1 | 0 | 0 | 1 | 1 | 1 | 0 | 0 | 0 | 0 | 1 |   | 1 | 0 | 0 | 0 | 0 | 0 | 0 | 0 | 0 | 0 |
| M 19 | 1 | 0 | 1 | 1 | 1 | 1 | 1 | 0 | 1 | 0 | 1 | 1 | 0 | 0 | 0 | 0 | 1 | 0 |   | 1 | 0 | 0 | 0 | 0 | 0 | 0 | 0 | 0 |
| M 20 | 1 | 0 | 1 | 0 | 1 | 1 | 1 | 0 | 0 | 0 | 1 | 1 | 0 | 0 | 0 | 0 | 0 | 0 | 1 |   | 1 | 0 | 1 | 0 | 0 | 0 | 1 | 1 |
| M 21 | 1 | 0 | 0 | 0 | 1 | 1 | 1 | 0 | 0 | 0 | 0 | 1 | 0 | 0 | 0 | 0 | 0 | 0 | 1 | 1 |   | 0 | 1 | 1 | 0 | 0 | 1 | 1 |
| M 22 | 1 | 0 | 0 | 0 | 1 | 1 | 1 | 0 | 0 | 1 | 1 | 0 | 0 | 0 | 0 | 0 | 0 | 0 | 0 | 1 | 1 |   | 1 | 1 | 0 | 0 | 1 | 1 |
| M 23 | 1 | 0 | 0 | 0 | 1 | 1 | 1 | 0 | 1 | 0 | 1 | 0 | 0 | 0 | 0 | 0 | 0 | 0 | 0 | 1 | 1 | 1 |   | 1 | 0 | 0 | 1 | 1 |
| M 24 | 1 | 0 | 0 | 0 | 1 | 1 | 1 | 0 | 0 | 0 | 1 | 0 | 0 | 0 | 0 | 0 | 0 | 0 | 0 | 1 | 1 | 1 | 1 |   | 1 | 0 | 1 | 1 |
| M 25 | 1 | 0 | 1 | 0 | 1 | 1 | 1 | 0 | 0 | 0 | 1 | 0 | 0 | 0 | 0 | 0 | 0 | 0 | 0 | 1 | 1 | 1 | 1 | 1 |   | 1 | 1 | 1 |
| M 26 | 1 | 0 | 0 | 0 | 1 | 1 | 1 | 0 | 0 | 0 | 1 | 0 | 0 | 0 | 0 | 0 | 0 | 0 | 0 | 1 | 1 | 1 | 1 | 1 | 1 |   | 1 | 1 |
| M 27 | 1 | 0 | 0 | 0 | 1 | 1 | 1 | 0 | 0 | 0 | 1 | 0 | 0 | 0 | 0 | 0 | 0 | 0 | 0 | 1 | 1 | 1 | 1 | 1 | 1 | 1 |   | 1 |
| M 28 | 1 | 0 | 0 | 0 | 1 | 0 | 1 | 0 | 1 | 0 | 1 | 0 | 0 | 0 | 0 | 0 | 0 | 0 | 0 | 1 | 1 | 1 | 1 | 1 | 1 | 1 | 1 |   |

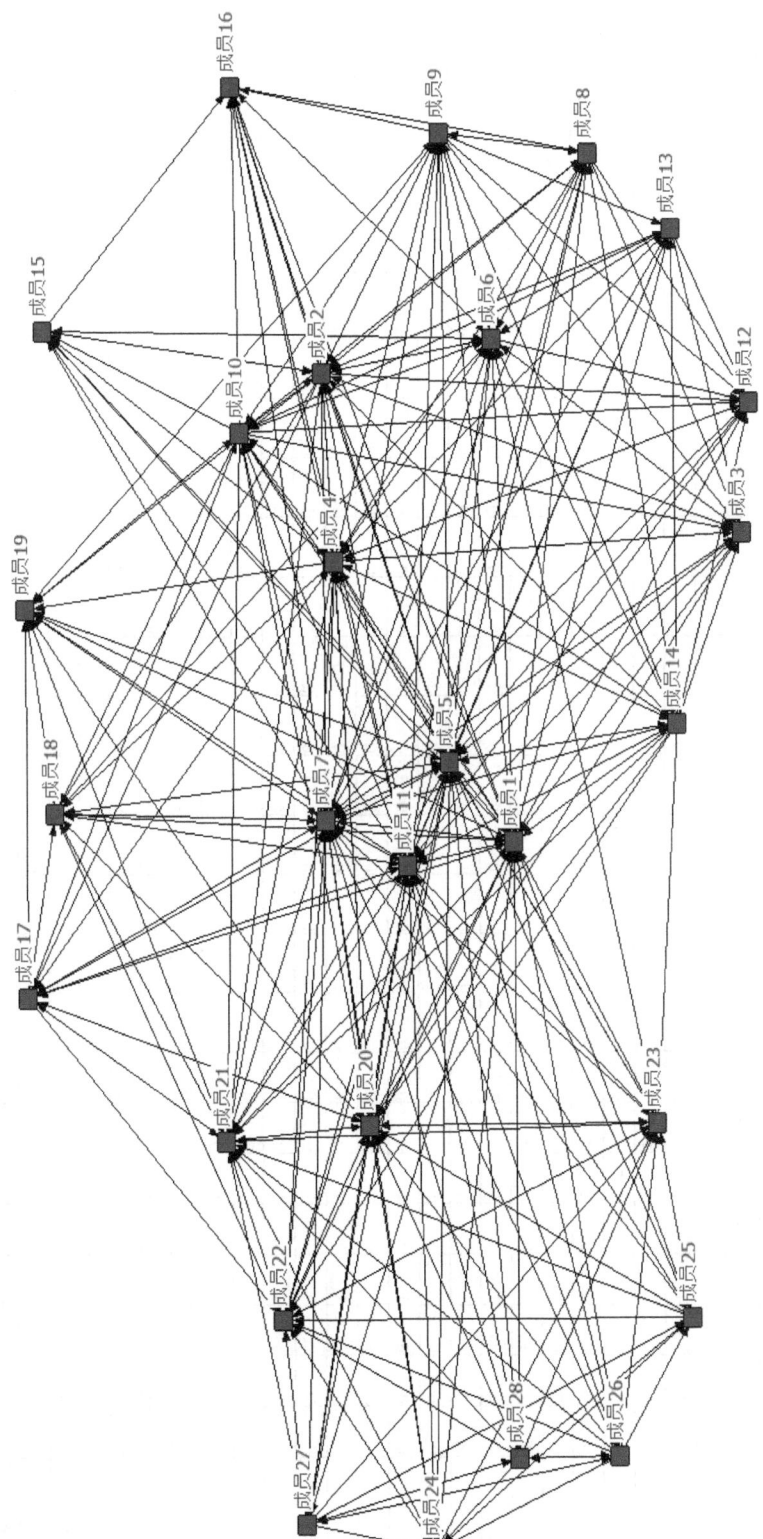

**Figure 3-2 Community chart of financial service task conflict**

**Table 3-4 Conflict matrix of financial service relationship**

| M | M1 | M2 | M3 | M4 | M5 | M6 | M7 | Ms8 | M9 | M10 | M11 | M12 | M13 | M14 | M15 | M16 | M17 | M18 | M19 | M20 | M21 | M22 | M23 | M24 | M25 | M26 | M27 | M28 |
|---|----|----|----|----|----|----|----|-----|----|-----|-----|-----|-----|-----|-----|-----|-----|-----|-----|-----|-----|-----|-----|-----|-----|-----|-----|-----|
| M1 |  | 0 | 1 | 0 | 0 | 0 | 1 | 0 | 1 | 1 | 0 | 0 | 1 | 1 | 0 | 0 | 0 | 0 | 0 | 0 | 0 | 0 | 0 | 0 | 0 | 0 | 0 | 0 |
| M2 | 0 |  | 0 | 1 | 1 | 1 | 1 | 0 | 0 | 0 | 0 | 0 | 0 | 0 | 0 | 1 | 0 | 0 | 0 | 1 | 0 | 0 | 0 | 0 | 0 | 0 | 0 | 0 |
| M3 | 1 | 0 |  | 1 | 1 | 1 | 1 | 0 | 0 | 0 | 1 | 0 | 0 | 0 | 0 | 0 | 0 | 0 | 1 | 1 | 0 | 0 | 0 | 0 | 0 | 0 | 0 | 0 |
| M4 | 0 | 1 | 1 |  | 1 | 1 | 1 | 0 | 0 | 0 | 0 | 0 | 0 | 0 | 0 | 0 | 1 | 1 | 0 | 1 | 0 | 1 | 1 | 1 | 0 | 0 | 0 | 0 |
| M5 | 0 | 1 | 0 | 1 |  | 1 | 1 | 0 | 0 | 0 | 1 | 0 | 0 | 0 | 0 | 0 | 1 | 0 | 1 | 0 | 1 | 1 | 1 | 0 | 0 | 0 | 0 | 0 |
| M6 | 0 | 1 | 1 | 1 | 1 |  | 1 | 1 | 0 | 0 | 1 | 1 | 0 | 0 | 0 | 0 | 0 | 0 | 0 | 1 | 0 | 0 | 1 | 0 | 0 | 0 | 1 | 1 |
| M7 | 1 | 1 | 1 | 1 | 1 | 1 |  | 1 | 1 | 1 | 1 | 1 | 1 | 1 | 0 | 1 | 0 | 1 | 1 | 1 | 1 | 1 | 1 | 1 | 1 | 1 | 1 | 1 |
| M8 | 0 | 0 | 0 | 1 | 1 | 1 | 1 |  | 1 | 1 | 0 | 0 | 0 | 0 | 0 | 0 | 0 | 0 | 0 | 0 | 0 | 0 | 0 | 0 | 0 | 0 | 0 | 0 |
| M9 | 0 | 0 | 0 | 0 | 0 | 0 | 1 | 0 |  | 0 | 1 | 1 | 0 | 0 | 1 | 0 | 0 | 0 | 0 | 0 | 0 | 0 | 0 | 0 | 0 | 0 | 0 | 0 |
| M10 | 0 | 0 | 0 | 0 | 0 | 1 | 1 | 0 | 0 |  | 0 | 0 | 0 | 0 | 0 | 0 | 1 | 1 | 1 | 1 | 1 | 0 | 0 | 0 | 0 | 0 | 1 | 0 |
| M11 | 0 | 0 | 1 | 0 | 1 | 0 | 1 | 1 | 1 | 0 |  | 0 | 0 | 0 | 0 | 0 | 1 | 0 | 1 | 1 | 0 | 0 | 0 | 0 | 0 | 0 | 0 | 0 |
| M12 | 0 | 0 | 0 | 1 | 1 | 0 | 1 | 0 | 1 | 1 | 0 |  | 0 | 0 | 0 | 0 | 0 | 0 | 1 | 1 | 1 | 0 | 0 | 0 | 0 | 0 | 0 | 0 |
| M13 | 0 | 1 | 0 | 1 | 1 | 1 | 1 | 1 | 1 | 0 | 1 | 0 |  | 1 | 0 | 1 | 1 | 1 | 0 | 0 | 1 | 1 | 1 | 0 | 0 | 0 | 0 | 0 |
| M14 | 0 | 0 | 0 | 0 | 0 | 0 | 1 | 0 | 0 | 0 | 0 | 0 | 1 |  | 0 | 0 | 0 | 0 | 0 | 0 | 0 | 0 | 0 | 0 | 0 | 0 | 0 | 0 |
| M15 | 0 | 0 | 0 | 0 | 0 | 0 | 1 | 0 | 0 | 0 | 0 | 0 | 0 | 0 |  | 1 | 0 | 1 | 1 | 0 | 1 | 1 | 0 | 0 | 0 | 0 | 0 | 0 |
| M16 | 0 | 1 | 0 | 1 | 1 | 0 | 1 | 0 | 0 | 0 | 0 | 0 | 0 | 0 | 0 |  | 0 | 0 | 1 | 1 | 1 | 0 | 0 | 0 | 0 | 0 | 0 | 0 |
| M17 | 0 | 0 | 0 | 1 | 1 | 0 | 1 | 0 | 0 | 0 | 0 | 0 | 0 | 0 | 0 | 0 |  | 1 | 1 | 0 | 1 | 0 | 0 | 0 | 0 | 0 | 0 | 0 |
| M18 | 0 | 0 | 0 | 0 | 1 | 0 | 1 | 0 | 0 | 0 | 0 | 0 | 0 | 0 | 0 | 0 | 1 |  | 0 | 0 | 1 | 0 | 0 | 0 | 0 | 0 | 0 | 0 |
| M19 | 0 | 0 | 0 | 0 | 0 | 0 | 1 | 0 | 0 | 0 | 0 | 0 | 0 | 0 | 0 | 0 | 0 | 0 |  | 0 | 0 | 0 | 0 | 0 | 0 | 0 | 0 | 0 |
| M20 | 0 | 0 | 1 | 0 | 1 | 0 | 1 | 0 | 0 | 0 | 0 | 0 | 0 | 0 | 0 | 0 | 1 | 0 | 0 |  | 0 | 0 | 0 | 0 | 0 | 0 | 1 | 1 |
| M21 | 0 | 0 | 0 | 0 | 1 | 1 | 1 | 0 | 0 | 0 | 0 | 0 | 0 | 0 | 0 | 0 | 1 | 0 | 0 | 1 |  | 0 | 0 | 1 | 0 | 0 | 0 | 1 |
| M22 | 0 | 0 | 0 | 0 | 0 | 0 | 1 | 0 | 0 | 0 | 0 | 0 | 0 | 0 | 0 | 0 | 0 | 0 | 0 | 0 | 0 |  | 0 | 0 | 0 | 0 | 0 | 1 |
| M23 | 0 | 0 | 0 | 0 | 1 | 1 | 1 | 0 | 0 | 0 | 0 | 0 | 0 | 0 | 0 | 0 | 0 | 0 | 0 | 0 | 0 | 0 |  | 1 | 0 | 0 | 1 | 1 |
| M24 | 0 | 0 | 0 | 0 | 0 | 0 | 1 | 0 | 0 | 0 | 0 | 0 | 0 | 0 | 0 | 0 | 0 | 0 | 0 | 1 | 0 | 0 | 0 |  | 1 | 0 | 1 | 1 |
| M25 | 0 | 0 | 0 | 0 | 1 | 1 | 1 | 0 | 0 | 0 | 0 | 0 | 0 | 0 | 0 | 0 | 0 | 0 | 0 | 0 | 1 | 1 | 1 | 1 |  | 1 | 1 | 1 |
| M26 | 0 | 0 | 0 | 0 | 1 | 0 | 1 | 0 | 0 | 0 | 0 | 0 | 0 | 0 | 0 | 0 | 0 | 0 | 0 | 0 | 0 | 1 | 0 | 0 | 1 |  | 1 | 1 |
| M27 | 0 | 0 | 0 | 0 | 1 | 1 | 1 | 0 | 0 | 0 | 0 | 0 | 0 | 0 | 0 | 0 | 0 | 0 | 0 | 0 | 0 | 0 | 1 | 1 | 1 | 1 |  | 1 |
| M28 | 0 | 0 | 0 | 0 | 0 | 0 | 1 | 0 | 0 | 0 | 0 | 0 | 0 | 0 | 0 | 0 | 0 | 0 | 0 | 0 | 0 | 0 | 0 | 0 | 1 | 1 | 1 |  |

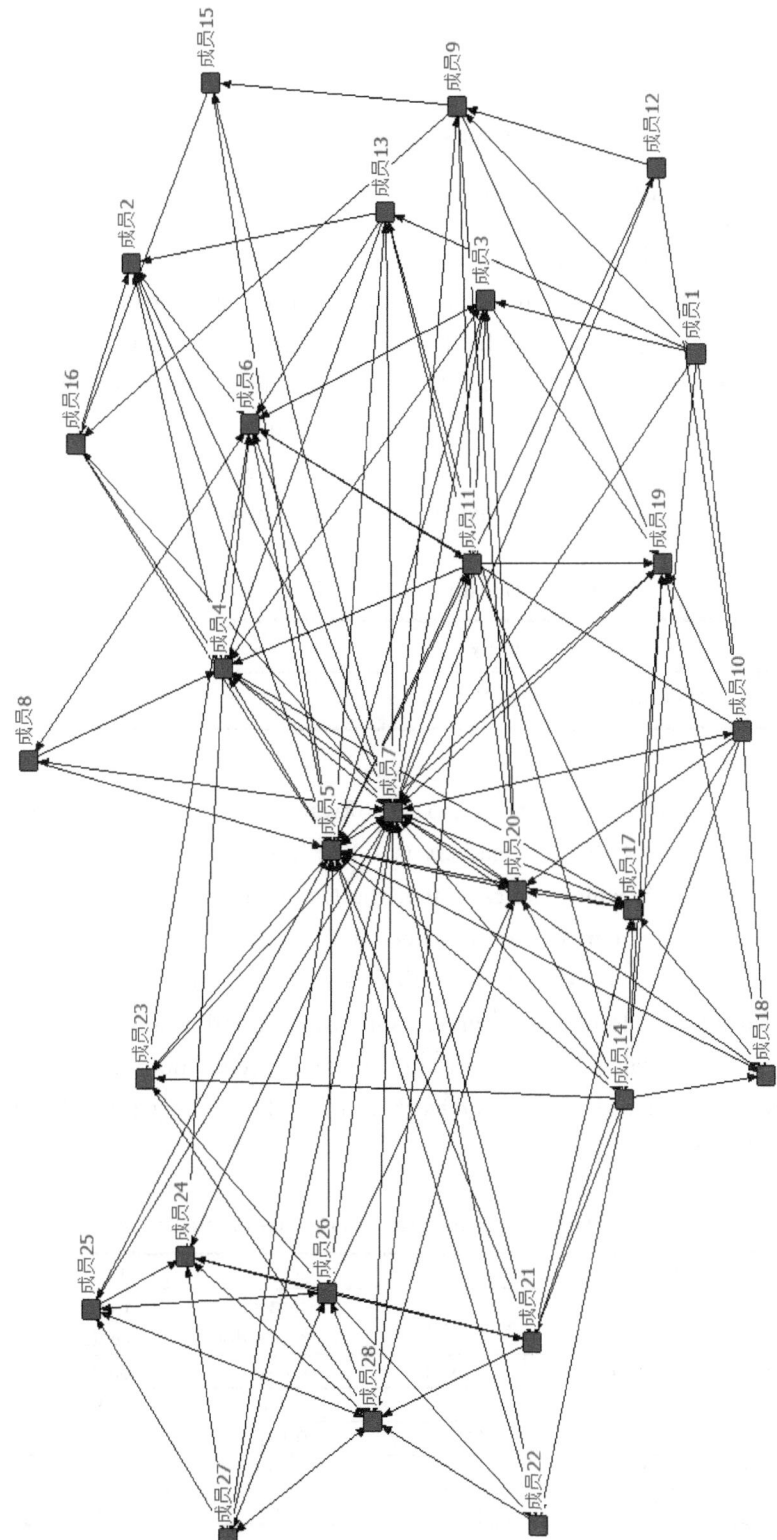

**Figure 3-3 Community chart of financial service relationship conflict**

### 3.1.3 Analysis of Conflict Network

### (1) Analysis of Task Conflict Network

1) Scale and density analysis. The scale refers to the number of all actors in the social network study, which is represented as the number of nodes in the community graph. The scale of the financial services task conflict network is 28. Density represents the strength and degree of interaction between members. The internal structure of a network can be close or distant. It can be seen from Table 3-5 that the density of financial service task conflict network is large, and there are many task conflicts and close connections among members.

**Table 3-5 Density of task conflict network**

| Type | Density | No. of Ties |
|------|---------|-------------|
| Task Conflict Network | 0.5093 | 385.0000 |

2) Distance analysis. According to the software analysis, the average distance between any two of the 28 members is 1.491; The cohesion index based on "distance" is 0.755, which indicates that the task conflict network has greater cohesion and more members are embedded in the task conflict network.

3) Centrality analysis. Centrality is the key content of social network analysis, which is often used to evaluate a person's importance and measure the position superiority or privilege of his position and social reputation. The centrality analysis results of task conflict network can be obtained by using UCINET software (Table 3-6, 3-7).

**Table 3-6 Centrality analysis results of the task conflict network**

| Index / Member | 1 Degree | 2 Closeness | 3 Betweenness centrality | 4 Eigenvector centrality |
|----------------|----------|-------------|--------------------------|--------------------------|
| Member 1 | 100.000 | 100.000 | 6.882 | 38.725 |
| Member 2 | 74.074 | 79.412 | 1.766 | 30.955 |
| Member 3 | 48.148 | 65.854 | 0.141 | 22.812 |
| Member 4 | 81.481 | 84.375 | 2.700 | 33.573 |
| Member 5 | 100.000 | 100.000 | 6.882 | 38.725 |

| Index / Member | 1 Degree | 2 Closeness | 3 Betweenness centrality | 4 Eigenvector centrality |
|---|---|---|---|---|
| Member 6 | 62.963 | 72.973 | 1.026 | 26.735 |
| Member 7 | 100.000 | 100.000 | 6.882 | 38.725 |
| Members 8 | 48.148 | 65.854 | 0.109 | 22.202 |
| Members 9 | 55.556 | 69.231 | 0.399 | 24.478 |
| Members 10 | 74.074 | 79.412 | 1.766 | 30.955 |
| Members 11 | 100.000 | 100.000 | 6.882 | 38.725 |
| Members 12 | 44.444 | 64.286 | 0.024 | 21.082 |
| Members 13 | 44.444 | 64.286 | 0.024 | 21.114 |
| Members 14 | 62.963 | 72.973 | 0.984 | 28.129 |
| Members 15 | 33.333 | 60.000 | 0.000 | 16.748 |
| Members 16 | 40.741 | 62.791 | 0.063 | 19.245 |
| Members 17 | 44.444 | 64.286 | 0.089 | 21.455 |
| Members 18 | 48.148 | 65.854 | 0.246 | 22.885 |
| Members 19 | 44.444 | 64.286 | 0.127 | 21.430 |
| Members 20 | 74.074 | 79.412 | 2.310 | 30.616 |
| Members 21 | 70.370 | 77.143 | 1.818 | 29.396 |
| Members 22 | 59.259 | 71.053 | 0.885 | 24.938 |
| Members 23 | 55.556 | 69.231 | 0.731 | 23.996 |
| Members 24 | 44.444 | 64.286 | 0.000 | 19.266 |
| Members 25 | 44.444 | 64.286 | 0.000 | 19.266 |
| Members 26 | 44.444 | 64.286 | 0.000 | 19.266 |
| Members 27 | 44.444 | 64.286 | 0.000 | 19.266 |
| Members 28 | 44.444 | 64.286 | 0.000 | 19.266 |

Table 3-7 Descriptive statistics of the results of network centrality analysis of task conflicts

| Project | 1 Degree | 2 Closeness | 3 Betweenness centrality | 4 Eigenvector centrality |
|---|---|---|---|---|
| mean value | 60.317 | 73.362 | 1.526 | 25.856 |
| standard deviation | 20.088 | 12.427 | 2.314 | 6.763 |
| the sum | 1688.889 | 2054.136 | 42.735 | 723.973 |
| variance | 403.544 | 154.440 | 5.357 | 45.744 |
| minimum value | 33.333 | 60.000 | 0.000 | 16.748 |
| Maximum | 100.000 | 100.000 | 6.882 | 38.725 |

It can be seen from the centrality index that the centrality of members 1, 5, 7 and 11 is 100, which indicates that these four members are at the center of the task conflict network, and they are the core members who have task conflicts with other members.

It can be seen from the list of members that member 1 is the leader of the financial services team, and members 5, 7 and 11 are outstanding members of the team, of which member 5 is the assistant director and member 7 is the director. They have been in the team for a long time and have rich experience; member 11 has been in the team for less than five years but has the most outstanding working ability, and often assists other members to complete their tasks. The degree centrality of member 15 is the lowest. According to the list the tenure of member 15 is less than three years, and his work efficiency is usually low, so it always follows the leadership's arrangement.

The closer an actor is to other actors, the easier it is to transmit information, and the more likely it is to be at the center of the network. Closeness centrality measures the closeness between one actor and other actors. If the distance between a node and other nodes is very short, it indicates that the node has a high closeness centrality. It can be seen from the value of closeness centrality that members 1, 5, 7 and 11 are in the center of the network and very close to other members.

The betweenness centrality measures the degree to which an individual is on the shortcut between any two other members, that is, the degree of resource control. It can be seen from the results of betweenness centrality that members 1, 5, 7 and 11 control most resources.

The calculation of eigenvectors focuses on the overall structure, rather than the partial structure, to find the most central actors. It can be seen from Table 3-6 that members 1, 5, 7 and 11 have a high centrality and are the core figures in the task conflict network. They also pose a high conflict risk to the team.

4) Cohesive subgroup analysis. Step 1: analysis of components. Through the analysis of the components of the task conflict network, it is found that no matter whether the component is weak or strong, the data has only one component and is composed of all members. Therefore, it is necessary to symmetrize the matrix to obtain more detailed analysis results. Step 2: symmetrical analysis. The original matrix is symmetrized according to the reciprocity relationship. Step 3: faction

analysis. This book stipulates that one faction is composed of 8 members, therefore there are 7 factions. The composition of these factions is shown in Table 3-8.

Table 3-8 Faction analysis results of the task conflict network

| Factions | Member |
|----------|--------|
| 1 | 1, 5, 7, 11, 17, 18, 19, 20, 21 |
| 2 | 1, 5, 7, 11, 20, 21, 22, 24 |
| 3 | 1, 2, 4, 5, 6, 7, 13, 14 |
| 4 | 1, 2, 4, 6, 7, 8, 9, 10 |
| 5 | 1, 2, 4, 6, 7, 9, 10, 14 |
| 6 | 1, 4, 6, 7, 8, 9, 10, 11 |
| 7 | 1, 4, 6, 7, 9, 10, 11, 14 |

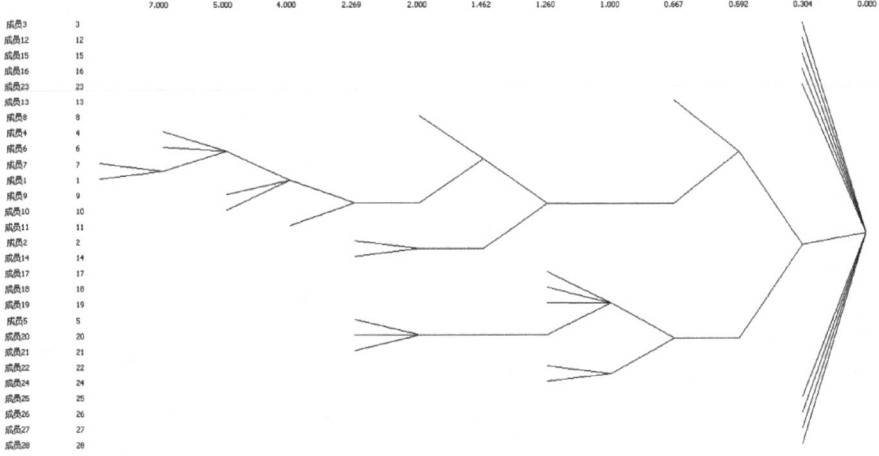

Figure 3-4 Faction analysis results of the task conflict network

According to the analysis in Table 3-8 and Figure 3-4, members 3, 12, 15, 16, 23, 25, 26, 27 and 28 do not belong to any faction, they are isolated; member 1 and member 7 are group sharing members, indicating that they are at the core of the task conflict network.

5) Structural holes analysis. According to the structural holes analysis results, the first column is the "effective size" of each member. The larger the value is, the

freer the member's action in the task conflict network is. However, because the individual network size of each member is different, combined with "efficiency" in the second column, we can see that the greater the efficiency is, the more efficient the member's action in the task conflict network is. It can be seen from Table 3-9 that member 1 and member 7 are the most efficient in their actions, followed by member 5, and member 12 is the least efficient.

From the result of "limit degree," the limit degree value of member 15 is the largest, indicating that the member is the most restricted in the task conflict network; it can be seen from the "level degree" that the level degree value of member 11 is the largest, indicating that this member is at the core of the network.

**Table 3-9 Structural holes analysis results of the task conflict network**

| Index \ Member | Effective scale | Efficiency | Limits | Grade |
|---|---|---|---|---|
| Member 1 | 14.741 | 0.546 | 0.146 | 0.044 |
| Member 2 | 7.530 | 0.377 | 0.202 | 0.052 |
| Member 3 | 2.405 | 0.185 | 0.294 | 0.026 |
| Member 4 | 9.346 | 0.425 | 0.183 | 0.051 |
| Member 5 | 14.712 | 0.545 | 0.147 | 0.049 |
| Member 6 | 6.047 | 0.356 | 0.229 | 0.041 |
| Member 7 | 14.741 | 0.546 | 0.146 | 0.044 |
| Member 8 | 2.273 | 0.175 | 0.294 | 0.025 |
| Member 9 | 3.700 | 0.247 | 0.259 | 0.034 |
| Member 10 | 7.065 | 0.353 | 0.204 | 0.052 |
| Member 11 | 14.167 | 0.525 | 0.151 | 0.059 |
| Member 12 | 1.647 | 0.137 | 0.321 | 0.027 |
| Member 13 | 1.868 | 0.156 | 0.319 | 0.026 |
| Member 14 | 5.074 | 0.298 | 0.235 | 0.046 |
| Member 15 | 1.267 | 0.141 | 0.409 | 0.019 |
| Member 16 | 1.639 | 0.149 | 0.343 | 0.023 |
| Member 17 | 2.477 | 0.206 | 0.311 | 0.018 |
| Member 18 | 2.833 | 0.218 | 0.297 | 0.034 |
| Member 19 | 2.659 | 0.222 | 0.307 | 0.012 |
| Member 20 | 8.273 | 0.414 | 0.202 | 0.055 |
| Member 21 | 7.267 | 0.382 | 0.213 | 0.056 |
| Member 22 | 4.958 | 0.310 | 0.253 | 0.058 |
| Member 23 | 4.659 | 0.311 | 0.264 | 0.048 |
| Member 24 | 2.675 | 0.223 | 0.315 | 0.026 |
| Member 25 | 2.250 | 0.188 | 0.324 | 0.034 |

| Member 26 | 2.471 | 0.206 | 0.321 | 0.033 |
| Member 27 | 2.556 | 0.213 | 0.319 | 0.031 |
| Member 28 | 2.556 | 0.213 | 0.319 | 0.031 |

## (2) Analysis of Relational Conflict Network

1) Scale and density analysis. The size of the relationship conflict network is also all 28 members. Table 3-10 shows that the density of the relationship conflict network is average.

### Table 3-10 Density of relationship conflict network

| Type | Density | No. of Ties |
| --- | --- | --- |
| Relationship Conflict Network | 0.2407 | 182.0000 |

2) Distance analysis. According to the analysis, the average distance between any two members in the relationship conflict network is 1.750, and the distance-based cohesion index is 0.603. Compared with the task conflict network, the average distance between any two members in the relationship conflict network is longer and the cohesion is lower.

3) Centrality analysis. The centrality analysis results of the relationship conflict network are shown in Tables 3-11 and 3-12.

### Table 3-11 Centrality analysis results of the relationship conflict network

| Index \ Member | 1 Degree | 2 Closeness | 3 Betweenness centrality | 4 Eigenvector centrality |
| --- | --- | --- | --- | --- |
| Member 1 | 22.222 | 56.250 | 0.577 | 16.618 |
| Member 2 | 22.222 | 56.250 | 0.142 | 19.429 |
| Member 3 | 29.630 | 58.696 | 0.620 | 25.465 |
| Member 4 | 44.444 | 64.286 | 2.840 | 32.451 |
| Member 5 | 81.481 | 84.375 | 17.223 | 49.971 |
| Member 6 | 37.037 | 61.364 | 1.726 | 27.729 |
| Member 7 | 100.000 | 100.000 | 31.160 | 58.569 |
| Member 8 | 14.815 | 54.000 | 0.000 | 15.531 |
| Member 9 | 29.630 | 58.696 | 1.550 | 19.478 |

| | | | | |
|---|---|---|---|---|
| Member 10 | 33.333 | 60.000 | 1.686 | 23.012 |
| Member 11 | 40.741 | 62.791 | 1.756 | 32.380 |
| Member 12 | 14.815 | 54.000 | 0.133 | 13.903 |
| Member 13 | 29.630 | 58.696 | 0.779 | 24.543 |
| Member 14 | 40.741 | 62.791 | 2.398 | 29.463 |
| Member 15 | 14.815 | 54.000 | 0.041 | 13.423 |
| Member 16 | 22.222 | 56.250 | 0.444 | 17.796 |
| Member 17 | 37.037 | 61.364 | 0.922 | 30.262 |
| Member 18 | 22.222 | 56.250 | 0.076 | 20.054 |
| Member 19 | 33.333 | 60.000 | 0.948 | 26.572 |
| Member 20 | 40.741 | 62.791 | 1.948 | 32.336 |
| Member 21 | 29.630 | 58.696 | 0.972 | 23.936 |
| Member 22 | 18.519 | 55.102 | 0.136 | 17.327 |
| Member 23 | 22.222 | 56.250 | 0.397 | 19.880 |
| Member 24 | 25.926 | 57.447 | 0.518 | 18.515 |
| Member 25 | 22.222 | 56.250 | 0.079 | 17.974 |
| Member 26 | 37.037 | 61.364 | 1.207 | 25.853 |
| Member 27 | 22.222 | 56.250 | 0.079 | 17.974 |
| Member 28 | 37.037 | 61.364 | 1.722 | 24.371 |

**Table 3-12 Descriptive statistics of the results of network centrality analysis of relationship conflicts**

| Project | 1 Degree | 2 Closeness | 3 Betweenness centrality | 4 Eigenvector centrality |
|---|---|---|---|---|
| mean value | 33.069 | 60.913 | 2.574 | 24.815 |
| standard deviation | 18.250 | 9.380 | 6.325 | 9.925 |
| the sum | 925.926 | 1705.569 | 72.080 | 694.815 |
| variance | 333.067 | 87.990 | 40.003 | 98.511 |
| minimum value | 14.815 | 54.000 | 0.000 | 13.423 |
| Maximum | 100.000 | 100.000 | 31.160 | 58.569 |

It can be seen from the degree centrality index that the degree centrality of member 5 and member 7 is 100 and 81.481 respectively, which indicates that these two members are in the center of the relationship conflict network. It can also be concluded that they are core members of the relationship conflict network because they have more relationship conflicts with other members. Member 5 and member 7 are also at the core of the task conflict network. On the one hand, they can cause more relationship conflicts due to more task conflicts; on the other hand, their interpersonal relationship with other members is indeed tense. According to the interviews with other members, member 5 is the assistant to the director, and member 7 is the director. They often discuss work with members. During this process, due to problems in mood, attitude and communication skills, members have a lot of complaints against them. The degree centrality of members 8, 12 and 15 is low, indicating that the three members have good interpersonal relationships with other members. It can also be seen from the closeness centrality, betweenness centrality and eigenvector centrality that member 5 and member 7 are in the center of the relationship network and very close to other members, which brings a high risk of relationship conflict to the team.

4) Cohesive subgroup analysis. Step 1: Analysis of components. By analyzing the components of the relationship conflict network, it is found that if the "weak component" is selected, the data has only one weak component, which is composed of all members; if the "strong component" is selected, the data includes a large strong component (consisting of 27 members, members 2, 3, 4, 5, 6, 7, 8, 9, 10, 11, 12, 13, 14, 15, 16, 17, 18, 19, 20, 21, 22, 23, 24, 25, 26, 27, 28) and a small strong component (consisting of member 1 alone) (Table 3-13). Step 2: symmetrical analysis. The original matrix is symmetrized according to the reciprocity relationship. Step 3: faction analysis. This book stipulates that one faction contains four members; therefore, seven factions can be obtained. The members of these factions are shown in Table 3-14.

**Table 3-13 The strong component analysis results of the relationship conflict network**

| Component | Number of nodes | Proportion |
| --- | --- | --- |
| 1 | 1 | 3.6% |
| 2 | 27 | 96.4% |

**Table 3-14 Faction analysis results of the relationship conflict network**

| Factions | Member |
| --- | --- |
| 1 | 4, 5, 7, 17 |
| 2 | 5, 7, 17, 18 |
| 3 | 5, 7, 17, 20 |

| 4 | 5, 7, 17, 21 |
|---|---|
| 5 | 2, 4, 5, 6, 7 |
| 6 | 3, 4, 6, 7 |
| 7 | 7, 25, 26, 27, 28 |

According to the analysis in Table 3-13 and Figure 3-5, members 1, 8, 9, 10, 11, 12, 13, 14, 15, 16, 19, 22, 23 and 24 do not belong to any faction. They are isolated members, which indicates that they have a good emotional relationship with other members and do not have relationship conflicts; member 7 is a group sharing member. He is at the core of the relationship conflict network, which indicates that he has a poor emotional relationship with other members and has many relationship conflicts with other members.

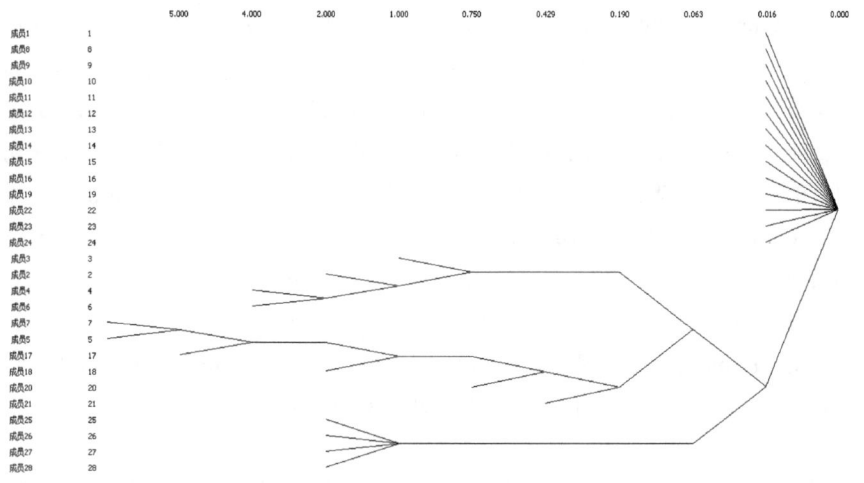

**Figure 3-5 Faction analysis results of the relationship conflict network**

5) Structural holes analysis. From the structural holes analysis results (Table 3-15), it can be seen that member 7 is the most efficient, followed by member 5, and member 8 is the least efficient; from the result of "Limits degree," it can be seen that the restriction degree value of Member 12 is the largest, indicating that the member is the most restricted in the relationship conflict network; it can be seen from the "grade degree" that the level degree value of member 9 is the largest, indicating that the member is at the core of the network.

**Table 3-15 Structural holes analysis results of the relationship conflict network**

| Member \ Index | Effective scale | Efficiency | Limits | Grade |
|---|---|---|---|---|
| Member 1 | 4.000 | 0.667 | 0.657 | 0.287 |
| Member 2 | 2.250 | 0.375 | 0.587 | 0.076 |
| Member 3 | 4.000 | 0.500 | 0.451 | 0.100 |
| Member 4 | 6.889 | 0.574 | 0.343 | 0.151 |
| Member 5 | 16.803 | 0.764 | 0.208 | 0.224 |
| Member 6 | 5.882 | 0.588 | 0.380 | 0.152 |
| Member 7 | 22.085 | 0.818 | 0.132 | 0.066 |
| Member 8 | 1.000 | 0.250 | 0.814 | 0.030 |
| Member 9 | 5.389 | 0.674 | 0.567 | 0.398 |
| Member 10 | 5.850 | 0.650 | 0.509 | 0.354 |
| Member 11 | 5.714 | 0.519 | 0.373 | 0.135 |
| Member 12 | 2.200 | 0.550 | 0.910 | 0.326 |
| Member 13 | 3.850 | 0.481 | 0.463 | 0.111 |
| Member 14 | 6.731 | 0.612 | 0.392 | 0.224 |
| Member 15 | 1.800 | 0.450 | 0.854 | 0.143 |
| Member 16 | 2.714 | 0.452 | 0.623 | 0.131 |
| Member 17 | 5.375 | 0.538 | 0.376 | 0.106 |
| Member 18 | 2.444 | 0.407 | 0.592 | 0.085 |
| Member 19 | 4.727 | 0.525 | 0.450 | 0.157 |
| Member 20 | 6.567 | 0.597 | 0.377 | 0.174 |
| Member 21 | 4.545 | 0.568 | 0.482 | 0.162 |
| Member 22 | 2.429 | 0.486 | 0.688 | 0.130 |
| Member 23 | 3.125 | 0.521 | 0.605 | 0.152 |
| Member 24 | 2.944 | 0.421 | 0.548 | 0.132 |
| Member 25 | 2.100 | 0.350 | 0.585 | 0.066 |
| Member 26 | 5.357 | 0.536 | 0.403 | 0.139 |
| Member 27 | 2.100 | 0.350 | 0.585 | 0.066 |
| Member 28 | 6.167 | 0.617 | 0.419 | 0.209 |

So far, this book has constructed the task conflict network and relationship conflict network within the financial service innovation team through the social network analysis method, and analyzed the structure of the two types of conflict networks from six aspects: scale, density, distance, centrality, cohesive subgroups and structural holes, so as to grasp the conflict situation of the team from a macro perspective.

### 3.1.4 Implementation Steps of Team Conflict Network

According to the relevant contents and methods of social network analysis, this book has achieved a relatively macro description of the internal conflict network of the financial service innovation team. It vividly revealed the complex and diverse conflict relationships within the innovation team, and tried to fill the gap between the conflict theory and the social network theory. In order to achieve a macro description of innovation team conflict in a wide range, this book proposes the implementation steps of using social networks to analyze team conflict networks (Figure 3-6).

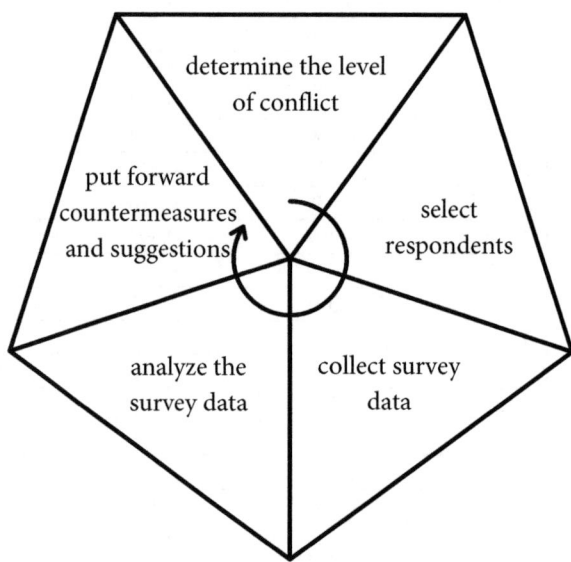

**Figure 3-6 Implementation steps of social network analysis team conflict network**

It can be seen from Figure 3-6 that to use the social network theory to analyze the conflict network within a team, five steps are needed: determining the level of conflict – selecting respondents – collecting survey data – analyzing survey data – putting forward countermeasures and suggestions.

Step 1: Determine the level of conflict. It is necessary to evaluate the level of conflict within the team before building a conflict network. If the level of conflict perceived by members is very low, it indicates that the level of conflict within the team is not serious, and most members may not be involved in the conflict network. This type of conflict network has more isolated points and fewer connections between nodes, which has little effect on analyzing the conflict relationship between members. Determining the team conflict level is mainly to let members evaluate the perceived conflict level. The scale developed by Jehn and Amason is more mature and widely used.

Step 2: Select respondents. Generally speaking, there are two research orientations of social network analysis: one is to focus on the individual network, and the other is to focus on all actors in the whole social network. To describe the conflict relationship between members of the innovation team from a macro perspective, this book believes that the second approach is more appropriate since taking all members of the team as the survey object can obtain a more accurate conflict interaction model. Therefore, in the phase of selecting respondents, all team members are included in the questionnaire.

Step 3: Collect survey data. Social network analysis can use different collection methods to obtain data, such as questionnaires, in-depth interviews, field observations, etc. When collecting data from the financial service innovation team, this book combines questionnaires and field observation to mutually verify the data through different channels. There is little relevant research on questionnaires relating to a conflict network. This book has translated the Team Conflict Network Questionnaire developed by Ching into Chinese, securing good reliability and validity. This book believes that in order to improve the reliability of data, multiple methods can be used comprehensively, such as using a questionnaire survey as the main method and in-depth interview and field observation as the auxiliary.

Step 4: Analyze the survey data. At present, social network analysis software is relatively mature, including UCINET, MultiNet, Negopy, etc., and can easily process data. General measurement indicators of the overall social network include scale, node degree, density, centrality, etc. In order to achieve the overall description of the conflict network of the financial service innovation team, this book mainly uses the conflict network matrix and community diagram. A detailed analysis from six aspects, including scale, density, distance, centrality, cohesive subgroups and structural holes, is made in order to more profoundly reveal the macro conflict relationship of the team.

Step 5: Put forward countermeasures and suggestions. Through the analysis of the fourth step, we can master the conflict relationship of innovation teams from a macro perspective, and researchers can propose corresponding management countermeasures according to the specific results of measurement indicators.

## 3.2 Analysis of Members' Influence on the Conflict Network

With the help of social network theory, we can achieve a macro description of the conflict relations among members of the innovation team, and can more vividly and intuitively reveal the complex and diverse conflict relations among members. In order to deepen the understanding of members' conflict relations, this chapter uses the complex system brittleness theory to analyze the influence of each member on the conflict network, so as to grasp members' conflict relations from the "individual and team" level.

### 3.2.1 Judgment Method of Influence Degree

In order to analyze the influence of each member on the conflict network from the perspective of "individual and team," this book mainly conducts research from two aspects: first, this book obtains team conflict network based on social network; Second, this book evaluates the level of brittleness source of complex system brittleness theory.

### (1) Grade of Brittleness Source

In the brittleness theory of complex systems, the brittleness source is defined as "the part (subsystem) of the complex system that first collapses due to the interference of the internal and external interferences," and the collapse of this part (subsystem) causes the collapse of other parts (subsystems). The grade of brittleness source is diverse among a complex system. Some brittleness sources' collapse will lead to the collapse of the whole system, while other brittleness sources' collapse will only lead to a minor collapse. According to the degree to which the brittleness source can cause the collapse of the whole complex system, it can be divided into 12 levels (Table 3-16).

## Table 3-16 Classification of brittle source

| Value of $M_m$ | Relationship between $a_m$, $b_m$, and $c_m$ | Grade | Explain |
|---|---|---|---|
| $M_m > 1$ $(a_m > b_m)$ | $a_m > b_m, c_m = 0$ | 1 | The system tends to collapse |
| | $a_m > b_m > c_m$ | 2 | The system tends to collapse |
| | $a_m > c_m \geq b_m$ | 3 | The system tends to collapse with a weak tendency |
| | $c_m \geq a_m > b_m$ | 4 | The system tends to collapse weakly |
| $M_m = 1$ $(a_m = b_m)$ | $a_m = b_m, c_m = 0$ | 5 | The tendency of the system to collapse is similar to that of the system far away from collapse |
| | $a_m = b_m > c_m$ | 6 | The tendency of the system to collapse is similar to that of opposites |
| | $a_m = b_m = c_m$ | 7 | The tendency of the system to collapse is similar to that of the opposite, but uncertain |
| | $c_m > a_m = b_m$ | 8 | The trend of system collapse is similar to the opposite trend, but it is weak due to the existence of uncertainty |
| $M_m < 1$ $(a_m < b_m)$ | $c_m > b_m > a_m$ | 9 | Due to the existence of uncertainty, the trend of the system away from collapse is weak |
| | $b_m > c_m > a_m$ | 10 | Weak tendency of the system away from collapse |
| | $b_m > a_m > c_m$ | 11 | The trend of system away from collapse is weak |
| | $a_m < b_m, c_m = 0$ | 12 | The system tends to stay away from collapse |

Note: $a_m$ is the brittleness identity, $b_m$ is the brittleness opposition, $c_m$ is the brittleness fluctuation, and $M_m$ is the tendency to collapse.

In Table 3-16, Grade 1 indicates that the brittleness source can cause the system to collapse to the largest extent, and Grade 12 indicates that the brittleness source can cause the system to collapse to the smallest extent. Among them, $a_m$ is brittleness identity, which means that when Subsystem $X$ collapses, the Subsystem $Y$ tends to collapse due to the brittleness connection between them; $b_m$ is brittleness opposition, which means that when the Subsystem $X$ collapses, the Subsystem $Y$ is far away from collapse due to the brittleness connection between them; $c_m$ is brittleness fluctuation, which means that when Subsystem $X$ collapses, Subsystem $Y$ tends to be the identity or opposite with time, and Subsystem $X$ and

Subsystem $Y$ are of brittleness fluctuation. In this way, subsystems related to Subsystem $X$ are divided into three categories.

Assume that the total number of subsystems which have brittleness connection with Subsystem $X$ is $l_m$. When Subsystem $X$ collapses, among $l_m$, there are $S_m$ systems that are of the same brittleness as Subsystem $X$, there are $Q_m$ systems that are of the opposite brittleness as Subsystem $X$, the remaining $P_m$ systems are of the brittleness fluctuation as Subsystem $X$, then the connection function of Subsystem $X$ is:

$$\mu_m = \frac{S_m}{l_m} + \frac{Q_m}{l_m}i + \frac{P_m}{l_m}j, (m = 1, 2, \cdots, l) \quad \text{Equation (3.1)}$$

$$S_m + Q_m + P_m = l_m, \quad a_m = \frac{S_m}{l_m}, \quad b_m = \frac{Q_m}{l_m}, \quad c_m = \frac{P_m}{l_m}, \quad i = -1, \quad j \in [-1, 1],$$

$a_m + b_m + c_m = 1$. Since $M_m$ is the tendency to collapse, then $M_m = \frac{a_m}{b_m}$; If

$M_m > 1$, it indicates that among $l_m$ subsystems, the number of subsystems tending to collapse, $S_m$, far exceeds the number of subsystems far away from collapse, $Q_m$.

## (2) Judgment Method

In this book, each member of the team is regarded as a subsystem. According to the analysis of grade of brittleness source, it can be seen that the grade of brittleness source of some team members is very small, that is, they have a great influence on the conflict network. Because of the complex task collaboration relationship or close emotional relationship in daily work, once they are embedded in the conflict network, the member can pass on the factors and risks of conflict through many ways, involving more members in the conflict network; However, some members have a high grade of brittleness source, that is, they have little influence on the conflict network. They have isolated working relationships, less work contact with other members, and infrequent informal emotional contact. Therefore, even if they are embedded in the conflict network, these members have few or no ways to spread conflict factors and risks, so it is impossible to involve other members in the conflict network.

From the observation at a certain point in time, it can be seen that there are either conflicts or no conflicts between members, and members can only judge the current conflict status during the data collection process. The influence of time evolution is one consideration for brittleness fluctuation. Since this book gives the conflict relationship between members at a certain time, the situation of brittleness fluctuation is not included, and only the conflict relationship between members is analyzed based on the brittleness identity and brittleness opposition.

This book provides the following methods to determine the impact of members on the conflict network.

Step 1: Draw the conflict matrix and conflict network community diagram.

To obtain the team conflict matrix and conflict network community diagram at the macro level, the first four steps in the social network analysis team conflict network implementation steps (Figure 3-6) need to be followed, that is, by determining the conflict level, selecting survey objects, collecting survey data and analyzing survey data, and then using social network analysis software to generate them.

Step 2: Determine the relationship function related to members.

Suppose that there are $n$ members in an innovation team. To calculate the impact of member A on the conflict network, we first need to determine the number of members with brittleness links to member $A$ according to the conflict matrix and the conflict network community diagram (the remaining $n-1$ members in the team either have conflict with member $A$ or do not have conflict with member $A$). If $s$ members conflict with member $A$, that is, they are of brittleness identity, then the members that do not have conflict with member $A$ and are of brittleness opposition are:

$$q = (n-1) - s \quad \text{Equation (3.2)}$$

Since this book shows the conflict relationship between members at a certain time point, and does not include the situation of brittle fluctuation, equation (3.1) becomes:

$$\mu_m' = \frac{s}{n-1} + \frac{q}{n-1}i + \frac{0}{n-1}j \quad \text{Equation (3.3)}$$

The formula represents the connection degree function related to member A. $i = -1$, $j \in [-1,1]$, $s + q = n-1$. $n-1$ represents the brittleness identity related to member $A$, $n-1$ represents the brittleness opposition related to member $A$, and $n-1$ represents the brittleness fluctuation related to member $A$ (its value is 0).

If $a = \dfrac{s}{n-1}$, $b = \dfrac{q}{n-1}$, $c = \dfrac{0}{n-1}$, $a$ indicates the brittleness identity related to member $A$, $b$ indicates the brittleness opposition related to member $A$, and $c$ indicates the brittleness fluctuation related to member $A$ (its value is 0), and $a + b = 1$.

The third step is to compare the value of $a$ and $b$ and obtain the results according to the classification of brittle source table.

The specific values of $a$ (brittleness identity) and $b$ (brittleness opposition) can be obtained through calculation, and the grade of member $A$ can be obtained according to the classification of brittle source table, that is, the degree of influence of member $A$ on the conflict network can be clarified.

## 3.2.2 Judgment of the Influence of Financial Service Team Members on the Conflict Network

### (1) Judgment of Members' Influence on the Task Conflict Network

Based on the above judgment methods, this book takes the financial service team as an example to judge the influence of members on the task conflict network. Suppose that member 1 is embedded in the task conflict network. Through the task conflict matrix (Table 3-3), it is found that there are 27 members who have work contact and task conflict with member 1, that is, these 27 members are likely to be embedded in the task conflict network because of member 1; there are 0 members who do not have task conflict with member 1. Therefore, by substituting formula (3-3), we conclude that $a = \dfrac{s}{n-1} = \dfrac{27}{27} = 1$, $b = \dfrac{q}{n-1} = \dfrac{0}{27} = 0$, $c = \dfrac{p}{n-1} = \dfrac{0}{27} = 0$, and $a_{M1} > b_{M1}, c_{M1} = 0$. It can be seen from the classification of brittle source table that the brittleness source grade of member 1 is 1, which means that member 1 has a great influence on the task conflict network.

Similarly, the brittle source grade of the remaining 27 members can be calculated (Table 3-17).

**Table 3-17 Judgement of financial service members' influence on the task conflict network**

| Member | Relationship between $a$, $b$, and $c$ | Brittleness source grade |
|--------|----------------------------------------|--------------------------|
| Member 1 | $a_{M1} = \dfrac{27}{27} = 1 > b_{M1} = \dfrac{0}{27} = 0, c_{M1} = 0$ | 1 |
| Member 2 | $a_{M2} = \dfrac{19}{27} = 0.704 > b_{M2} = \dfrac{8}{27} = 0.296, c_{M2} = 0$ | 1 |
| Member 3 | $a_{M3} = \dfrac{7}{27} = 0.259 < b_{M3} = \dfrac{20}{27} = 0.741, c_{M3} = 0$ | 12 |
| Member 4 | $a_{M4} = \dfrac{21}{27} = 0.778 > b_{M4} = \dfrac{6}{27} = 0.222, c_{M4} = 0$ | 1 |
| Member 5 | $a_{M5} = \dfrac{24}{27} = 0.889 > b_{M5} = \dfrac{3}{27} = 0.111, c_{M5} = 0$ | 1 |
| Member 6 | $a_{M6} = \dfrac{15}{27} = 0.556 > b_{M6} = \dfrac{12}{27} = 0.444, c_{M6} = 0$ | 1 |
| Member 7 | $a_{M7} = \dfrac{26}{27} = 0.963 > b_{M7} = \dfrac{1}{27} = 0.037, c_{M7} = 0$ | 1 |
| Member 8 | $a_{M8} = \dfrac{10}{27} = 0.370 < b_{M8} = \dfrac{17}{27} = 0.630, c_{M8} = 0$ | 12 |
| Member 9 | $a_{M9} = \dfrac{14}{27} = 0.519 > b_{M9} = \dfrac{13}{27} = 0.481, c_{M9} = 0$ | 1 |
| Member 10 | $a_{M10} = \dfrac{19}{27} = 0.704 > b_{M10} = \dfrac{8}{27} = 0.296, c_{M10} = 0$ | 1 |
| Member 11 | $a_{M11} = \dfrac{21}{27} = 0.778 > b_{M11} = \dfrac{6}{27} = 0.222, c_{M11} = 0$ | 1 |
| Member 12 | $a_{M12} = \dfrac{4}{27} = 0.148 < b_{M12} = \dfrac{23}{27} = 0.852, c_{M12} = 0$ | 12 |
| Member 13 | $a_{M13} = \dfrac{9}{27} = 0.333 < b_{M13} = \dfrac{18}{27} = 0.667, c_{M13} = 0$ | 12 |
| Member 14 | $a_{M14} = \dfrac{16}{27} = 0.593 > b_{M14} = \dfrac{11}{27} = 0.407, c_{M14} = 0$ | 1 |
| Member 15 | $a_{M15} = \dfrac{7}{27} = 0.259 < b_{M15} = \dfrac{20}{27} = 0.741, c_{M15} = 0$ | 12 |
| Member 16 | $a_{M16} = \dfrac{7}{27} = 0.259 < b_{M16} = \dfrac{20}{27} = 0.741, c_{M16} = 0$ | 12 |
| Member 17 | $a_{M17} = \dfrac{10}{27} = 0.370 < b_{M17} = \dfrac{17}{27} = 0.630, c_{M17} = 0$ | 12 |
| Member 18 | $a_{M18} = \dfrac{9}{27} = 0.333 < b_{M18} = \dfrac{18}{27} = 0.667, c_{M18} = 0$ | 12 |
| Member 19 | $a_{M19} = \dfrac{9}{27} = 0.333 < b_{M19} = \dfrac{18}{27} = 0.667, c_{M19} = 0$ | 12 |

| Member 20 | $a_{M20} = \dfrac{12}{27} = 0.444 < b_{M20} = \dfrac{15}{27} = 0.556, c_{M20} = 0$ | 12 |
|---|---|---|
| Member 21 | $a_{M21} = \dfrac{10}{27} = 0.370 < b_{M21} = \dfrac{17}{27} = 0.630, c_{M21} = 0$ | 12 |
| Member 22 | $a_{M22} = \dfrac{7}{27} = 0.259 < b_{M22} = \dfrac{20}{27} = 0.741, c_{M22} = 0$ | 12 |
| Member 23 | $a_{M23} = \dfrac{6}{27} = 0.222 < b_{M23} = \dfrac{21}{27} = 0.778, c_{M23} = 0$ | 12 |
| Member 24 | $a_{M24} = \dfrac{8}{27} = 0.296 < b_{M24} = \dfrac{19}{27} = 0.703, c_{M24} = 0$ | 12 |
| Member 25 | $a_{M25} = \dfrac{8}{27} = 0.296 < b_{M25} = \dfrac{19}{27} = 0.703, c_{M25} = 0$ | 12 |
| Member 26 | $a_{M26} = \dfrac{11}{27} = 0.407 < b_{M26} = \dfrac{16}{27} = 0.593, c_{M26} = 0$ | 12 |
| Member 27 | $a_{M27} = \dfrac{11}{27} = 0.407 < b_{M27} = \dfrac{16}{27} = 0.593, c_{M27} = 0$ | 12 |
| Member 28 | $a_{M28} = \dfrac{11}{27} = 0.407 < b_{M28} = \dfrac{16}{27} = 0.593, c_{M28} = 0$ | 12 |

It can be seen from Table 3-17 that, of the 28 members, 10 members (1, 2, 4, 5, 6, 7, 9, 10, 11, 14) have a grade of brittleness source of 1, indicating that once these members are embedded in the task conflict network, they are more likely to pull other members into the task conflict network because they have more complex task collaboration relationships with other members and they have more ways to broadcast task conflict factors and risks, which has a great impact on the task conflict network. The grade of brittleness source of the remaining 18 members is 12, which indicates that they have very little influence on the task conflict network. Even though they have been embedded in the task conflict network, they have fewer ways to transmit task conflict factors and risks, so they have less influence on the whole task conflict network.

## (2) Judgment of Members' Influence on the Relationship Conflict Network

Similar to the above analysis process, this book analyzes the influence of members on the relationship conflict network. Suppose that member 1 is embedded in the relationship conflict network. Since there are only six members who have emotional ties and relationship conflicts with him (Table 3-4), we conclude

$$a = \frac{s}{n-1} = \frac{6}{27} = 0.222 \ , \ b = \frac{q}{n-1} = \frac{21}{27} = 0.778 \ , \ c_m = \frac{0}{n-1} = \frac{0}{27} = 0 \ , \ \text{and} \ a_{M1} < b_{M1}, c_{M1} = 0 \ .$$

By checking the classification of brittle source table, it can be seen that the brittleness source grade of member 1 is 12, indicating that member 1 has very little influence on the relationship conflict network.

Similarly, the grade of brittleness source of other members can be calculated (Table 3-18).

Table 3-18 Judgement of the influence degree of financial service members on the relationship conflict network

| Member | Relationship between $a$, $b$, and $c$ | Brittleness source grade |
|---|---|---|
| Member 1 | $a_{M1} = \dfrac{6}{27} = 0.222 < b_{M1} = \dfrac{21}{27} = 0.778, c_{M1} = 0$ | 12 |
| Member 2 | $a_{M2} = \dfrac{4}{27} = 0.148 < b_{M2} = \dfrac{23}{27} = 0.852, c_{M2} = 0$ | 12 |
| Member 3 | $a_{M3} = \dfrac{7}{27} = 0.259 < b_{M3} = \dfrac{20}{27} = 0.741, c_{M3} = 0$ | 12 |
| Member 4 | $a_{M4} = \dfrac{8}{27} = 0.296 < b_{M4} = \dfrac{19}{27} = 0.704, c_{M4} = 0$ | 12 |
| Member 5 | $a_{M5} = \dfrac{12}{27} = 0.444 < b_{M5} = \dfrac{15}{27} = 0.556, c_{M5} = 0$ | 12 |
| Member 6 | $a_{M6} = \dfrac{8}{27} = 0.296 < b_{M6} = \dfrac{19}{27} = 0.704, c_{M6} = 0$ | 12 |
| Member 7 | $a_{M7} = \dfrac{26}{27} = 0.963 > b_{M7} = \dfrac{1}{27} = 0.037, c_{M7} = 0$ | 1 |
| Member 8 | $a_{M8} = \dfrac{4}{27} = 0.148 < b_{M8} = 23 = 0.852, c_{M8} = 0$ | 12 |
| Member 9 | $a_{M9} = \dfrac{6}{27} = 0.222 < b_{M9} = \dfrac{21}{27} = 0.778, c_{M9} = 0$ | 12 |
| Member 10 | $a_{M10} = \dfrac{7}{27} = 0.259 < b_{M10} = \dfrac{20}{27} = 0.741, c_{M10} = 0$ | 12 |
| Member 11 | $a_{M11} = \dfrac{8}{27} = 0.296 < b_{M11} = \dfrac{19}{27} = 0.704, c_{M11} = 0$ | 12 |
| Member 12 | $a_{M12} = \dfrac{4}{27} = 0.148 < b_{M12} = \dfrac{23}{27} = 0.852, c_{M12} = 0$ | 12 |
| Member 13 | $a_{M13} = \dfrac{7}{27} = 0.259 < b_{M13} = \dfrac{20}{27} = 0.741, c_{M13} = 0$ | 12 |
| Member 14 | $a_{M14} = \dfrac{10}{27} = 0.370 < b_{M14} = \dfrac{17}{27} = 0.630, c_{M14} = 0$ | 12 |
| Member 15 | $a_{M15} = \dfrac{3}{27} = 0.111 < b_{M15} = \dfrac{24}{27} = 0.889, c_{M15} = 0$ | 12 |

| Member 16 | $a_{M16} = \dfrac{4}{27} = 0.148 < b_{M16} = \dfrac{23}{27} = 0.852, c_{M16} = 0$ | 12 |
|---|---|---|
| Member 17 | $a_{M17} = \dfrac{7}{27} = 0.259 < b_{M17} = \dfrac{20}{27} = 0.741, c_{M17} = 0$ | 12 |
| Member 18 | $a_{M18} = \dfrac{4}{27} = 0.148 < b_{M18} = \dfrac{23}{27} = 0.852, c_{M18} = 0$ | 12 |
| Member 19 | $a_{M19} = \dfrac{2}{27} = 0.074 < b_{M19} = \dfrac{25}{27} = 0.926, c_{M19} = 0$ | 12 |
| Member 20 | $a_{M20} = \dfrac{5}{27} = 0.185 < b_{M20} = \dfrac{22}{27} = 0.815, c_{M20} = 0$ | 12 |
| Member 21 | $a_{M21} = \dfrac{5}{27} = 0.185 < b_{M21} = \dfrac{22}{27} = 0.815, c_{M21} = 0$ | 12 |
| Member 22 | $a_{M22} = \dfrac{3}{27} = 0.111 < b_{M22} = \dfrac{24}{27} = 0.889, c_{M22} = 0$ | 12 |
| Member 23 | $a_{M23} = \dfrac{3}{27} = 0.111 < b_{M23} = \dfrac{24}{27} = 0.889, c_{M23} = 0$ | 12 |
| Member 24 | $a_{M24} = \dfrac{2}{27} = 0.074 < b_{M24} = \dfrac{25}{27} = 0.926, c_{M24} = 0$ | 12 |
| Member 25 | $a_{M25} = \dfrac{6}{27} = 0.222 < b_{M25} = \dfrac{21}{27} = 0.778, c_{M25} = 0$ | 12 |
| Member 26 | $a_{M26} = \dfrac{10}{27} = 0.370 < b_{M26} = \dfrac{17}{27} = 0.630, c_{M26} = 0$ | 12 |
| Member 27 | $a_{M27} = \dfrac{6}{27} = 0.222 < b_{M27} = \dfrac{21}{27} = 0.778, c_{M27} = 0$ | 12 |
| Member 28 | $a_{M28} = \dfrac{5}{27} = 0.185 < b_{M28} = \dfrac{22}{27} = 0.815, c_{M28} = 0$ | 12 |

It can be seen from Table 3-18 that only one of the 28 members (member 7) has a brittleness source grade of 1, indicating that the member has the greatest influence on the relationship conflict network. Once the member is embedded in the relationship conflict network, because he has relatively complex interpersonal conflicts with other members, he is likely to pull other members into the relationship conflict network. Since relationship conflict always plays a negative role in team effectiveness, team leaders should pay attention to improving the communication skills of the member, and try to reduce the tense interpersonal relationship between him and other members, so as to effectively control the level of relationship conflict.

## 3.3 Analysis and Evaluation of the Relevance of Conflicts among

## Members

Through the above analysis, this book has realized the analysis of the conflict relationship between members from the "team-individual and team" level. As for the specific conflict correlation between members from the "individual and individual" level, it needs to be further analyzed using catastrophe theory. When judging the influence degree of members on the conflict network, this chapter has preliminarily analyzed three kinds of brittleness relationships that may exist among members: brittleness identity, brittleness opposition and brittleness fluctuation. Now we will make a specific analysis.

### 3.3.1 Evaluation Method of Membership Conflict Relevance

In order to realize the analysis and evaluation of the conflict relationship between members at the micro level, this book conducts research based on the relevant content of the brittleness relevance of complex systems. When a subsystem in a complex system collapses due to the interference of internal and external factors, it is worth discussing whether other subsystems will be affected and what kind of impact they will meet. The relationship between these subsystems can be analyzed by the brittleness correlation and brittle connection function between subsystems.

### (1) Brittleness Correlation

Suppose that there are three subsystems $X,Y,Z$ , $X=\{x_1,x_2,\cdots x_i\cdots,x_n\}$ , $1<i<n$; $Y=\{y_1,y_2,\cdots y_j\cdots,y_n\}$ , $Z=\{z_1,z_2,\cdots z_j\cdots,z_n\}$ , $1\le j\le n$.

The number of measurable states in the state vector set of Subsystem $Y$ and Subsystem $Z$ is $n$, and the change degree of these $n$ state vectors under the action of internal and external factors will play a key role in the normal operation of the entire subsystem.

If Subsystem $X$ collapses under the interference of internal and external factors, and at least one of the state vectors of the associated Subsystem $Y$, that is, $y_j(1<j<n)$ , changes due to the influence of brittleness correlation, then Subsystem $y_j$ is said to be of brittleness identity to Subsystem $X$; other

unaffected state vectors are of brittleness opposition to Subsystem $X$; as time changes, some state vectors tend to be identical or opposite, and these state vectors are of brittleness fluctuation to Subsystem $X$. The brittleness correlation between subsystems $Z$ and $X$, and is consistent with the analysis of Subsystem $Y$.

## (2) Brittle Connection Function

Assume that the brittleness weight coefficient vector, $\beta = \{\beta_1, \beta_2, \cdots \beta_j \cdots, \beta_n\}$, is respectively relative to each state vector of Subsystem $Y$, indicating the extent to which each state vector of Subsystem $Y$ collapses independently when the Subsystem $X$ collapses. When the brittleness of state vector $y_i$ is of brittleness identity to Subsystem $X$, the weight coefficient is 1; the weight coefficient of brittleness opposition is 0; the weight coefficient of brittleness fluctuation is between 0 and 1. The degree of transmission and amplification of brittleness between subsystems is related to the brittleness connection function between subsystems. The brittleness connection function can be measured by the brittleness identity, brittleness opposition and brittleness fluctuation between subsystem states.

According to the meaning of brittleness correlation and brittleness weight coefficient vector, it can be seen that:

1)  the brittleness identity of Subsystem $Y$ at Moment $t$ is $a = \sum_{j=1}^{k} \beta_j(t), 1 < k < n$. If no state vector is identical to Subsystem $X$, then $a = 0$;

2)  the brittleness opposition of Subsystem $Y$ at Moment $t$ is $b = \sum_{j=1}^{h} \beta_j(t), 1 < h < n$. If no state vector is opposite to Subsystem $X$, then $b = 0$;

3) the brittleness fluctuation of Subsystem $Y$ at Moment $t$ is $c = \sum_{j=1}^{n-k-h} \beta_j(t)$.

If no state vector fluctuates as Subsystem $X$, then $c = 0$;

The brittle connection function between Subsystem $X$ and Subsystem $Y$ is:

$$F = f(a,b,c) \quad \text{Equation (3.4)}$$

$a,b,c$ represent respectively the brittleness identity, brittleness opposition and brittleness fluctuation between the two subsystems at Time $t$.

## (3) Catastrophe Progression Method

On the basis of the catastrophe progression method, the cusp catastrophe model is used to evaluate the brittleness to explain that when a subsystem collapses under interference, the brittleness relationship between the non-collapsing subsystem and the collapsing subsystem is evaluated according to their degree of identity, degree of opposition and degree of fluctuation. In catastrophe theory, each kind of catastrophe is determined by a potential energy function. The control parameter is $u, v, w, t$ in the potential energy function, and the state variable is $x, y$; the equilibrium surface is the set of all points that satisfy that the first derivative (or two first partial derivatives) of the potential energy function is zero; the whole picture of a certain type of catastrophe process can be described by the corresponding equilibrium surface. Thom has proved that when the control variables are no more than four, there are at most seven types of catastrophe, namely fold catastrophe, cusp catastrophe, swallowtail catastrophe, elliptical umbilical catastrophe, hyperbolic umbilical catastrophe, butterfly catastrophe and parabolic umbilical catastrophe[104]. The potential function of cusp catastrophe is:

$$V(x) = x^4 + ux^2 + vx \quad \text{Equation (3.5)}$$

The specific steps of the catastrophe progression method are:

the first step is to build an indicator system. The evaluation indicators are grouped according to the evaluation purpose to obtain indicators that are easy to quantify. Generally, there are no more than four control variables of elementary catastrophe state variables, so the decomposition of indicators at each level generally does not exceed four. The phase space of cusp catastrophe potential function is three-dimensional, and its equilibrium surface M is:

$$4x^3 + 2ux + v = 0 \quad \text{Equation (3.6)}$$

The singular point set, namely a subset I of M, is:

$$12x^2 + 2u = 0 \quad \text{Equation (3.7)}$$

Eliminate $x$, the bifurcation equation $B$ is:

$$8u^3 + 27v^2 = 0 \quad \text{Equation (3.8)}$$

The bifurcation equation in decomposition form is:

$$\begin{cases} u = -6x^2 \\ v = 8x^3 \end{cases} \quad \text{Equation (3.9)}$$

Suppose $v$ is a conservative force of a certain quality state of the system, which keeps the system in its original quality state. When comparing $u$ with $v$, $v$ is the main aspect of a contradiction, which determines the original quality of the system and is a regular factor; When $u$ continues to develop and gradually becomes the main aspect of the contradiction, once the bifurcation set of $u,v$ is reached, a qualitative catastrophe occurs, and $u$ becomes a partial factor. $u$ divides M into abrupt and gradual catastrophe part. In terms of evaluation, it is usually taken $x$ as evaluation decision variables (affirmative, negative, choice, rejection, etc.) and as objectives (criteria, requirements, etc.); Take $u$ as the main objective requirement, because it is the main aspect of a contradiction, which causes qualitative changes in evaluation and decision-making; take $v$ as a secondary goal, because it is a secondary aspect of the contradiction. The relationship between control variables and state variables in cusp catastrophe model is shown in Figure 3-7:

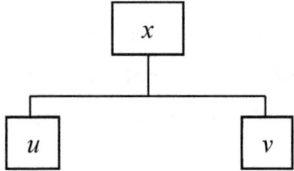

**Figure 3-7 Schematic diagram of cusp catastrophe system**

The second step is the normalization of catastrophe progression. According to the bifurcation set equation in the form of cusp catastrophe decomposition, we can get:

$$x_u = \sqrt{\frac{u}{-6}} \quad \text{Equation (3.10)}$$

$$x_v = \sqrt[3]{\frac{v}{8}} \quad \text{Equation (3.11)}$$

$x_u$ and $x_v$ represent the corresponding values of $u$ and $v$ respectively. If the absolute value of $x$ is 1, then $u = -6, v = 8$, that is, the value range of the state variable $x$ and the control variable $u,v$ is determined. In the actual operation, for the convenience of the operation, continue to limit the value range of the state variable and control variable to 0 to 1. If $x =1$(absolute value), then $u =6$ (absolute value), if the value of $u$ is reduced by one sixth, so that the range of $u$ is between 0 and 1, that is, $u = 1 \times 6$, then $x_u = \sqrt{\dfrac{u}{-6}} = \sqrt{\dfrac{1 \times 6}{-6}} = \sqrt{u}$ . Similarly, if the value of

$v$ is reduced by one eighth, that is, $v = 1 \times 8$, then $x_v = \sqrt[3]{\dfrac{v}{8}} = \sqrt[3]{\dfrac{1 \times 8}{8}} = \sqrt[3]{v}$ .

The normalization formula of cusp catastrophe model is:

$$\begin{cases} x_u = \sqrt{u} \\ x_v = \sqrt[3]{v} \end{cases} \quad \text{Equation (3.12)}$$

## (4) Operating Steps

In this book, each member of the team is regarded as a subsystem, and the evaluation of conflict correlation among members is established based on the catastrophe progression method, that is, the brittle relationship between the members of the team who have embedded the conflict network and the members who have not embedded the conflict network is evaluated according to their identity, opposition and fluctuation. The situation of brittleness fluctuation is derived from the evolution of time, but this book considers the conflict relationship that has been formed between members at a certain point in time. Therefore, the conflict relationship between members is only analyzed based on brittleness identity and brittleness opposition.

Suppose that an innovation team has $m$ members. Member $A$ has been involved in a conflict network, thus the conflict correlation between member $A$ and member $B$ can be calculated by the cusp catastrophe progression method since the brittleness fluctuation is not considered.

Firstly, the brittleness identity ($u$) and brittleness opposition ($v$) between member $B$ and member $A$ are calculated. According to the definition of brittleness correlation and brittleness weight coefficient vector, the brittleness identity degree of member $B$ and member $A$ is $a = \sum\limits_{j=1}^{k} \beta_j(t), 1 < k < n$ , and the brittleness

opposition degree is $b = \sum\limits_{j=1}^{h} \beta_j(t), 1 < h < n$. In the actual investigation, it is very

difficult to obtain the state vector and its weight coefficient vector of each member, so we can refer to the method of Weiqi. Assign the brittleness identity ($u$) and brittleness opposition ($v$) as $u + v = 1$ . This book believes that due to the uniqueness of social science research, the degree of brittleness identity and brittleness opposition can be assigned by means of expert interviews, questionnaires, and viewing raw materials.

Secondly, the cusp catastrophe normalization formula is substituted for calculation. On the basis of obtaining the values of brittleness identity degree ($u$) and brittleness opposition degree ($v$), the values are substituted into the cusp catastrophe normalization formula. If $u=p$ and $v=q$, Formula (3.12) can be rewritten as:

$$\begin{cases} B_u = \sqrt{u} = \sqrt{p} \\ B_v = \sqrt[3]{v} = \sqrt[3]{q} \end{cases} \quad \text{Equation (3.13)}$$

$B_u$ is the brittleness identity of Member B. $B_v$ is the brittleness opposition of Member B. And $p + q = 1$.

Finally, according to the principle of "reserving the smaller one among the large," the conflict relevance between member $B$ and member $A$ is obtained. According to the value of $\sqrt{p}$ and $\sqrt[3]{q}$, analyze the relationship between $B_u$ and $B_v$. Finally get the final result according to the principle of "reserving the smaller one among the large."

### 3.3.2 Evaluation of Financial Services Team Members' Conflict Relevance

### (1) Evaluation of the Relevance of Member Conflicts in the Task Conflict Network

To study the relevance of member conflicts in the task conflict network, 3 members can be selected from 28 members for analysis. Randomly select member 1 as Subsystem X. Assuming that member 1 has been involved in the task conflict network, select member 11 and member 20 as Subsystem Y,Z respectively, indicating that these two members have not been involved in the task conflict network. As this book only considers the degree of identity and the degree of opposition, the cusp catastrophe progression method is used for evaluation (Table 3-19).

**Table 3-19 The degree of identity and opposition of task conflicts between members 11 and 20 and member 1**

| Member | (Identity degree) | (Opposition degree) |
|---|---|---|
| 11 | 0.5 | 0.5 |
| 20 | 0.6 | 0.4 |

In Table 3-19, the values of the degree of identity and opposition of members 11, 20 and 1 come from two sources: first, read the two-week observation notes of the financial service innovation team; second, discuss with the team leader on the basis of the roughly set values.

Substituting into the normalization formula of cusp catastrophe (Formula (3.13)),

member 11: $\begin{cases} \text{Member11}_u = \sqrt{u} = \sqrt{0.5} = 0.7071 \\ \text{Member11}_v = \sqrt[3]{v} = \sqrt[3]{0.5} = 0.7937 \end{cases}$

According to the principle of "reserving the smaller one among the large," $\text{Member11}_u < \text{Member11}_v$. Therefore, $x_{M11} = 0.7071$, that is, the brittleness correlation between member 11 and member 1 is 0.7071.

Member 20: $\begin{cases} \text{Member20}_u = \sqrt{u} = \sqrt{0.6} = 0.7746 \\ \text{Member20}_v = \sqrt[3]{v} = \sqrt[3]{0.4} = 0.7368 \end{cases}$

According to the principle of "reserving the smaller one among the large," $\text{Member20}_u > \text{Member20}_v$. Therefore, $x_{M20} = 0.7368$, that is, the brittleness correlation between member 20 and member 1 is 0.7368.

Since $x_{成员11} < x_{成员20}$, it can be seen that the degree of brittleness correlation between member 20 and member 1 is greater than that between member 11 and member 1.

## (2) Evaluation of the Relevance of Member Conflicts in the Relationship Conflict Network

In this book, 3 of the 28 members are randomly selected to evaluate the conflict relevance of the members of the relationship conflict network, and member 5 is randomly selected as Subsystem $X$, assuming that member 5 has been involved in the relationship conflict network; member 11 and member 20 are still selected as Subsystem $Y$、$Z$ respectively, indicating that these two members have not been involved in the relationship conflict network. As this book only considers the degree of identity and the degree of opposition, the cusp catastrophe progression method is used for evaluation (Table 3-20).

**Table 3-20 The degree of identity and opposition of the relationship conflicts between members 11 and 20 and member 5**

| Member | (Identity degree) | (Opposition degree) |
|--------|-------------------|---------------------|
| 11 | 0.3 | 0.7 |
| 20 | 0.5 | 0.5 |

In Table 3-20, the values of the degree of identity and opposition of members 11, 20 and 5 still come from two sources: first, reading of the two-week observation notes of the financial service innovation team; second, discussion with the team leader on the basis of the roughly set values. Substituting into the normalization formula of cusp catastrophe (Formula (3.13)),

$$\text{Member 11: } \begin{cases} \text{Member11}_u = \sqrt{u} = \sqrt{0.3} = 0.5477 \\ \text{Member11}_v = \sqrt[3]{v} = \sqrt[3]{0.7} = 0.8879 \end{cases}$$

According to the principle of "reserving the smaller one among the large," since $\text{Member11}_u < \text{Member11}_v$, so $x_{M11} = 0.5477$.

$$\text{Member 20: } \begin{cases} \text{Member20}_u = \sqrt{u} = \sqrt{0.5} = 0.7071 \\ \text{Member20}_v = \sqrt[3]{v} = \sqrt[3]{0.5} = 0.7937 \end{cases}$$

According to the principle of "reserving the smaller one among the large," since $\text{Member20}_u > \text{Member20}_v$, so $x_{M20} = 0.7071$.

Since $x_{M11} < x_{M20}$, it can be seen that the degree of brittleness correlation between member 20 and member 5 is greater than that between member 11 and member 5.

So far, through the application of social network theory and complex system brittleness theory, this book has realized the research on the conflict relationship of innovation team members from the three levels of "team-individual and team-individual and individual," and based on this, it has constructed the research model of "team-individual and team-individual and individual" for the conflict relationship of innovation team members, providing a new idea and method for the research on the conflict relationship of members (Figure 3-8).

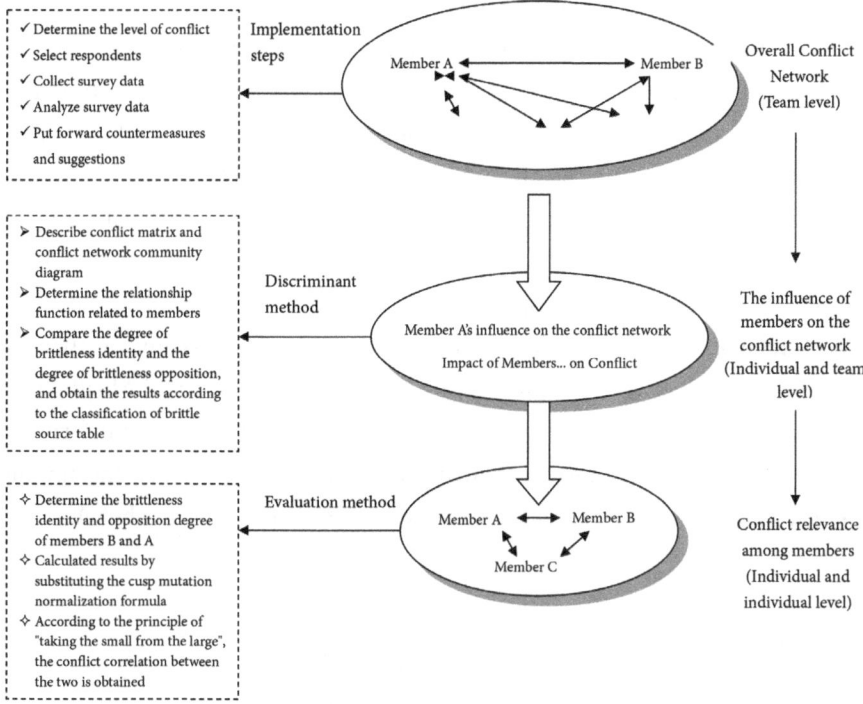

**Figure 3-8 The "team – individual and team – individual and individual" research model of the conflict relationship of innovation team members**

It can be seen from Figure 3-8 that in order to achieve an all-round study of the conflict relationship between members of an innovation team, it is necessary to start from the three levels of "team – individual and team – individual and individual":

At the "team" level, the social network theory is mainly used to build and analyze the conflict network within the team, which requires five steps: determining the level of conflict → selecting respondents → collecting survey data → analyzing survey data → putting forward countermeasures and suggestions. With the help of social network theory, we can achieve a macro description of the conflict relations among members of the innovation team, and can more vividly and intuitively reveal the complex and diverse conflict relations among members.

At the level of "individual and team," the brittleness theory of complex systems is mainly used to analyze the influence of each member on the conflict network. The specific classification method includes three steps: depicting the conflict matrix and the conflict network community diagram of the innovation team → determining the relationship function related to a member → comparing the brittleness identity and brittleness opposition of the member, and obtaining the results according to the classification of brittle source table.

At the level of "individual and individual," the brittleness theory of complex system is still used to analyze the conflict relevance of each member, so as to clarify the specific conflict relationship between members. The specific evaluation method includes three steps: determine the brittleness identity and brittleness opposition degree between member $B$ and member $A$ → substitute the brittleness identity and opposition degree into the cusp catastrophe normalization formula for calculation → according to the principle of "reserving the smaller one among the large," obtain the conflict relevance between member $B$ and member $A$.

## 3.4 Summary

This chapter aims to realize systematic research on the conflict relationship among members of the innovation team from the three levels of "team-individual and team-individual and individual" in the "process" stage of team operation, and constructs the "team-individual and team-individual and individual" research model of the conflict relationship among members of the innovation team, providing a new idea and method for the research on the conflict relationship among members. Firstly, from the perspective of the entire innovation team, the social network analysis method is used to build the innovation team conflict network, and then the structural characteristics of the conflict network are analyzed in detail from the aspects of scale, density, distance, centrality, cohesive subgroups, structural holes, and related factors. In order to realize the macro description of the innovation team conflict, this chapter proposes the implementation steps of the team conflict network. Secondly, combined with the content of determining the grade of brittleness source of complex systems, the paper gives a method to determine the impact of members on the conflict network and takes the financial service innovation team as an example to analyze, which realizes the analysis of member conflict relationship at the "individual and team" level.

Finally, taking the conflict relevance among members as the foothold, using the cusp catastrophe model to propose an evaluation method for the conflict relevance of members, and taking the financial service innovation team as an example for analysis, the analysis of member conflict relationship at the "individual and individual" level is realized.

# CHAPTER 4

# The Impact of Innovation Team Conflicts on Team Effectiveness

The existing literature tends to study the effect of team conflicts in different types. The research conclusions on the relationship between relationship conflict and team effectiveness are consistent, and believe that relationship conflict always damages team effectiveness. As for the effect of task conflict on team effectiveness, the academic world has not reached a consensus so far, and there are even contrary conclusions. Scholars all believe that task conflict is a "double-edged sword" and it is necessary to explore the impact of task conflict on team effectiveness in different research situations. In order to clarify the impact of innovation team conflict on team effectiveness, this book tries to explore the relationship between team conflict and team effectiveness from different research perspectives and different research situations in the "output" phase of team operation. It means that the moderating effects of team's emotional intelligence and conflict network density on the relationship between team conflict and team effectiveness are considered according to the emotion theory and the content of conflict network. In this way, on the one hand, the research on the effects of team conflict can be enriched, and on the other hand, conflict can be better recognized and managed.

## 4.1 The Construction of Conceptual Model of Innovation Team Conflict Affecting Team Effectiveness

### 4.1.1 Formation of the Conceptual Model

The existing literature has relatively consistent conclusions on the effect of relationship conflict, but there are different opinions on the effect of task conflict. Relevant scholars point out that the effect of task conflict varies in different research situations. Therefore, this book attempts to discuss the impact of innovation team conflict on team effectiveness in a new research situation. On the one hand, considering that conflict is the product of interaction among members, conflict theory has some relations with social network theory, of which conflict network density plays a certain role. On the other hand, since conflict is essentially an emotional response, people have always put too much emphasis on team behavior and interpret it from a cognitive level, while neglecting emotion and other irrational factors. Therefore, the effect of team emotional intelligence should be considered.

Figure 4-1 shows the conceptual model of innovation team conflict affecting team effectiveness formed in this book. Task conflict is the independent variable; team effectiveness is the dependent variable; relationship conflict is the mediating variable; team emotional intelligence, the density of task conflict network and relationship conflict network are the moderating variables. According to the study of Wen Zhonglin[105], this model is a moderated mediating effect model.

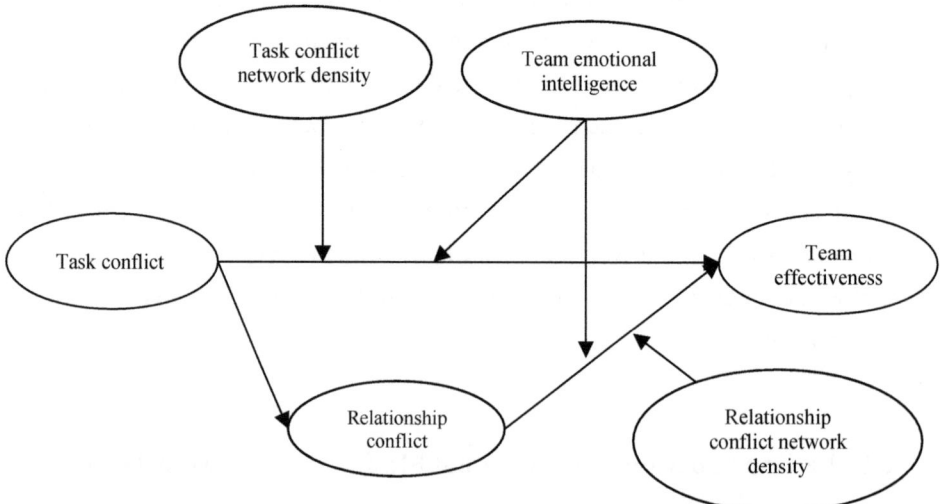

**Figure 4-1 Conceptual model of innovation team conflict affecting team effectiveness**

## 4.1.2 The Relationship between Team Conflict and Team Effectiveness

### (1) The Impact of Relationship Conflict on Team Effectiveness

Researchers agree that relationship conflict is harmful in various research situations. This book argues that there are two reasons for relationship conflict damaging team outcomes, members' emotional acceptance and sustainable development capability. One is that anxiety and various bad feelings caused by relationship conflict interfere with members' normal cognition, making them fail to take all job information into account. On the other hand, hostility arising from relationship conflict may cause tension in the interpersonal relationship, making it impossible for members to accept others' useful ideas or information. More seriously, when relationship conflict occurs, members may spend a lot of time and energy defending others, thus they cannot concentrate time and energy to task-related problems. It may also adversely affect member satisfaction and continued cooperation among members, and damage the sustainable development of the team.

Based on the above analysis, the book proposes:

**H1. Relationship conflict in innovation team has a negative effect on team effectiveness.**

H1a. Relationship conflict in innovation team has a negative effect on team outcomes.

H1b. Relationship conflict in innovation team has a negative effect on member satisfaction.

H1c. Relationship conflict in innovation team has a negative effect on the sustainable development capability of team.

### (2) The Impact of Task Conflict on Team Effectiveness

As for the effect of task conflict, there is still no consensus, and contrary research findings even appear. Scholars who believe that task conflict is beneficial to hold that task conflict promotes the integration of cognitive resources, and this information processing process is often superior to the personal information processing process. At the same time, it can avoid group thinking, thus helping to achieve better performance. Other scholars hold that task conflict is harmful, for it will intensify the pressure of members, divert their attention, and adversely affect team performance. Some scholars hold that the effect of task conflict is more complex, that's to say, the relationship between task conflict and its outcome variables is different in various research situations, and task conflict is a "double-edged sword."

The third view is more comprehensive and realistic, that is, the relationship between task conflict and outcome variables is different in different research situations. (1) Task conflicts of different levels have different effects on team outcomes. (2) Task conflict has different effects on team performance at different stages of team development. For example, in the middle stage of team development, teams with a higher level of task conflict usually achieve high performance, while cases are different at other stages. (3) Task conflicts of different task types have different effects. For example, moderate task conflict plays a positive role in the unconventional task, while it is harmful in a conventional task. (4) Many scholars also studied the effects of other mediating variables or moderating variables. For example, Bisseling studied the impact of task conflict on team performance and member satisfaction in two countries with completely different cultures (Brazil and the Netherlands). The results showed that task conflict was negatively correlated with member satisfaction and team performance in Brazil. However, no significant correlation was found between task conflict and member satisfaction and team performance in the Netherlands[106]. Other variables, such as conflict management style, leadership style, member attribution style, team atmosphere and team orientation, are mediating variables or moderating variables between task conflict and its outcome variables.

The main job of innovation team is scientific and technological innovation, knowledge innovation, or all creative activities related to the development of technology. Since most activities are unconventional tasks, moderate task conflict is of great importance. The reason is that moderate task conflict is beneficial to strengthen members' collective learning and integration of cognitive resources, which may improve team outcomes. But if the task conflict is at an unduly high level, its positive effect will be lost, because the cognitive load of members is increased and the information processing is hindered at this moment. Therefore, the book argues that there is an inverted-U relationship between task conflict and team outcome. As for the relationship between task conflict and member satisfaction and the sustainable development capability of team, the book believes that task conflict has a negative effect on both of them. That's because previous studies confirmed that task conflict has a negative effect on various working attitudes of members, such as identity, emotional acceptance of the team and other members, satisfaction, and related factors, especially in Chinese relationship-oriented culture.

Based on the above analysis, the book proposes:

**H2. Task conflict in innovation team has different effects on team effectiveness.**

H2a. There is an inverted-U relationship between task conflict and team outcome, that is, moderate task conflict is beneficial to team outcome.

H2b. Task conflict in innovation team has a negative effect on member satisfaction.

H2c. Task conflict in innovation team has a negative effect on the sustainable development capability of team.

### (3) The Mediating Effect of Relationship Conflict

During the theoretical analysis and empirical research, many scholars have found that task conflict is positively associated with relationship conflict to a certain extent, that is, task conflict will lead to relationship conflict under certain circumstances, with an average correlation coefficient of 0.47. The reason for the positive correlation between task conflict and relationship conflict lies in the fact that rationality and emotion cannot be completely separated in the process of conflict interaction, and different cognition of task may cause fierce debate among members. When harsh words appear in this process, task conflict and relationship conflict may appear simultaneously. If a member feels disappointed or irritated with others, he may be inclined to doubt the opinions of others because angry people are less patient and less likely to compromise than happy people[107].

In addition, Simons et al. analyzed the reasons for their correlation in detail. The first reason is the wrong attribution. Members usually interpret and evaluate the behavior of others, while task conflict may induce people to use biased information processing in the attribution process and amplify the bias. The second aspect is the impact of behavior. If the strategy adopted to deal with task conflict is too aggressive or irrational, it can cause a matter-of-fact discussion to escalate into a degree of personal attack, which will bring participants emotional discomfort even if the conflict is only related to task. Based on a Chinese cultural background, it is found that due to the misunderstanding of reasons, members often produce a negative emotional response, which turns task conflict into relationship conflict. Similarly, if the task conflict has not been solved for a long time, it is easy to cause the misattribution of the conflict by the parties, which leads to the escalation of the conflict and wrong interpretation of the task conflict as a relationship conflict. In the Chinese context, task conflict and relationship conflict tend to occur together, and the correlation between them is higher[108]. If handled improperly, task conflict will develop into relationship conflict[109].

Based on the above analysis, the book argues that:

**H3. Relationship conflict in innovation team acts as a mediator between task conflict and team effectiveness.**

### 4.1.3 The Moderating Effect of Team Emotional Intelligence and Conflict Network Density

#### (1) The Moderating Effect of Team Emotional Intelligence

In team life, through communication and interaction with each other, members will produce and experience various emotional experiences. In addition, emotions are contagious and empathic, and members may intentionally or unintentionally imitate some emotional behaviors of others to have the same or similar emotions. In their earlier study, Jehn and Levine pointed out that task conflict and relationship conflict may be the premise of negative emotions such as fear, anxiety and hostility, or these negative emotions lead to conflict. Conflict is essentially an emotional response, and it often occurs when members cannot effectively understand and control their or other members' emotions. Therefore, as an important variable in the process of team interaction, conflict is inevitably closely related to emotion. According to the theory of emotion, team emotional intelligence refers to the capability of a team to perceive, understand, evaluate, share, coordinate, standardize and manage its emotions comprehensively, which is the result of the final integration of individual emotional intelligence. Team emotional intelligence is an important way to identify team entities, which is of great necessity to understand the process of team interaction and its effectiveness.

Therefore, the moderating effect of team emotional intelligence is considered in this book when explaining the relationship between team conflict and team effectiveness.

1) The relationship between team emotional intelligence and team effectiveness

Aristotle, who found the cognitive theory of emotion, pointed out that emotion affects people's behavior to some extent[110], and it is impossible to fully understand work-related behaviors without taking emotion into account[111]. The role of team emotional intelligence is mainly to improve the integration effect and team vitality, generate the emotional drive for members and improve team performance[112]. The results of empirical research also show that team emotional intelligence is closely related to team-related outcome variables; for example, team emotional intelligence has a positive impact on team members and team performance[113]. Besides, team emotional intelligence is significantly positively correlated with team satisfaction[114] and team performance. Chinese scholar Zhang Huihua took Chinese samples as an example and found that team emotional intelligence is highly positively correlated with team performance, which is a valuable variable in the workplace and has varying degrees of predictability for valid working variables[115]. Chen Quan found that team emotional intelligence is one of the core psychological characteristics of the senior management team, which has a significant impact on team operation processes and strategic decisions. It is conducive to resolving team conflict, promoting behavioral integration, team operation process and strategic performance[116].

2) The relationship between team emotional intelligence and team conflict

As for the relationship between team emotional intelligence and team conflict, many scholars believe that the former contributes to the management of the latter. For example, people with higher emotional intelligence have more sophisticated conflict management skills, commitment to cooperation, and the ability to control and use emotion to find solutions that meet the needs of both parties in conflict. Groups with high emotional intelligence can solve conflicts more effectively and bring better group performance than those with low emotional intelligence[117]. Through experimental studies, Barsade found that emotions can spread among members, and positive emotional contagion was significantly correlated with the generation of intra-team cooperation, reduction of conflict and team task performance[118]. George pointed out that emotional intelligence enables groups to invent new ways to argue and prevent arguments from escalating into conflicts. The higher the group's emotional intelligence is, the better it can detect vicious emotional cycles and respond to potential negative harm, which prevents members from transferring task conflicts to individual interpersonal relationships[119]. Wolff et al. studied the role of emotional intelligence in self-managed teams and found that empathy in emotional intelligence can help to correctly understand the emotional needs of team members and promote the development of cognitive and emotional processes[120]. The Chinese scholar Hu Ruishan's research showed that task conflict, relationship conflict and team performance are negatively correlated, and team emotional intelligence plays a moderating role in the relationship between team conflict and team performance[121]. Wei Xuhua revealed that group emotional intelligence has a significant impact on the group decision-making process, and groups with high emotional intelligence have lower relationship conflict[122]. Chen Quan's research found that emotional intelligence has a significant impact on conflict of top management team, and plays a partial mediating role in the transition from task conflict to relationship conflict. Relationship conflict and task conflict are lower when emotional intelligence is higher.

This book argues that team emotional intelligence plays an important moderating role in the relationship between innovation team conflict and team effectiveness. The reason is that team emotional intelligence is the ability of the team to perceive, recognize, understand and manage the emotions of the whole team, which is very effective in regulating and managing destructive emotions. The team with higher emotional intelligence tends to devote more resources to managing and regulating emotions, which will help reduce team pressure and enable members to have a more positive attitude towards the team.

Based on the existing conclusions and the above analysis, the book holds that:

**H4. Team emotional intelligence plays a moderating role among task conflict, relationship conflict and team effectiveness:**

H4a. The positive correlation between moderate task conflict and team outcome is stronger and the negative correlation between task conflict and member satisfaction and sustainable development capability is weaker when the team emotional intelligence is higher.

H4b. The negative correlation between relationship conflict and team outcome, member satisfaction and sustainable development capability is weaker when the team emotional intelligence is higher.

## (2) Moderating Effect of Conflict Network Density

Network density describes the strength of connections and interactions between members, which is one of the important indexes to show the characteristics of network structure. Higher network density means greater connections that any member has with others in the network. Most studies show that the higher the density of positive social network relationships (such as a counseling network and emotional network), the more interactions between members, the more information and resource interaction, and the more inclination to share common values, beliefs or goals. Therefore, it is conducive to knowledge acquisition, sharing, transfer, mining, fusion, reconstruction and integration[123]. It also has a significant positive impact on organizational learning ability and technological innovation performance. Some scholars pointed out that excessively high network density may inhibit the organization's capacity to acquire resources and weaken learning ability[124]. That's because members in a dense network disperse the time and effort necessary for creative activities in order to maintain the interaction[125]. In addition, members in a dense network tend to have the same views and ideas, and the less differentiated views are detrimental to the cultivation of creative ideas[126]. Similarly, the book believes that once the social network relationship is negative, the higher its density, and the more destructive it will be. That's because in a high-density negative network, it is easier for network nodes to contact each other, and it is relatively easy for harmful information and bad emotions to transfer and spread. For a task conflict network, higher density means that there are more different opinions and oppositions on task-related issues among the members of the network. In such a network with high density, the members are "over-embedded," which will hinder their effective cognition of the task. For a relational conflict network, higher density means more emotional opposition and interpersonal friction among the members of the network, and wider spread of harmful emotions.

Based on the above analysis, the book argues that:

**H5. Conflict network density plays a moderating role among task conflict, relationship conflict and team effectiveness:**

H5a. The positive correlation between moderate task conflict and team outcome is weaker and the negative correlation between task conflict and team satisfaction and sustainable development capability is stronger when the density of task conflict network is higher.

H5b. The negative correlation between relationship conflict and team outcome, member satisfaction and sustainable development capability is stronger when the density of relationship conflict network is higher.

In conclusion, the book forms 11 hypotheses to be tested (Table 4-1).

**Table 4-1 Summary of research hypotheses**

| Number | Content of Hypotheses |
|--------|------------------------|
| H1a | Relationship conflict in innovation teams has a negative effect on team outcomes. |
| H1b | Relationship conflict in innovation teams has a negative effect on member satisfaction. |
| H1c | Relationship conflict in innovation teams has a negative effect on sustainable development capability. |
| H2a | There is an inverted-U relationship between task conflict and team outcome, that is, moderate task conflict is beneficial to team outcome. |
| H2b | Task conflict in innovation teams has a negative effect on member satisfaction. |
| H2c | Task conflict in innovation teams has a negative effect on sustainable development capability. |
| H3 | Relationship conflict in innovation team acts as the mediator between task conflict and team effectiveness. |
| H4a | The positive correlation between moderate task conflict and team outcome is stronger and the negative correlation between task conflict and member satisfaction and sustainable development capability is weaker when the team emotional intelligence is higher. |
| H4b | The negative correlation between relationship conflict and team outcome, member satisfaction and sustainable development capability is weaker when the team emotional intelligence is higher. |
| H5a | The positive correlation between moderate task conflict and team outcome is weaker and the negative correlation between task conflict and team satisfaction and sustainable development capability is stronger when the density of task conflict network is higher. |
| H5b | The negative correlation between relationship conflict and team outcome, member satisfaction and sustainable development capability is stronger when the density of relationship conflict network is higher. |

## 4.2 Measurement of Related Variables and Small Sample Test

### 4.2.1 Formation of the Questionnaire

The book designs the questionnaire so as to obtain research material and collect data with a unified questionnaire. Firstly, a literature review is carried out, and the measurement status of research variables is summarized and analyzed. Considering the reliability and validity of the scale, mature scales at home and abroad are selected. Secondly, "translation-back translation" is carried out for the English version of scale to ensure the consistency of content expression between the Chinese version and the original version. Finally, relevant experts and innovation team leaders and members are interviewed to improve the content or expression.

### 4.2.2 Measurement of Variables

The variables in this study include task conflict in innovation team, relationship conflict, team emotional intelligence, team effectiveness, the density of task conflict network and relationship conflict network. There has been productive research on the measurement of the first four variables, and the book uses the existing mature scale for reference. Since these variables are measured at the team level, the book mainly asks members to record their perceptions of a particular feature or state of the team, and adds up their individual opinions. The measurement of conflict network density has been discussed in the previous chapter, and this chapter continues to use the traditional method of social network measurement.

#### (1) Task Conflicts and Relationship Conflicts in Innovation Team

The measurement items of task conflict and relationship conflict are analyzed in the above two chapters, which will continue to be used in this chapter.

#### (2) Team Emotional Intelligence

The original team emotional intelligence was proposed and measured by Druskat, but with numerous items, the scale was very inconvenient to measure. After revision by Hamme, the content was reduced from the original 13 dimensions to

9 dimensions and the corresponding measurement tool ECGN (Emotional Competency Group norms) was developed[127], but this scale still contained too many items and too broad definition of team emotional intelligence. The scale developed by Jordan et al. is WEIP, with 16 items of 4 dimensions[128]. Liu Dong, a Chinese scholar, believes that team emotional intelligence should be composed of three elements: members' level of emotional intelligence, ability to deal with team conflict and team's learning ability[129]. Wang Liang et al. proposed that team emotional intelligence should include cognition of team role, team conflict management, team value consensus and team interpersonal relationships[130], but neither study developed nor verified the scale.

Since there is no consensus on the dimensional composition of team emotional intelligence, the measurement of this variable still needs to be explored. This book measures team emotional intelligence from four dimensions: a team's ability of emotional cognition, emotional interaction and sharing, emotional evaluation and coordination, and emotional regulation. Among them, team emotional cognition includes two items; for example, "members in team can always understand each other's emotions"; team emotional interaction includes four items, one is that members can understand the signals from team's emotions; team emotional evaluation and coordination includes three items, one is that the team can clearly and timely feel the general emotion of members; team emotional regulation includes four items, one is that teams tend to create positive general emotion.

### (3) The Effectiveness of the Innovation Team

Despite different emphases on the expression of team effectiveness, scholars at home and abroad believe that it should be a multidimensional concept covering both the extrinsic indicator of team performance and internal indicators of team viability, such as member behavior, attitude, and development potential in the future. Therefore, some scholars have suggested that member satisfaction and sustainable development capability of team can express this part. The book believes that innovation team effectiveness is the result of the final activities of the innovation team, which can be evaluated from three aspects, that is, outcomes, member satisfaction and capacity for sustainable development. Therefore, the measurement of innovation team effectiveness can also be divided into three dimensions, and the specific items of each dimension are compiled with reference to the scale of Hackman[131], Kirkman et al.[132] and other scales widely used in China. Among them, the team outcome consists of four items, for example, "team objectives achieved well"; member satisfaction consists of three items, for example, "working in a team makes me feel very satisfied"; sustainable development capability of team consists of three items, for example, "I am willing to sacrifice my personal interests for the success of the team."

### (4) The Density of Task Conflict Network and Relationship Conflict Network

In the previous chapter, a questionnaire was produced to measure the task conflict network and relationship conflict network of innovation teams. From it, the task conflict network contains three items, such as "In order to complete the task, who do you often have to discuss about the task with?." The relationship conflict network contains three items, such as "In a team, who do you often get angry or dissatisfied with?." In this chapter, we continue to use this questionnaire and use UCINET to automatically calculate the task conflict network density and relationship conflict network density according to the traditional method of social network survey.

### 4.2.3 Small Sample Test

The measurement clauses in the testing questionnaire of small sample (Appendix E) are designed by integrating relevant scales of different scholars, so there may be mismatched clauses. Therefore, the small sample is tested before the formal survey. In order to improve the reliability and validity of the scale, CITC analysis, α reliability coefficient method and exploratory factor analysis were used to purify the scale. As the data of conflict network density are directly calculated by UCINET, aggregation test and reliability and validity analysis of data on the team level are not performed[133].

### (1) Sampling and Basic Sample Information

Considering the convenience of the survey scope, the small sample survey was mainly carried out in Nanjing, covering universities, biomedicine, electronic appliances and software development.

There are 31 items for the measurement of four research variables, such as task conflict. According to the principle that the number of copies should be five times the items in a single questionnaire, a total of 155 copies of questionnaires should be issued for a small sample survey. Due to the difference in team size, 163 questionnaires were collected from 13 innovation teams in this survey, of which 147 questionnaires were valid (a questionnaire with more than 10% unanswered questions and all questions with the same score were invalid). Because of the special survey method of conflict network density and the sensitive survey content, after confirming 13 innovation teams, we went to each team for on-site distribution and filling to ensure the quality of the questionnaire: firstly, to obtain a list of team members from the Human Resources Department or the human resources office, and then gather them in a conference room, stating in advance that each questionnaire is only accessible to the researcher and no member's name will appear in the final research results. A total of 147 conflict network questionnaires were collected from 13 teams through on-the-spot distribution and filling.

**(2) Analysis Process**

1) Descriptive statistics

Descriptive statistics of data include maximum value, minimum value, mean value, standard deviation, skewness and kurtosis (Table 4-2).

**Table 4-2 Descriptive statistical results of small sample survey data**

| Items | Minimum Value | Maximum Value | Mean Value | Standard Deviation | Skewness | | Kurtosis | |
|-------|---------------|---------------|------------|--------------------|----------|----------|----------|----------|
| | | | | | Statistic | Standard Error | Statistic | Standard Error |
| TC1 | 1 | 5 | 2.89 | .587 | -.598 | .200 | 3.010 | .397 |
| TC2 | 1 | 4 | 2.93 | .722 | -.329 | .200 | .007 | .397 |
| TC3 | 1 | 5 | 2.93 | .703 | .105 | .200 | -.255 | .397 |
| TC4 | 1 | 5 | 2.59 | .826 | .072 | .200 | -.205 | .397 |
| RC1 | 1 | 4 | 2.01 | .993 | .483 | .200 | -.977 | .397 |
| RC2 | 1 | 4 | 2.23 | .892 | .114 | .200 | -.857 | .397 |
| RC3 | 1 | 5 | 2.24 | .902 | .249 | .200 | -.457 | .397 |
| RC4 | 1 | 4 | 2.27 | .909 | .058 | .200 | -.923 | .397 |

| Items | Minimum Value | Maximum Value | Mean Value | Standard Deviation | Skewness | | Kurtosis | |
|---|---|---|---|---|---|---|---|---|
| | | | | | Statistic | Standard Error | Statistic | Standard Error |
| EI1 | 1 | 5 | 3.28 | .774 | .008 | .200 | -.034 | .397 |
| EI2 | 2 | 5 | 3.70 | .645 | -.089 | .200 | -.102 | .397 |
| EI3 | 2 | 5 | 3.50 | .716 | -.296 | .200 | -.220 | .397 |
| EI4 | 2 | 5 | 3.34 | .745 | .262 | .200 | -.126 | .397 |
| EI5 | 1 | 4 | 3.18 | .750 | -.513 | .200 | -.416 | .397 |
| EI6 | 1 | 5 | 3.02 | .910 | -.151 | .200 | -.296 | .397 |
| EI7 | 1 | 5 | 3.22 | .748 | -.193 | .200 | .282 | .397 |
| EI8 | 2 | 5 | 3.34 | .687 | -.047 | .200 | -.279 | .397 |
| EI9 | 2 | 5 | 3.19 | .715 | .158 | .200 | -.192 | .397 |
| EI10 | 1 | 5 | 3.35 | .809 | -.262 | .200 | -.330 | .397 |
| EI11 | 2 | 5 | 3.44 | .653 | -.307 | .200 | -.312 | .397 |
| EI12 | 2 | 5 | 3.20 | .740 | -.243 | .200 | -.933 | .397 |
| EI13 | 1 | 5 | 3.54 | .743 | -.842 | .200 | 1.016 | .397 |
| GE1 | 1 | 5 | 3.54 | .742 | -.256 | .200 | .342 | .397 |
| GE2 | 1 | 5 | 3.45 | .733 | -.298 | .200 | .839 | .397 |
| GE3 | 1 | 5 | 3.33 | .814 | -.221 | .200 | .023 | .397 |
| GE4 | 1 | 5 | 3.34 | .832 | -.203 | .200 | .649 | .397 |
| GE5 | 1 | 5 | 3.28 | .905 | .035 | .200 | -.401 | .397 |
| GE6 | 1 | 5 | 3.29 | .776 | -.102 | .200 | .311 | .397 |
| GE7 | 2 | 5 | 3.82 | .722 | -.262 | .200 | -.037 | .397 |
| GE8 | 1 | 5 | 3.41 | .826 | -.094 | .200 | -.211 | .397 |
| GE9 | 2 | 5 | 3.76 | .696 | -.506 | .200 | .444 | .397 |
| GE10 | 1 | 5 | 3.52 | .814 | -.078 | .200 | -.076 | .397 |

Note: Task conflict is TC, relationship conflict is RC, emotional intelligence is EI, and group effectiveness is GE.

It can be seen from Table 4-2 that the absolute value of skewness is less than 3 and the absolute value of kurtosis is less than 10, and the score of each item complies with the data requirements of normal distribution.

Reflecting the structural characteristics of team conflict, conflict network density is calculated on a team basis. The conflict network density of 13 teams can be calculated by UCINET (Table 4-3).

**Table 4-3 Descriptive statistical results of conflict network density**

| Team | Task Conflict Network Density | Relationship Conflict Network Density |
|---|---|---|
| 1 | 0.24 | 0.17 |
| 2 | 0.34 | 0.29 |
| 3 | 0.37 | 0.28 |
| 4 | 0.27 | 0.30 |
| 5 | 0.21 | 0.19 |
| 6 | 0.15 | 0.10 |
| 7 | 0.28 | 0.21 |
| 8 | 0.31 | 0.22 |
| 9 | 0.53 | 0.51 |
| 10 | 0.33 | 0.27 |
| 11 | 0.36 | 0.28 |
| 12 | 0.29 | 0.17 |
| 13 | 0.56 | 0.67 |
| Minimum Value | 0.15 | 0.17 |
| Maximum Value | 0.56 | 0.67 |
| Mean Value | 0.326 | 0.290 |
| Standard Deviation | 0.115 | 0.144 |
| Skewness | 0.870 | 1.953 |
| Kurtosis | 0.777 | 3.604 |

2) CITC analysis and internal consistency reliability analysis

There are two standards for project purification. Firstly, when the correlation coefficient of the revised project is less than 0.3, the item should be removed. Secondly, for items with CITC values between 0.3 and 0.5, if the deletion of it can significantly increase the Cronbach's α coefficient on the whole, the item should be deleted. The test results of the measurement scale of each research variable were obtained by SPSS analysis (Table 4-4).

**Table 4-4 CITC analysis and internal consistency reliability analysis of the variable measurement scale**

| Variable | Item | Total Correlation of Corrected Item | Cronbach's Alpha Value of Deleted Item | Overall Cronbach's Alpha Value |
|---|---|---|---|---|
| Task Conflict | TC1 | .618 | .724 | 0.788 |
| | TC2 | .671 | .695 | |
| | TC3 | .513 | .783 | |
| | TC4 | .610 | .737 | |
| Relationship Conflict | RC1 | .573 | .851 | 0.852 |
| | RC2 | .772 | .779 | |
| | RC3 | .678 | .818 | |
| | RC4 | .755 | .784 | |
| Team Emotional Intelligence | EI1 | .532 | .811 | 0.828 |
| | EI2 | .480 | .815 | |
| | EI3 | .489 | .814 | |
| | EI4 | .405 | .820 | |
| | EI5 | .201 | .836 | |
| | EI6 | .513 | .813 | |
| | EI7 | .649 | .802 | |
| | EI8 | .653 | .803 | |
| | EI9 | .552 | .810 | |
| | EI10 | .564 | .808 | |
| | EI11 | .558 | .810 | |
| | EI12 | .515 | .813 | |
| | EI13 | .074 | .844 | |
| Team Effectiveness | GE1 | .641 | .793 | 0.823 |
| | GE2 | .658 | .792 | |
| | GE3 | .565 | .801 | |
| | GE4 | .497 | .810 | |
| | GE5 | .480 | .810 | |
| | GE6 | .589 | .798 | |
| | GE7 | .477 | .810 | |
| | GE8 | .453 | .813 | |
| | GE9 | .386 | .818 | |
| | GE10 | .346 | .822 | |

It can be seen from Table 4-4 that both task conflict and relationship conflict have 4 measurement items, and the total correlation coefficients of the corrected items are all greater than 0.5. The overall Cronbach's α coefficients are 0.788 and 0.852, and deleting any item cannot significantly increase the overall Cronbach's α coefficient, so the original measurement items of task conflict and relationship conflict are retained.

There are 13 items for measuring team emotional intelligence, among which the total correlation value of corrected items EI5 and EI13 is less than 0.3. If these two items are deleted, the overall Cronbach's α coefficient will increase significantly, so it should be deleted. It can be seen from another CITC analysis and internal consistency reliability analysis that the overall Cronbach's α coefficient increased to 0.856 after the deletion of these two items, and the CITC values of other items all met the conditions. Therefore, there are 11 measurement items remaining in the team emotional intelligence scale.

There are 10 items for measuring team effectiveness, and the total correlation values of the corrected items are all greater than 0.3. The overall Cronbach's α coefficient is 0.823, and deleting any item cannot significantly increase the overall Cronbach's α coefficient, so 10 measurement items of the innovation team effectiveness scale are retained.

3) Exploratory factor analysis

An exploratory factor analysis was performed in this book to determine the extent to which each scale measured theoretical concepts and characteristics.

Innovation team conflict scale. According to exploratory factor analysis (Table 4-5), KMO is 0.788 and Bartlett's test of sphericity has a significance probability of 0.000, indicating strong correlation between variables. It also turns down the hypothesis that each variable is independent. The common factor variance of 8 items is greater than 0.4. By extracting factors through principal component analysis and selecting characteristic roots greater than 1, it can be seen that the cumulative variance contribution rate of the two factors is 61.282%, indicating the good structural validity of the questionnaire[263]. Innovation team conflict is composed of task conflict and relationship conflict.

**Table 4-5 Exploratory factor analysis results of innovation team conflicts**

| Items | Rotating Component Matrix | | Common Factor Variance |
|---|---|---|---|
| | Factor1 | Factor2 | |
| RC1 | .778 | | .620 |
| RC3 | .772 | | .603 |
| RC2 | .762 | | .620 |
| RC4 | .671 | | .489 |
| TC2 | | .866 | .754 |
| TC1 | | .820 | .684 |
| TC3 | | .676 | .492 |
| TC4 | | .669 | .641 |
| Cumulative Account for Total Variance Variation | 61.282% | | |
| Sufficient Sample of Kaiser-Meyer-Olkin Measurement | 0.788 | | |
| Bartlett's Test of Sphericity | Approx. Chi-Square | 1418.761 | |
| | df | 28 | |
| | Sig. | .000 | |

The scale of emotional intelligence of the innovation team. CITC analysis and internal consistency reliability analysis showed that EI5 and EI13 in the team emotional intelligence scale were deleted because they did not meet the requirements. According to exploratory factor analysis (Table 4-6), KMO is 0.710 and the significance probability of the Bartlett sphericity test is 0.000. The common factor variance of 11 items is greater than 0.5. By extracting factors through principal component analysis and selecting characteristic roots greater than 1, it can be seen that the cumulative variance contribution rate of the four factors is 72.502%, indicating the good structural validity of the questionnaire.

**Table 4-6 Exploratory factor analysis results of emotional intelligence of the innovation team**

| Items | Rotating Component Matrix | | | | Common Factor Variance |
|---|---|---|---|---|---|
| | Factor1 | Factor 2 | Factor 3 | Factor 4 | |
| EI11 | .870 | | | | .814 |
| EI10 | .814 | | | | .770 |
| EI12 | .660 | | | | .622 |
| EI8 | | .828 | | | .767 |
| EI9 | | .791 | | | .779 |
| EI7 | | .643 | | | .612 |
| EI1 | | | .856 | | .745 |
| EI2 | | | .751 | | .711 |
| EI6 | | | | .842 | .800 |
| EI4 | | | | .792 | .708 |
| EI3 | | | | .552 | .649 |
| Cumulative Account for Total Variance Variation | 72.502% | | | | |
| Sufficient Sample of Kaiser-Meyer-Olkin Measurement | 0.710 | | | | |
| Bartlett's Test of Sphericity | Approx. Chi-Square | 599.376 | | | |
| | df | 55 | | | |
| | Sig. | .000 | | | |

Innovation team effectiveness. According to exploratory factor analysis, KMO is 0.779 and the significance probability of the Bartlett sphericity test is 0.000, with common factor variance of 10 items greater than 0.5. By extracting factors through principal component analysis and selecting characteristic roots greater than 1, it can be seen that the cumulative variance contribution rate of the three factors is 69.545%, indicating the good structural validity of the questionnaire. (Table 4-7).

Table 4-7 Exploratory factor analysis results of innovation team effectiveness

| Items | Rotating Component Matrix | | | Common Factor Variance |
|---|---|---|---|---|
| | Factor 1 | Factor 2 | Factor 3 | |
| GE2 | .823 | | | .754 |
| GE4 | .817 | | | .687 |
| GE3 | .772 | | | .641 |
| GE1 | .685 | | | .629 |
| | | .848 | | .734 |
| GE6 | | .840 | | .785 |
| GE5 | | .705 | | .567 |
| GE9 | | | .896 | .821 |
| GE10 | | | .865 | .755 |
| GE8 | | | .691 | .580 |
| Cumulative Account for Total Variance Variation | 69.545% | | | |
| Sufficient Sample of Kaiser-Meyer-Olkin Measurement | 0.779 | | | |
| Bartlett's Test of Sphericity | Approx. Chi-Square | 589.215 | | |
| | df | 45 | | |
| | Sig. | .000 | | |

Through small sample testing, the fifth and thirteenth items of the team emotional intelligence scale are deleted in this book, and the revised scale has good internal consistency and validity. The formal questionnaire formed after small sample testing is shown in Appendix F.

## 4.3 The Revision of Conceptual Model of Innovation Team Conflict Affecting Team Effectiveness

### 4.3.1 Data Collection and Aggregation Validation

#### (1) Data Collection and Description of Statistical Characteristics

1) Selection of research objects

The research object of this book is innovation teams in knowledge-intensive industries such as universities, software development, bio-medicine, electronics and electrical appliances. The respondents were members of an innovation team, and the data at the individual level were summed up for specific analysis.

2) Determination of sample size

Taking the opinions of different scholars into account, this book intends to survey 200 innovation teams of different sizes.

3) Sampling method and process

During a period of five months, the survey was conducted in two ways: on the spot and online. They were sent out to universities in Nanjing, Suzhou, Changzhou, Shanghai, Anhui and Wuhan, software development, biomedicine, electronics and electrical appliances and other knowledge-intensive industries. For the questionnaire distribution and completion on the spot, one should first contact the human resources staff of the organization to select an innovation team and gather all members in a conference room. Before filling in the questionnaire, the survey objective, survey content and confidentiality provisions were introduced, and then the questionnaires were distributed and collected on the spot. Due to geographical restrictions, an electronic questionnaire was also adopted. Firstly, the staff of the human resources department of the organization was contacted, and then the website was sent to the members of the selected innovation team. After filling in the answers, the members directly submitted their answers.

The collection of conflict network data was the same as the small sample survey. After confirming valid questionnaires and teams, the questionnaires were sent to enterprises or universities nearby for filling on the spot. If the area was far away, relevant teachers from Hohai University, the University of Science and Technology of China, and Wuhan University were entrusted by the author to fill and collect the questionnaire in enterprises or universities.

4) Collection of questionnaire and description of statistical characteristics

There are two principles for screening valid questionnaires in this book: eliminate questionnaires with more than 10% uncompleted answers and questionnaires with the same score for all questions. A total of 767 questionnaires from 159 innovation teams were collected in this survey, 703 of which were valid after preliminary screening.

The statistical characteristics of the samples are shown in Table 4-8.

**Table 4-8 Basic information of formal survey samples**

| Survey Items | Category | Number of people | Proportion |
|---|---|---|---|
| Gender | Male | 494 | 72.3% |
| | Female | 209 | 27.7% |
| Age | 20 to 29 years old | 358 | 50.9% |
| | 30 to 39 | 234 | 33.3% |
| | 40 to 49 | 79 | 11.2% |
| | 50 or higher | 32 | 4.6% |
| Degree of Education | Junior college and below | 37 | 5.3% |
| | Undergraduate | 91 | 12.9% |
| | Masters | 319 | 45.4% |
| | PhD degrees | 256 | 36.4% |
| Team Size | less than 5 | 61 | 11.4% |
| | 6 to10 | 173 | 32.5% |
| | 11 to 15 | 202 | 37.9% |
| | 15 or more | 97 | 18.2% |
| Established Time | less than 3 years | 65 | 9.2% |
| | 4 to 6 years | 124 | 17.6% |
| | 7 to 9 years | 167 | 23.8% |
| | 10 to 12 years | 117 | 16.6% |
| | 13 years or more | 230 | 32.8% |

## (2) Test of Common Method Variance

Due to the special data collection method of conflict network density, this book does not carry out a test of common method variance. The measurement items of four variables, such as task conflict, were answered by individual members, which may lead to the problem of common method variance. In order to test the deviation that may lead to the expansion of the correlation between concepts, the book puts 29 measurement items together for factor analysis. It can be seen from the result of unrotated factor analysis that 8 factors explain 77.598% of the total variation of all variables, among which the first principal component only explains 16.094% of the total variation. Therefore, the homology deviation of data obtained in this survey is not significant.

## (3) Sum of Data

Conflict network density represents the structural characteristics of team conflict relations, and it is already a variable at the team level. This book only needs to sum up the data of four research variables, such as task conflict. Firstly, it is necessary to sum up the data at the individual level and judge the effectiveness of its integration. Secondly, if the scores of individual members converge to an acceptable level, the mean value of individual measurements is adopted to represent the measurement value of the team.

The rationality of data summation is verified by $r_{WG}$. $r_{WG}$ index is the ratio of the mean of scoring variance to the expected variance, which is used to examine the degree of consistency in the ratings of two or more individuals on one or more items. Since this index evaluates the intraclass variance through pair comparison of measured values and is not affected by the number of team samples, it can effectively evaluate the degree of intra-team convergence. The value range of $r_{WG}$ is (0,1), and the closer it is to 1, the more the scores within the group converge. When its value is 0.7 or above, it is acceptable to sum data from the individual level to the team level, and the calculation formula of $r_{WG}$ is as follows:

$$r_{WG}(J) = \frac{J[1-\left(\dfrac{\overline{S_{xj}^2}}{\sigma_{EU}^2}\right)]}{J[1-\left(\dfrac{\overline{S_{xj}^2}}{\sigma_{EU}^2}\right)]+\left(\dfrac{\overline{S_{xj}^2}}{\sigma_{EU}^2}\right)} , \sigma_{EU}^2 = \frac{A^2-1}{12} \quad \text{Equation (4.1)}$$

In this formula, $J$ is the number of measurement items, $\overline{S_{xj}^2}$ is the mean of all team variances, $\sigma_{EU}^2$ is the expected variance, $A$ is the number of measurement grades (The book adopts Richter 5-point scale, $A = 5$). Due to the large sample size and the large number of innovation teams involved, the $r_{WG}$ value of each variable corresponding to 159 teams is not listed in this book, but the average $r_{WG}$ value of each research variable is reported (Table 4-9).

Table 4-9 The total test of each research variable data in formal survey

| Variable | Dimension | The Average $r_{WG}$ Value |
|---|---|---|
| Innovation Team Conflict | Task Conflict | 0.943 |
| | Relationship Conflict | 0.959 |
| Innovation Team Emotional Intelligence | Emotional Recognition Ability | 0.883 |
| | Emotional Interaction Ability | 0.943 |
| | Emotional Evaluation Ability | 0.929 |
| | Emotional Specification Ability | 0.926 |
| Innovation Team Effectiveness | Team Outcome | 0.945 |
| | Member Satisfaction | 0.926 |
| | Sustainable Development Capability of Team | 0.930 |

It can be seen from Table 4-9 that the average $r_{WG}$ values of all dimensions of variables are above 0.7, which meets the conditions for data summing at the team level.

## (4) Descriptive Statistics

Since individual data meets the condition of data summing at a team level, the book uses the mean value of individual measured values to represent the measured values of the team, and the value of conflict network density is directly calculated by UCINET. The correlation coefficient matrix of all variables is shown in Table 4-10. It can be seen from the table that there is a certain degree of correlation between variables.

Table 4-10 The correlation coefficient matrix of each research variable in formal survey

| Variable | Task Conflict | Relationship Conflict | Team Outcome | Satisfaction | Continuing Cooperation | Emotional Recognition | Emotional Interaction | Emotional Assessment | Emotional Specification | Task Conflict Network Density | Relationship Conflict Network Density |
|---|---|---|---|---|---|---|---|---|---|---|---|
| Task Conflict | 1 | | | | | | | | | | |
| Relationship Conflict | .612** | 1 | | | | | | | | | |
| Team Outcome | -.505** | -.528** | 1 | | | | | | | | |
| Satisfaction | -.441** | -.462** | .608** | 1 | | | | | | | |
| Continuing Cooperation | -.509** | -.552** | .648** | .592** | 1 | | | | | | |
| Emotional Recognition | -.408** | -.424** | .744** | .606** | .599** | 1 | | | | | |
| Emotional Interaction | -.414** | -.411** | .738** | .621** | .562** | .962** | 1 | | | | |
| Emotional Assessment | -.377** | -.398** | .693** | .576** | .519** | .924** | .934** | 1 | | | |
| Emotional Specification | -.391** | -.403** | .707** | .599** | .542** | .944** | .951** | .966** | 1 | | |
| Task Conflict Network Density | .505** | .674** | -.627** | -.463** | -.508** | -.521** | -.485** | -.462** | -.466** | 1 | |
| Relationship Conflict Network Density | .585** | .660** | -.662** | -.527** | -.574** | -.560** | -.525** | -.498** | -.497** | .939** | 1 |

**. Significant correlation was found at.01 level (bilateral).

Table 4-11 shows the descriptive statistics.

**Table 4-11 Descriptive statistical results of team-level data for each research variable in formal survey**

| Item | Minimum Value | Maximum Value | Mean Value | Standard Deviation | Skewness | | Kurtosis | |
|---|---|---|---|---|---|---|---|---|
| | | | | | Statistic | Standard Error | Statistic | Standard Error |
| Task Conflict | 2 | 5 | 3.10 | .729 | 1.310 | .302 | 1.567 | .595 |
| Relationship Conflict | 2 | 5 | 3.27 | .578 | .406 | .302 | .279 | .595 |
| Emotional Recognition | 2 | 5 | 3.53 | .602 | -.011 | .302 | .039 | .595 |
| Emotional Interaction | 2 | 5 | 3.56 | .507 | -.516 | .302 | .092 | .595 |
| Emotional Assessment | 2 | 5 | 3.24 | .599 | -.096 | .302 | .333 | .595 |
| Emotional Specification | 2 | 5 | 3.37 | .651 | -.416 | .302 | -.328 | .595 |
| Team Outcome | 2 | 5 | 3.18 | .609 | -.379 | .302 | .183 | .595 |
| Satisfaction | 2 | 5 | 3.37 | .651 | -.416 | .302 | -.328 | .595 |
| Sustainable Development | 2 | 5 | 3.46 | .534 | -.362 | .302 | -.174 | .595 |
| Task Conflict Network Density | 0.15 | 0.77 | 0.42 | 0.132 | 0.464 | 0.192 | -0.686 | 0.383 |
| Relationship Conflict Network Density | 0.10 | 0.79 | 0.38 | 0.138 | 0.364 | 0.192 | -0.346 | 0.383 |

It can be seen from Table 4-11 that the absolute value of data skewness is less than 3 and the absolute value of kurtosis is less than 10. The data follows normal distribution and can be processed later.

## 4.3.2 Data Analysis and Hypothesis Testing

### (1) Reliability Analysis

Task conflict and other variables were analyzed by referring to CITC and internal consistency reliability analysis (Table 4-12).

**Table 4-12 CITC analysis and internal consistency reliability analysis results of the formal survey scale**

| Variable | Item | Total Correlation of Corrected Item | Cronbach's Alpha Value of Deleted Item | Overall Cronbach's Alpha Value |
|---|---|---|---|---|
| Task Conflict | TC1 | .618 | .724 | 0.788 |
| | TC2 | .671 | .695 | |
| | TC3 | .513 | .783 | |
| | TC4 | .610 | .737 | |
| Relationship Conflict | RC1 | .592 | .686 | 0.760 |
| | RC2 | .595 | .688 | |
| | RC3 | .566 | .701 | |
| | RC4 | .493 | .740 | |
| Team Emotional Intelligence | EI1 | .418 | .799 | 0.809 |
| | EI2 | .407 | .800 | |
| | EI3 | .475 | .794 | |
| | EI4 | .540 | .788 | |
| | EI5 | .440 | .798 | |
| | EI6 | .446 | .797 | |
| | EI7 | .413 | .801 | |
| | EI8 | .535 | .787 | |
| | EI9 | .540 | .789 | |
| | EI10 | .563 | .790 | |
| | EI11 | .497 | .792 | |
| Team Effectiveness | GE1 | .597 | .938 | 0.938 |
| | GE2 | .668 | .936 | |
| | GE3 | .728 | .933 | |
| | GE4 | .817 | .929 | |
| | GE5 | .743 | .933 | |
| | GE6 | .834 | .928 | |
| | GE7 | .743 | .933 | |
| | GE8 | .742 | .933 | |
| | GE9 | .823 | .928 | |
| | GE10 | .827 | .928 | |

It can be seen from Table 4-12 that the total correlation values corrected by 29 measurement items were all greater than 0.4, and deleting any item could not significantly increase the Cronbach's α coefficient of each item, indicating that the scale met the requirements of reliability measurement.

## (2) Validity Analysis

Validity of scale can be measured through convergent validity and discriminant validity. The former studies the aggregation phenomenon of the measurement with the same feature. It is a state evaluation of whether there a significant high correlation between one indicator variable and other indicator variables that measure the same latent variable. Average variance extracted can be used to evaluate it. AVE evaluates the total variance explained by the latent variable relative to the measurement error. The extracted mean variance is 0.5 or above, indicating that the latent variable measurement has sufficient convergence validity. AVE measurement formula is:

$$AVE = \frac{\sum \lambda^2}{\sum \lambda^2 + \sum \varepsilon_j} \quad \text{Equation (4.2)}$$

Among them, $\lambda$ is the standardized factor load, and $\varepsilon_j$ is the measurement error of item J.

Discriminant validity refers to the degree of distinguishing different features when using the same measurement method to measure or construct, that is, there should be no high correlation between the measurement results of different features. It can be judged by examining whether the correlation coefficient between two latent variables is less than the AVE root mean square of the two latent variables.

1) Validity analysis of task conflict scale

Figure 4-2 shows that this measurement model has a better fitting result, and the standardized factor load of all obvious variables is significant and greater than 0.5. All fitting optimization indexes (Table 4-13) meet the standards and AVE values exceed the lower limit of 0.5, representing good convergent validity.

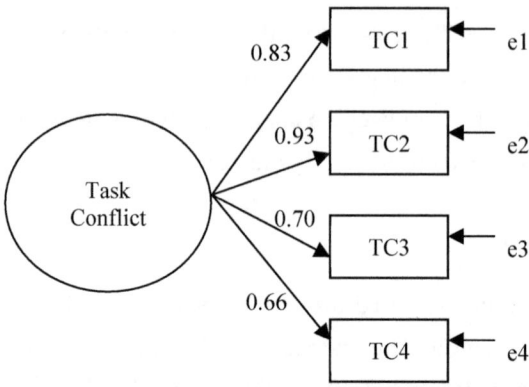

**Figure 4-2 Confirmatory factor analysis model of task conflict in innovation team**

**Table 4-13 Confirmatory factor analysis results of task conflict in innovation team**

| Dimension | Measurement Items | Normalized Factor Load | Standard Error | Critical Ratio (C.R.) | AVE |
|---|---|---|---|---|---|
| | TC1 | .834 | —— | —— | |
| Task Conflict | TC2 | .928 | .069 | 17.071 | 0.651 |
| | TC3 | .705 | .066 | 13.501 | |
| | TC4 | .659 | .055 | 12.360 | |

Fitting Optimization Index:

$\chi^2/df$ =2.260, NFI=0.997, CFI=0.998, IFI=0.998, TLI=0.988, RMSEA=0.064

2) Validity analysis of relationship conflict scale

Figure 4-3 shows that this measurement model has a better fitting result, and the standardized factor load of all obvious variables is greater than or equal to 0.5 and significant. All fitting optimization indexes (Table 4-14) meet the standards and AVE values exceed the lower limit of 0.5, representing good convergent validity.

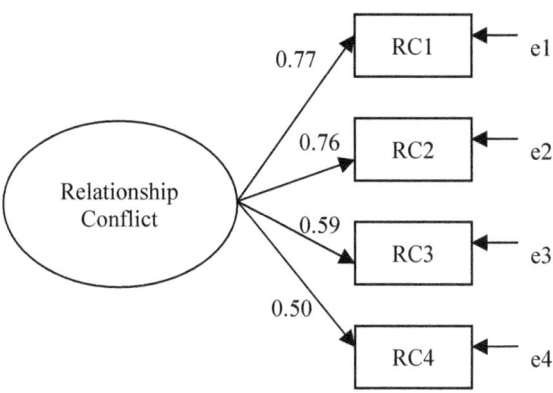

**Figure 4-3 Confirmatory factor analysis model of relationship conflict in innovation team**

**Table 4-14 Confirmatory factor analysis results of relationship conflict in innovation team**

| Dimension | Measurement Items | Normalized Factor Load | Standard Error | Critical Ratio (C.R.) | AVE |
|---|---|---|---|---|---|
| Relationship Conflict | RC1 | .766 | —— | —— | |
| | RC2 | .759 | .075 | 12.410 | 0.512 |
| | RC3 | .585 | .077 | 11.052 | |
| | RC4 | .505 | .074 | 9.647 | |

Fitting Optimization Index:

$\chi^2/df$ =1.513, NFI=0.997, CFI=0.999, IFI=0.999, TLI=0.994, RMSEA =0.031

3) Validity analysis of the team emotional intelligence scale

According to the results of the confirmatory factor analysis, the fitting result of this measurement model is good. The specific confirmatory factor analysis model and results are shown in Figure 4-4 and Table 4-15.

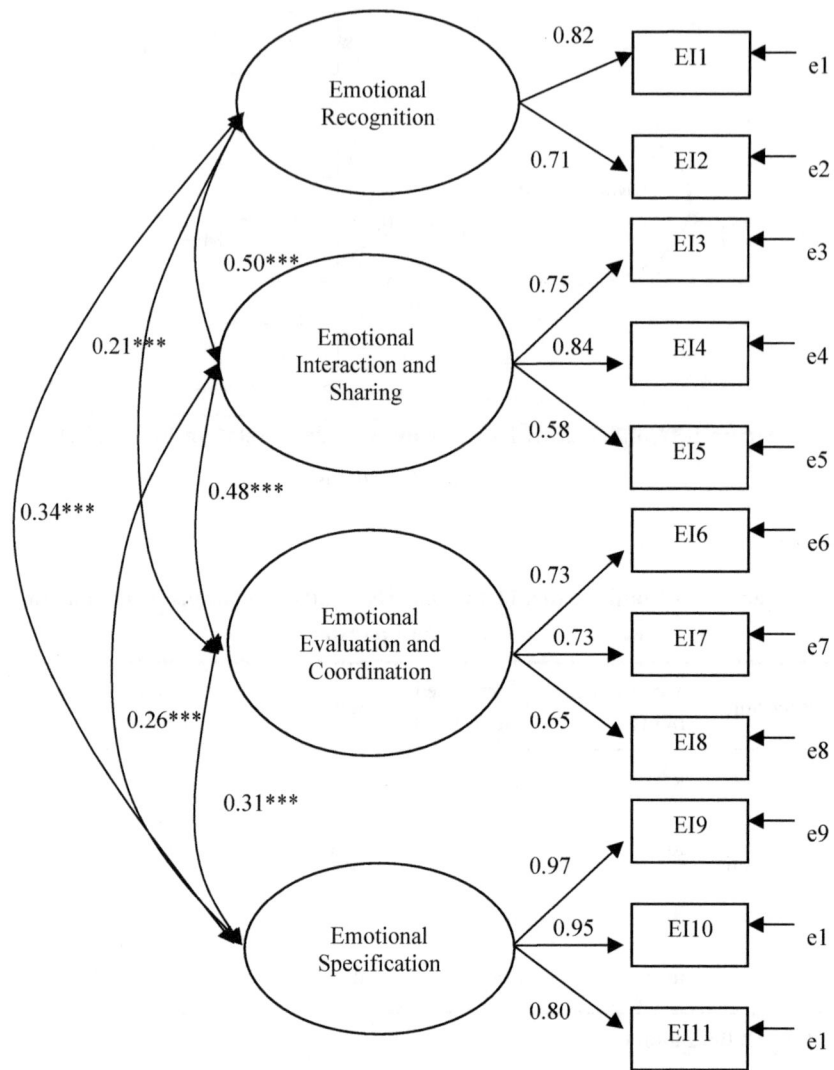

**Figure 4-4 Confirmatory factor analysis model of emotional intelligence of**

**innovation team**

Table 4-15 shows that the scale of team emotional intelligence has better analysis result with all fitting optimization indexes exceeding the proposed value. The standardized factor load of all obvious variables is significant and greater than 0.5. AVE values exceed the lower limit of 0.5, representing good convergent validity. Since team emotional intelligence contains four dimensions, this book studies the discriminant validity of its measurement questionnaire (Table 4-16).

**Table 4-15 Confirmatory factor analysis results of emotional intelligence of innovation team**

| Dimension | Measurement Items | Normalized Factor Load | Standard Error (S.E.) | Critical Ratio (C.R.) | AVE |
|---|---|---|---|---|---|
| Emotional Recognition | EI1 | .823 | —— | —— | 0.688 |
| | EI2 | .707 | .077 | 11.135 | |
| Emotional Interaction and Sharing | EI3 | .752 | —— | —— | 0.599 |
| | EI4 | .836 | .059 | 18.049 | |
| | EI5 | .579 | .058 | 14.523 | |
| Emotional Evaluation | EI6 | .733 | —— | —— | 0.541 |
| | EI7 | .734 | .068 | 14.879 | |
| | EI8 | .647 | .065 | 14.398 | |
| Emotional Specification | EI9 | .969 | —— | —— | 0.911 |
| | EI10 | .946 | .016 | 52.404 | |
| | EI11 | .798 | .025 | 33.163 | |

Fitting Optimization Index

$\chi^2/df$ =2.925, NFI=0.979, CFI=0.986, IFI=0.986, TLI=0.974, RMSEA=0.051

From Table 4-16, the values in the diagonal brackets are the square root of AVE of each dimension, and the values on the non-diagonal lines are the correlation coefficients between two dimensions. Because the square root of AVE is greater than the correlation coefficient of the non-diagonal lines on the row and column, there are clear differences among the four dimensions of team emotional intelligence.

**Table 4-16 Discriminant validity test of the measurement dimension of innovation team emotional intelligence**

| Dimension | Average Value | Standard Deviation | Emotional Recognition | Emotional Interaction and Sharing | Emotional Evaluation | Emotional Specification |
|---|---|---|---|---|---|---|
| Emotional Recognition | 4.0560 | 0.7259 | (0.8295) | | | |
| Emotional Interaction and Sharing | 3.5551 | 0.7098 | 0.345** | (0.7740) | | |
| Emotional Evaluation | 3.3531 | 0.7435 | 0.177** | 0.378** | (0.7355) | |
| Emotional Specification | 4.1595 | 0.6079 | 0.294** | 0.216** | 0.270** | (0.9545) |

4) Validity analysis of the team effectiveness scale

According to the results of confirmatory factor analysis, the model of team effectiveness measurement has a better fitting result. The specific model and results are shown in Figure 4-5 and Table 4-17. Table 4-17 shows that the analysis result of team effectiveness scale is good with all fitting optimization indexes exceeding the proposed value. The standardized factor load of all obvious variables is significant and greater than 0.5. AVE values all exceed the lower limit of 0.5, representing good convergent validity.

The discriminant validity of the team effectiveness scale is studied here. Table 4-18 shows that AVE square roots are all greater than their correlation coefficients, so there are clear differences among the three dimensions of innovation team effectiveness.

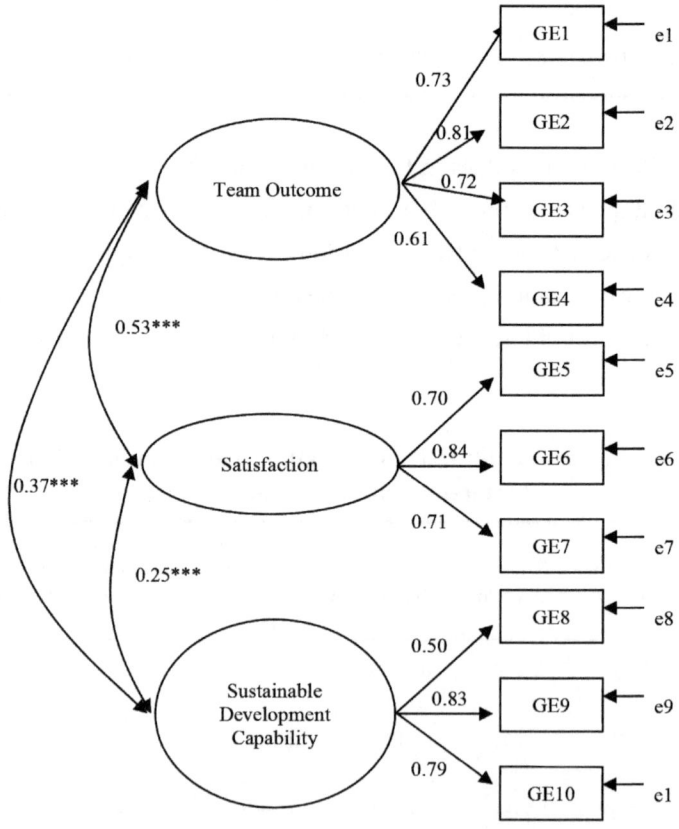

**Figure 4-5 Confirmatory factor analysis model of innovation team effectiveness**

**Table 4-17 Confirmatory factor analysis results of innovation team effectiveness**

| Dimension | Measurement Items | Normalized Factor Load | Standard Error (S.E.) | Critical Ratio (C.R.) | AVE |
|---|---|---|---|---|---|
| Team Outcome | GE1 | .730 | —— | —— | 0.629 |
| | GE2 | .814 | .076 | 13.461 | |
| | GE3 | .717 | .075 | 12.886 | |
| | GE4 | .610 | .075 | 14.081 | |
| Satisfaction | GE5 | .697 | —— | —— | 0.720 |
| | GE6 | .844 | .084 | 15.300 | |
| | GE7 | .706 | .062 | 13.978 | |
| Sustainable Development Capability | GE8 | .503 | —— | —— | 0.640 |
| | GE9 | .829 | .143 | 10.386 | |
| | GE10 | .788 | .144 | 10.641 | |

Fitting Optimization Index:

$\chi^2/df$ =2.606, NFI=0.973, CFI=0.983, IFI=0.983, TLI=0.964, RMSEA=0.055

**Table 4-18 Discriminant validity test of the measurement dimension of innovation team's effectiveness**

| Dimension | Average Value | Standard Deviation | Team Outcome | Satisfaction | Sustainable Development Capability |
|---|---|---|---|---|---|
| Team Outcome | 3.1332 | 0.6187 | (0.7931) | | |
| Satisfaction | 3.3427 | 0.6095 | 0.412** | (0.8485) | |
| Sustainable Development Capability | 3.4559 | 0.5480 | 0.266* | 0.321** | (0.8000) |

5) Validity analysis of the overall measurement model

This book conducts confirmatory factor analysis on the overall model of task conflict, relationship conflict, team emotional intelligence and team effectiveness of innovation teams (Figure 4-6, Table 4-19). As can be seen from Table 4-19, the analysis results of the overall measurement model are good, with each fitting optimization index exceeding the proposed value, the standardized factor load of each obvious variable is significant and greater than 0.5, and the AVE value exceeding the lower limit of 0.5.

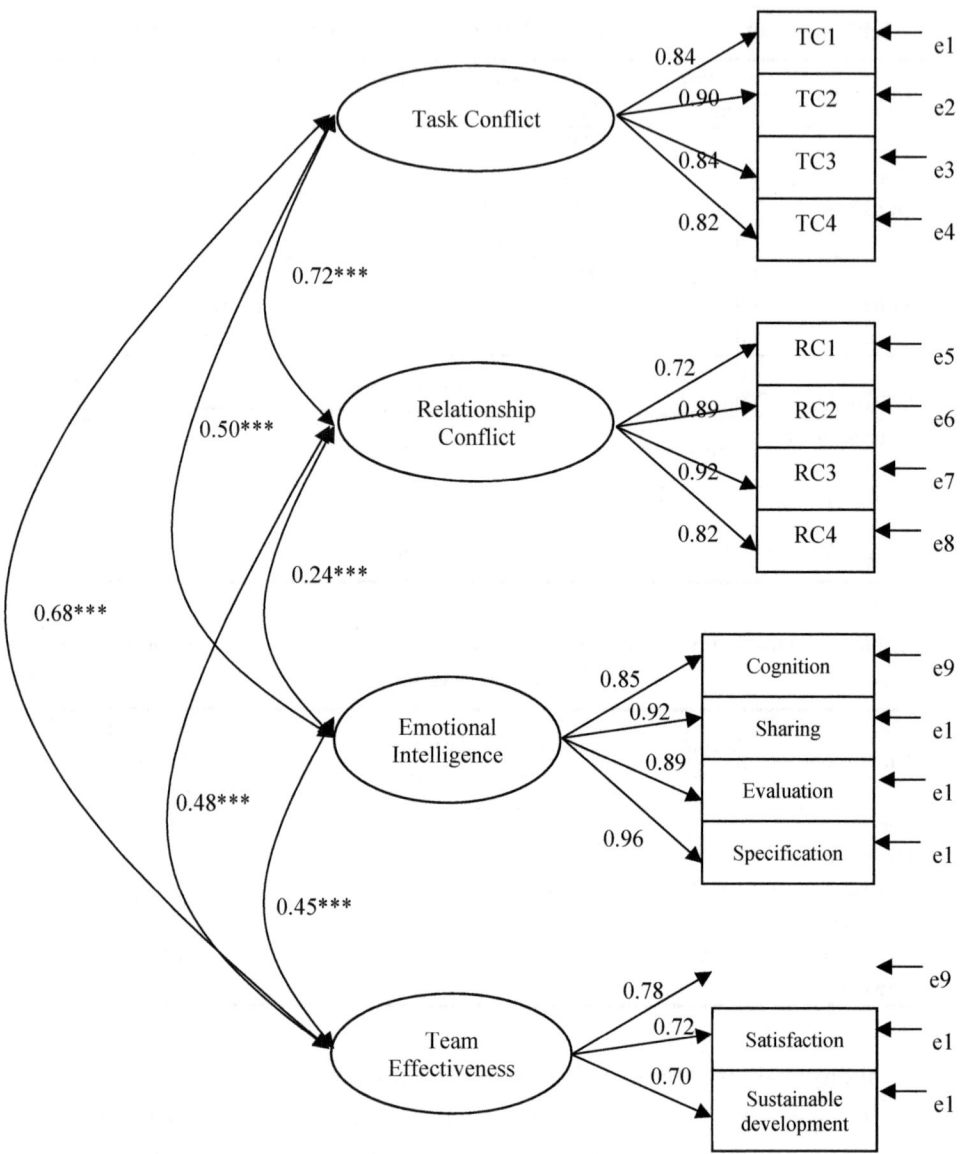

**Figure 4-6 Confirmatory factor analysis model of the overall model**

**Table 4-19 Confirmatory factor analysis results of the overall model**

| Variable | Measurement Items | Normalized Factor Load | Standard Error (S.E.) | Critical Ratio (C.R.) | AVE |
|---|---|---|---|---|---|
| Task Conflict | TC1 | .844 | —— | —— | 0.686 |
| | TC2 | .896 | .047 | 21.486 | |
| | TC3 | .839 | .050 | 19.325 | |
| | TC4 | .825 | .052 | 18.776 | |
| Relationship Conflict | RC1 | .724 | —— | —— | 0.678 |
| | RC2 | .892 | .094 | 11.842 | |
| | RC3 | .919 | .092 | 11.998 | |
| | RC4 | .822 | .089 | 11.320 | |
| Emotional Intelligence | Cognition | .852 | —— | —— | 0.626 |
| | Interaction and Sharing | .924 | .048 | 23.423 | |
| | Evaluation and Coordination | .887 | .051 | 21.817 | |
| | Specification | .856 | .052 | 20.468 | |
| Team Effectiveness | Team Outcome | .784 | —— | —— | 0.507 |
| | Satisfaction | .720 | .066 | 11.930 | |
| | Sustainable Development Capability | .696 | .081 | 11.616 | |

Fitting Optimization Index:

$\chi^2/df$ =2.982, NFI=0.935, CFI=0.956, IFI=0.956, TLI=0.937, RMSEA=0.076

From Table 4-20, AVE square roots are all greater than the correlation coefficient of the non-diagonal lines on the row and column, so there are clear differences among the dimensions of the overall model.

**Table 4-20 Discriminant validity test table for research variables of the overall model**

| Dimension | Average Value | Standard Deviation | Task Conflict | Relationship Conflict | Team Emotional Intelligence | Team Effectiveness |
|---|---|---|---|---|---|---|
| Task Conflict | 5.79 | 0.969 | (0.8283) | | | |
| Relationship Conflict | 6.20 | 0.927 | 0.722 | (0.8234) | | |
| Team Emotional Intelligence | 4.91 | 1.315 | 0.504 | 0.243 | (0.7912) | |
| Team Effectiveness | 5.49 | 1.204 | 0.681 | 0.484 | 0.450 | (0.7120) |

### (3) The Impact of Control Variables

The control variables pertain to categorical independent variables, and each control variable has more than two categories. The variables at the team level include team size and team establishment time. This book examines the influence of control variables on mediating and outcome variables through a single factor analysis of variance. Individual variables such as gender are not the focus of this study, so they are not considered in this book.

1) The impact of team size
It is clear that there is no significant difference in three dimensions of relationship conflict and team effectiveness in teams of different sizes.

**Table 4-21 The impact of team size on mediating variable and outcome variable**

| Dimension | F-measure | Significance Probability | Whether it is significant |
|---|---|---|---|
| Relationship Conflict | .437 | .727 | NO |
| Team Outcome | .271 | .846 | NO |
| Satisfaction | .120 | .948 | NO |

| Dimension | F-measure | Significance Probability | Whether it is significant |
|---|---|---|---|
| Sustainable Development Capability | .374 | .772 | NO |

2) Team establishment time

As shown in Table 4-22, different establishment time of the team has no significant influence on three dimensions of relationship conflict and team effectiveness.

**Table 4-22 The impact of team establishment time on mediating variable and outcome variable**

| Dimension | F-measure | Significance Probability | Whether it is significant |
|---|---|---|---|
| Relationship Conflict | .943 | .442 | No |
| Team Outcome | 1.040 | .390 | No |
| Satisfaction | .209 | .933 | No |
| Sustainable Development Capability | .496 | .738 | No |

## (4) Verification of Hypothesis

This conceptual model is a moderated mediating effect model. Therefore, the mediating effect of relationship conflict should be tested first, and then the moderating effect of conflict network density and team emotional intelligence should be tested.

1) The mediating effect test of relationship conflict

The first is to build the relationship model of the impact of task conflict on relationship conflict. It can be seen from Table 4-23 that all fitting indexes meet the requirements, and the standardized path coefficient of task conflict and relationship conflict is 0.680 and significant at 0.001 level.

**Table 4-23 Analysis of the impact of task conflict on relationship conflict**

| Regression Path of Hypothesis | Standardized Path Coefficient | Significance Probability | Whether the hypothesis is supported |
|---|---|---|---|
| Relationship Conflict←Task Conflict | 0.680 | *** | Yes |

Fitting Optimization Index:

$\chi^2\!/_{df}$ =1.560, NFI=0.912, CFI=0.965, IFI=0.966, TLI=0.946, RMSEA=0.070

Note: *** P <0.001, ** P <0. 01, * P <0.05 the same below

Second, the book argues that task conflict has different effects on team effectiveness when assuming the influence of task conflict on team effectiveness. That is to say, task conflict has a negative effect on member satisfaction and sustainable development capability, but there is an inverted-U relationship between task conflict and team outcome, so the book first tests the relationship between task conflict and team outcome. The test results using multiple regression are shown in Table 4-24.

**Table 4-24 Analysis of the impact of task conflict on outcomes**

| Variable | Team Outcome | |
|---|---|---|
| | Model 1 | Model 2 |
| Task Conflict (TC) | -0.505*** | -0.492 |
| Quadratic Term of Task Conflict (TC2) | | 0.020 |
| $R^2$ | 0.255 | 0.255 |
| (S)$R^2$ | 0.255*** | 0.000 |
| F | 30.137*** | 0.026 |

In Model 1, the centralized task conflict was substituted into the equation, where (S)$R^2$ was 0.255 and significant at P<0.001, colinear diagnosis VIF<2, there was a significant negative relationship between task conflict and team outcome, and the regression coefficient was –0.505 and significant at P<0.001. In Model 2, after substituting the quadratic term of the centralized task conflict into the equation, the model did not improve significantly. The regression coefficient of the quadratic term of task conflict was 0.020, which was not significant. Therefore, the hypothesis of an inverted-U relationship between task conflict and team outcome is not valid.

This book continues to construct the relationship model of the impact of task conflict on team effectiveness. Since the hypothesis of an inverted-U relationship between task conflict and team outcome is not valid, this book attempts to verify the linear negative correlation between them. As can be seen from Table 4-25, all fitting indexes meet the requirements, and the standardized path coefficients between task conflict and outcomes, satisfaction and sustainable development capability are significant.

**Table 4-25 Analysis of the impact of task conflict on team effectiveness**

| Regression Path of Hypothesis | Standardized Path Coefficient | Significance Probability | Whether the hypothesis is supported |
| --- | --- | --- | --- |
| Outcomes←Task Conflict | -0.615 | *** | No |
| Satisfaction←Task Conflict | -0.541 | *** | Yes |
| Sustainable Development Capability←Task Conflict | -0.488 | *** | Yes |
| Fitting Optimization Index | | | |
| $\chi^2 / df$ =1.347, NFI=0.850, CFI=0.952, IFI=0.953, TLI=0.941, RMSEA=0.062 | | | |

Then, the relationship model of the impact of relationship conflict on team effectiveness is constructed. Table 4-26 shows that all fitting indexes meet the requirements.

**Table 4-26 Analysis of the impact of relationship conflict on team effectiveness**

| Regression Path of Hypothesis | Standardized Path Coefficient | Significance Probability | Whether the hypothesis is supported |
| --- | --- | --- | --- |
| Outcomes←Relationship Conflict | -0.414 | *** | Yes |
| Satisfaction←Relationship Conflict | -0.554 | *** | Yes |

| | | | |
|---|---|---|---|
| Sustainable Development Capability←Relationship Conflict | -0.603 | *** | Yes |

Fitting Optimization Index

$\chi^2/df$ =1.212, NFI =0.8573, CFI=0.974, IFI=0.975, TLI=0.968, RMSEA=0.049

Through the above analysis, on the basis of satisfying the first three conditions of mediating effect, this book verifies the mediating effect of relationship conflict by constructing two competition models.

First, a complete mediation model was constructed, and the fitting results are shown in Table 4-27.

**Table 4-27 Fitting results of the complete mediation model of relationship conflict**

| Regression Path of Hypothesis | Standardized Path Coefficient | Significance Probability |
|---|---|---|
| Relationship Conflict←Task Conflict | 0.739 | *** |
| Outcomes←Relationship Conflict | -0.592 | *** |
| Satisfaction←Relationship Conflict | -0.574 | *** |
| Sustainable Development Capability←Relationship Conflict | -0.601 | *** |

Fitting Optimization Index:

$\chi^2/df$ =1.356, NFI =0.830, CFI=0.948, IFI=0.949, TLI=0.939, RMSEA=0.063

From Table 4-27 and Figure 4-7, the complete mediation model of relationship conflict has better fitting results, and the standardized path coefficients of task conflict and relationship conflict, as well as the standardized path coefficients of relationship conflict and outcomes, satisfaction and sustainable development capability are significant at 0.001 level.

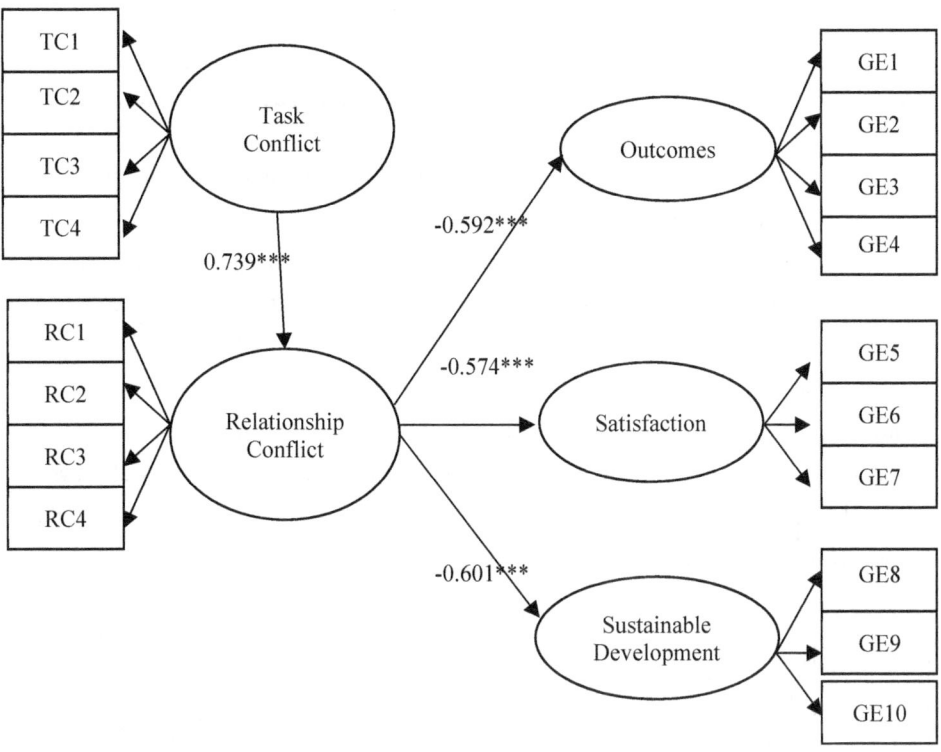

**Figure 4-7 The complete mediation model of relationship conflict**

Then, a partial mediation model is constructed, and the fitting results are shown in Table 4-28.

**Table 4-28 Fitting results of partial mediation model of relationship conflict**

| Regression Path of Hypothesis | Standardized Path Coefficient | Significance Probability |
|---|---|---|
| Relationship Conflict←Task Conflict | 0.779 | *** |
| Outcomes←Task Conflict | -0.440 | *** |
| Satisfaction←Task Conflict | -0.206 | 0.173 |
| Sustainable Development Capability←Task Conflict | -0.361 | 0.012 |
| Outcomes←Relationship Conflict | -0.513 | *** |
| Satisfaction←Relationship Conflict | -0.644 | *** |
| Sustainable Development Capability←Relationship Conflict | -0.508 | *** |

Fitting Optimization Index

$$\chi^2 \big/ df = 1.205,\ NFI = 0.902,\ CFI = 0.982,\ IFI = 0.982,\ TLI = 0.977,\ RMSEA = 0.048$$

As shown in Table 4-28, the fitting indexes of the partial mediation model are better than those of the complete mediation model. Compared with the complete mediation model, the partial mediation model can explain more variance of team effectiveness (0.426VS0.311). The relationship between task conflict and relationship conflict was significant (0.779, P <0.001). Relationship conflict has a significant correlation with three dimensions of team effectiveness, and the correlation between task conflict, satisfaction and sustainable development is insignificant. The book believes that relationship conflict plays a partial mediating role between task conflict and team effectiveness, and the partial mediation model formed is shown in Figure 4-8.

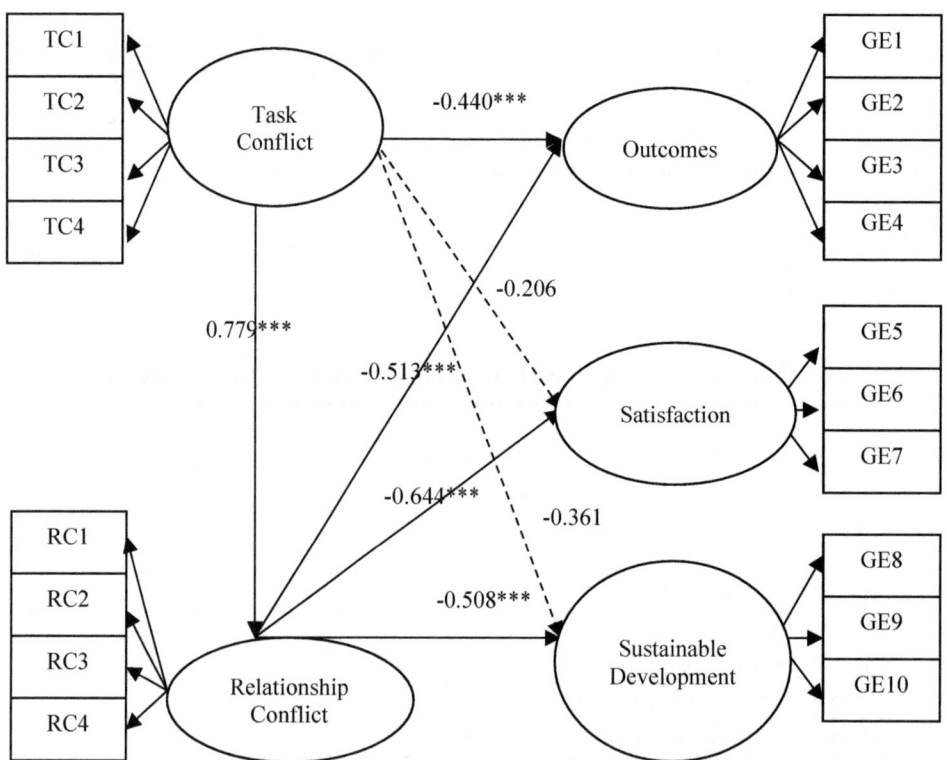

**Figure 4-8 Partial mediation model of relationship conflict**

Figure 4-8 shows that the standardized path coefficient of task conflict and relationship conflict is 0.779 (P<0.001). Relationship conflict plays a partial mediating role between task conflict and outcomes. The normalized path coefficient between task conflict and outcomes was –0.440 (P<0.001), and the normalized path coefficient between relationship conflict and outcomes was –0.513 (P<0.001). The direct effect of task conflict on satisfaction and sustainable development capability was not significant, but relationship conflict plays a completely mediating role in the relationship between task conflict, satisfaction and sustainable development capability. The standardized path coefficients of relationship conflict, satisfaction and sustainable development capability were –0.644 (P<0.001) and –0.508 (P<0.001).

According to the output results of structural equation models, the total standardized effect value of task conflict on outcomes, satisfaction and sustainable development capability is –0.840 (standardized direct effect value being –0.440, and standardized indirect effect value being –0.400), –0.708 (standardized direct effect value being –0.206, and standardized indirect effect value being –0.502) and –0.757 (standardized direct effect value being –0.361 and standardized indirect effect value being –0.396) respectively. The total standardized effect of relationship conflict on outcomes, satisfaction and sustainable development capability was –0.513, –0.644 and –0.508, respectively.

1) The moderating effect test of task conflict network density

According to the above analysis, relationship conflict plays a complete mediating role between task conflict and satisfaction and sustainable development capability, and a partial mediating role between task conflict and outcomes. Therefore, this book only considers whether the relationship between task conflict and outcomes is moderated by the density of task conflict network.

It can be seen from Table 4-29 that Model 2 is significantly improved compared with Model 1, $(S)R2=0.019$ (P<0.001). Combined with the moderating effect diagram (Figure 4-9), it can be seen that the higher the value of task conflict network density, the stronger the negative correlation between task conflict and outcomes.

**Table 4-29 Analysis of the moderating effect of task conflict network density on task conflict and outcomes**

| Variable | Outcomes | |
|---|---|---|
| | Model 1 | Model 2 |
| Task Conflict | -0.359*** | -0.246** |
| Task Conflict Network Density | -0.631*** | -0.684*** |
| Task Conflict × Task Conflict Network Density | | -0.167** |
| $R^2$ | 0.791 | 0.803 |
| $(S)R^2$ | 0.791*** | 0.019** |
| Modification of F | 164.337 | 8.681 |

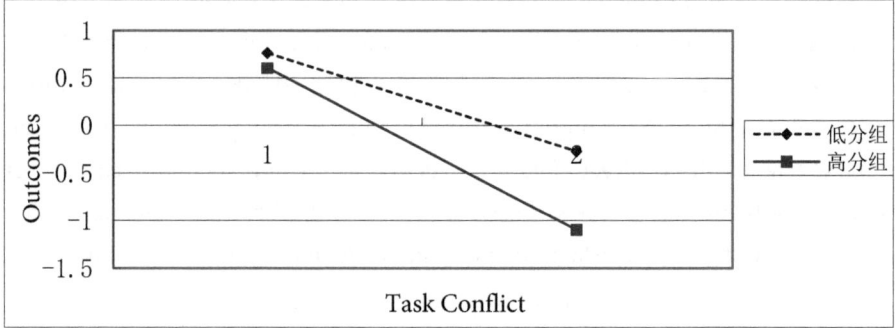

**Figure 4-9 The moderating effect of task conflict network density on task conflict and outcomes**

This book examines the moderating effect of relationship conflict network density on relationship conflict and team effectiveness. Table 4-30 shows that the density of relationship conflict network has a positive moderating effect on relationship conflict, outcomes, satisfaction and sustainable development capability. That is to say, the higher the relationship conflict network density, the stronger the negative correlation between relationship conflict and outcomes, satisfaction and sustainable development capability.

**Table 4-30 Analysis results of the moderating effect of relationship conflict network density on relationship conflict and team effectiveness**

| Variable | Outcomes | | Satisfaction | | Sustainable Development Capability | |
|---|---|---|---|---|---|---|
| | Model 1 | Model 2 | Model 1 | Model 2 | Model 1 | Model 2 |
| Relationship Conflict | -0.323*** | -0.226** | -0.247** | -0.091 | -0.314*** | -0.168* |
| Relationship Conflict Network Density | -0.661*** | -0.709*** | -0.661*** | -0.739*** | -0.624*** | -0.697*** |
| Relationship Conflict ×Relationship Conflict Network Density | | -0.140** | | -0.226*** | | -0.212*** |
| $R^2$ | 0.832 | 0.846 | 0.721 | 0.758 | 0.756 | 0.789 |
| (S)$R^2$ | 0.832*** | 0.014** | 0.721*** | 0.037*** | 0.756*** | 0.033*** |
| Modification of F | 214.818 | 7.923 | 112.379 | 13.271 | 135.127 | 13.310 |

This book examines the moderating effects of team emotional intelligence on task conflict, relationship conflict and team effectiveness. Since team emotional intelligence contains four dimensions, the moderating effects of the four dimensions are analyzed and tested respectively in order to avoid the multicollinearity bias caused by the co-entry into equation. Before hierarchical regression, the multicollinearity between variables is judged first. It is generally believed that when the tolerance is greater than 0.1, namely VIF is less than 10, there is basically no multicollinearity between the independent variables. Through SPSS analysis, the results show that there is no multicollinearity between variables. The mediating effect test of relationship conflict shows that relationship conflict fully mediates the relationship between task conflict, satisfaction and sustainable development capability, and partially mediates the relationship between task conflict and outcomes. Therefore, only whether the relationship between task conflict and outcomes is moderated by team emotional intelligence is considered in the book.

Multiple regression results (Table 4-31 and Table 4-32) show that the emotional cognitive dimension plays a significant negative moderating role between task conflict and outcomes, relationship conflict and team effectiveness.

**Table 4-31 Analysis results of the moderating effect of emotional cognition on task conflict and outcomes**

| Variable | Outcomes | |
|---|---|---|
| | Model 1 | Model 2 |
| Task Conflict | -0.242** | -0.292*** |
| Emotional Cognition | 0.645*** | 0.714*** |
| Task Conflict ×Emotional Cognition | | -0.183** |
| $R^2$ | 0.602 | 0.625 |
| $(S)R^2$ | 0.602*** | 0.023** |
| Modification of F | 65.813 | 5.325 |

**Table 4-32 Analysis results of the moderating effect of emotional cognition on relationship conflict and team effectiveness**

| Variable | Outcomes | | Satisfaction | | Sustainable Development Capability | |
|---|---|---|---|---|---|---|
| | Model 1 | Model 2 | Model 1 | Model 2 | Model 1 | Model 2 |
| Relationship Conflict | -0.260** | -0.255** | -0.250** | -0.245** | -0.363*** | -0.358*** |
| Emotional Cognition | 0.634*** | 0.755*** | 0.500*** | 0.613*** | 0.445*** | 0.559** |
| Relationship Conflict× Emotional Cognition | | -0.239** | | -0.222* | | -0.225* |
| $R^2$ | 0.609 | 0.651 | 0.418 | 0.455 | 0.467 | 0.505 |
| $(S)R^2$ | 0.609*** | 0.043** | 0.418*** | 0.037* | 0.467*** | 0.038* |
| Modification of F | 67.657 | 10.514 | 31.286 | 5.819 | 38.068 | 6.565 |

The results of multiple regression analysis (Table 4-33 and Table 4-34) show that emotional interaction and sharing plays a significant negative moderating role between task conflict and outcomes, relationship conflict and team effectiveness.

**Table 4-33 Analysis results of the moderating effect of emotional interaction on task conflict and outcomes**

| Variable | Outcomes | |
|---|---|---|
| | Model 1 | Model 2 |
| Task Conflict | -0.241** | -0.286*** |
| Interaction and sharing | 0.639*** | 0.729*** |
| Task Conflict × Interaction and Sharing | | -0.212** |
| $R^2$ | 0.593 | 0.624 |
| (S)$R^2$ | 0.593*** | 0.031** |
| Modification of F | 63.449 | 7.133 |

**Table 4-34 Analysis results of the moderating effect of emotional interaction on relationship conflict and team effectiveness**

| Variable | Outcomes | | Satisfaction | | Sustainable Development Capability | |
|---|---|---|---|---|---|---|
| | Model 1 | Model 2 | Model 1 | Model 2 | Model 1 | Model 2 |
| Relationship Conflict | -0.271*** | -0.269*** | -0.248** | -0.246** | -0.386*** | -0.384*** |
| Interaction and sharing | 0.627*** | 0.710*** | 0.519*** | 0.631*** | 0.403*** | 0.508*** |
| Task Conflict × Interaction and Sharing | | -0.167* | | -0.226* | | -0.212* |
| $R^2$ | 0.606 | 0.627 | 0.437 | 0.476 | 0.439 | 0.474 |
| (S)$R^2$ | 0.606*** | 0.021* | 0.437*** | 0.039* | 0.439*** | 0.034* |
| Modification of F | 66.921 | 4.905 | 33.791 | 6.352 | 34.086 | 5.594 |

The results of multiple regression analysis (Table 4-35 and Table 4-36) show that emotional evaluation and coordination plays a significant negative moderating role between task conflict and outcomes, relationship conflict and team effectiveness.

**Table 4-35 Analysis results of the moderating effect of emotional evaluation and coordination on task conflict and outcomes**

| Variable | Outcomes | |
|---|---|---|
| | Model 1 | Model 2 |
| Task Conflict | -0.284*** | -0.333*** |
| Evaluation and Coordination | 0.586*** | 0.648*** |
| Task Conflict × Evaluation and Coordination | | -0.177* |
| $R^2$ | 0.550 | 0.573 |
| $(S)R^2$ | 0.550*** | 0.023* |
| Modification of F | 53.085 | 4.609 |

**Table 4-36 Analysis results of the moderating effect of emotional evaluation and coordination on relationship conflict and team effectiveness**

| Variable | Outcomes | | Satisfaction | | Sustainable Development Capability | |
|---|---|---|---|---|---|---|
| | Model 1 | Model 2 | Model 1 | Model 2 | Model 1 | Model 2 |
| Relationship Conflict | -0.300*** | -0.293*** | -0.276** | -0.261** | -0.410*** | -0.399*** |
| Evaluation and Coordination | 0.574*** | 0.670*** | 0.466*** | 0.656*** | 0.356*** | 0.492*** |
| Relationship Conflict × Evaluation and Coordination | | -0.174* | | -0.343*** | | -0.246* |
| $R^2$ | 0.556 | 0.578 | 0.396 | 0.461 | 0.411 | 0.453 |
| $(S)R^2$ | 0.556*** | 0.022* | 0.396*** | 0.084*** | 0.411*** | 0.043* |
| Modification of F | 54.482 | 4.392 | 28.499 | 13.809 | 30.297 | 6.744 |

The results of multiple regression analysis (Table 4-37 and Table 4-38) show that emotional evaluation and coordination play a significant negative moderating role between task conflict and outcomes, relationship conflict and team effectiveness.

**Table 4-37 Analysis results of the moderating effect of emotional specification on task conflict and outcomes**

| Variable | Outcomes | |
|---|---|---|
| | Model 1 | Model 2 |
| Task Conflict | -0.269** | -0.324*** |
| Emotional Specification | 0.602*** | 0.683*** |
| Task Conflict×Emotional Specification | | -0.200* |
| $R^2$ | 0.562 | 0.589 |
| (S)$R^2$ | 0.562*** | 0.027* |
| Modification of F | 55.812 | 5.615 |

**Table 4-38 Analysis results of the moderating effect of emotional specification on relationship conflict and team effectiveness**

| Variable | Outcomes | | Satisfaction | | Sustainable Development Capability | |
|---|---|---|---|---|---|---|
| | Model 1 | Model 2 | Model 1 | Model 2 | Model 1 | Model 2 |
| Relationship Conflict | -0.291*** | -0.290*** | -0.263** | -0.262** | -0.398*** | -0.397*** |
| Emotional Specification | 0.590*** | 0.685*** | 0.493*** | 0.649*** | 0.382 | 0.490 |
| Relationship Conflict ×Emotional Specification | | -0.175* | | -0.288** | | -0.201** |
| $R^2$ | 0.571 | 0.593 | 0.417 | 0.475 | 0.426 | 0.455 |
| (S)$R^2$ | 0.571*** | 0.022* | 0.417*** | 0.058** | 0.426*** | 0.028** |
| Modification of F | 57.982 | 4.554 | 31.102 | 9.588 | 32.310 | 4.482 |

In conclusion, different dimensions of emotional intelligence of innovation team moderate the relationship between task conflict and outcomes, relationship conflict and team effectiveness to varying degrees.

## 4.3.3 Revision of the Conceptual Model

Based on the above analysis, the corresponding test results of hypothesis are summarized in Table 4-39.

Table 4-39 Test results of research hypothesis

| Number | Content of Hypotheses | Test Result |
|---|---|---|
| H1a | Relationship conflict in innovation teams has a negative effect on team outcomes. | Support |
| H1b | Relationship conflict in innovation teams has a negative effect on member satisfaction. | Support |
| H1c | Relationship conflict in innovation teams has a negative effect on sustainable development capability. | Support |
| H2a | There is an inverted-U relationship between task conflict and team outcomes, that is, moderate task conflict is beneficial to team outcomes. | Nonsupport |
| H2b | Task conflict in innovation teams has a negative effect on member satisfaction. | Support |
| H2c | Task conflict in innovation teams has a negative effect on sustainable development capability. | Support |
| H3 | Relationship conflict in innovation teams acts as the mediator between task conflict and team effectiveness. | Support |
| H4a | The positive correlation between moderate task conflict and team outcomes is stronger and the negative correlation between task conflict and member satisfaction and sustainable development capability is weaker when the team emotional intelligence is higher. | Partially Supported |
| H4b | The negative correlation between relationship conflict and team outcomes, member satisfaction and sustainable development capability is weaker when the team emotional intelligence is higher. | Support |
| H5a | The positive correlation between moderate task conflict and team outcomes is weaker and the negative correlation between task conflict and team satisfaction and sustainable development capability is stronger when the density of task conflict network is higher. | Partially Supported |
| H5b | The negative correlation between relationship conflict and team outcomes, member satisfaction and sustainable development capability is stronger when the density of relationship conflict network is higher. | Support |

Based on the test results, this book revises the conceptual model in Figure 4-1 and constructs the relationship model between innovation team conflict and team effectiveness (Figure 4-10).

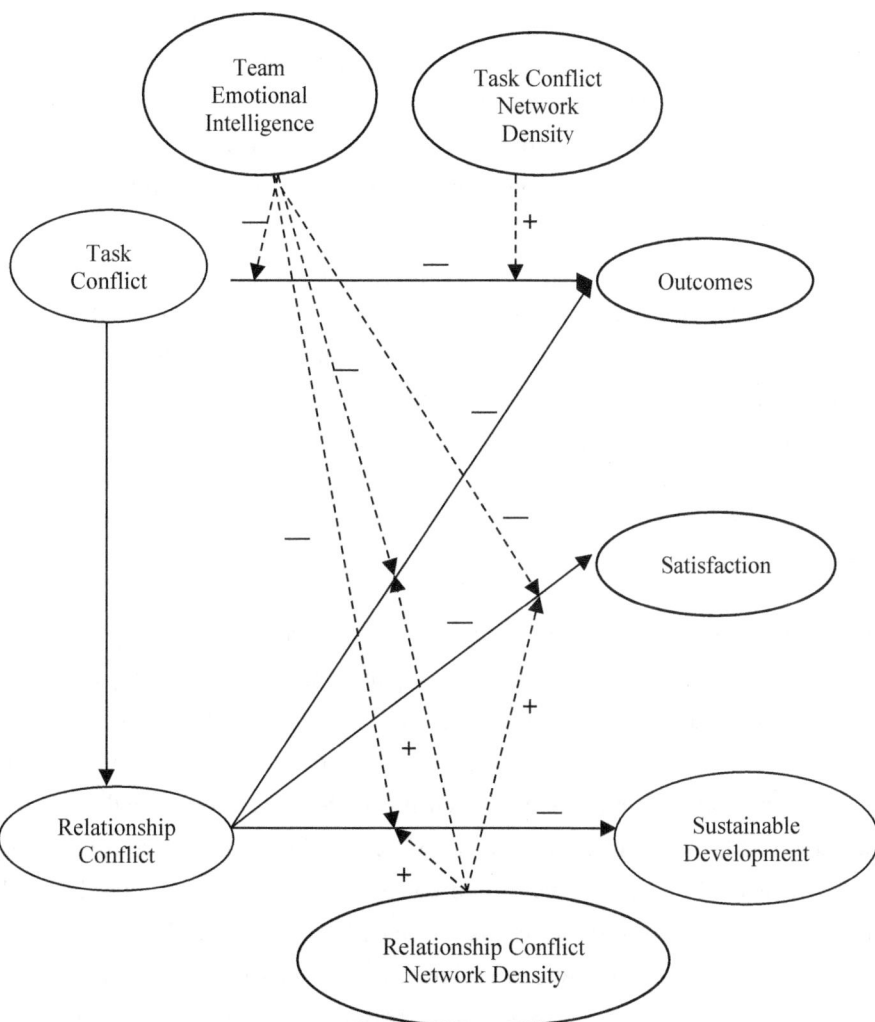

**Figure 4-10 Relationship model between innovation team conflict and team effectiveness**

Figure 4-10 shows that: firstly, task conflict in innovation teams is positively correlated with relationship conflict. Secondly, task conflict has a negative impact on team outcomes, and relationship conflict has a negative impact on all three dimensions of team effectiveness. Thirdly, relationship conflict acts as a mediator between task conflict and team effectiveness. Specifically speaking, it plays a complete mediating role in relationship between task conflict and satisfaction and sustainable development capability, and a partial mediating role in relationship between task conflict and team outcomes. Fourthly, the different dimensions of team emotional intelligence negatively moderate the relationship between task conflict and outcomes, relationship conflict and team effectiveness to varying degrees. Fifthly, task conflict network density plays a positive moderating role between task conflict and outcomes. Sixthly, relationship conflict network density plays a positive moderating role between relationship conflict and three dimensions of team effectiveness.

## 4.4 Summary

This chapter aims to study the impact of innovation team conflict on team effectiveness in the "output" phase of team operation. In order to clarify the effect of team conflict, a new research scenario was designed according to the research content in the preceding chapters and the theory of emotion, namely, the moderating effects of conflict network density and team emotional intelligence on the relationship between team conflict and team effectiveness were considered simultaneously. Firstly, hypotheses and conceptual models are proposed, based on theoretical analysis and the results in the existing literature. Secondly, initial analysis of the questionnaire was carried out through small sample testing. Finally, formal questionnaires were formed and distributed on a large scale, hypotheses were verified through data analysis, and a relationship model between innovation team conflict and team effectiveness was constructed. The empirical results show that: (1) task conflict is positively correlated with relationship conflict in innovation teams; (2) task conflict has a negative impact on team outcomes, while relationship conflict has a negative impact on all three dimensions of team effectiveness; (3) relationship conflict acts as a mediator between task conflict and team effectiveness. Specifically speaking, it plays a complete mediating role in relationship between task conflict and satisfaction and sustainable development capability, and a partial mediating role in relationship between task conflict and team outcomes; (4) different dimensions of team emotional intelligence negatively moderate the relationship between task conflict and outcomes, relationship conflict and team effectiveness to varying degrees; (5) task conflict network density plays a positive moderating role between task conflict and outcomes; (6) relationship conflict network density plays a positive moderating role between relationship conflict and three dimensions of team effectiveness.

# CHAPTER 5

# Simulation and Management Countermeasures of Innovation Team Conflict

The three chapters above study innovation team conflict from the input-process-output phases of team operation respectively, and analyze this problem systematically. The brittleness model of innovation team conflict can be further improved by studying the antecedent variables of innovation team conflict, the conflict relations between members and the impact of team conflict on team effectiveness. This chapter mainly uses Matlab software to simulate the brittleness model of innovation team conflict, so as to further verify the foregoing research conclusions. Meanwhile, corresponding countermeasures and suggestions are put forward for the management of innovation team conflict according to the above research content and results.

## 5.1 Simulation of the Brittleness Model of Innovation Team Conflict

According to the research content of the three chapters above, the brittleness model of innovation team conflict (Figure 2-3) is revised in this book to form a modified model (Figure 5-1).

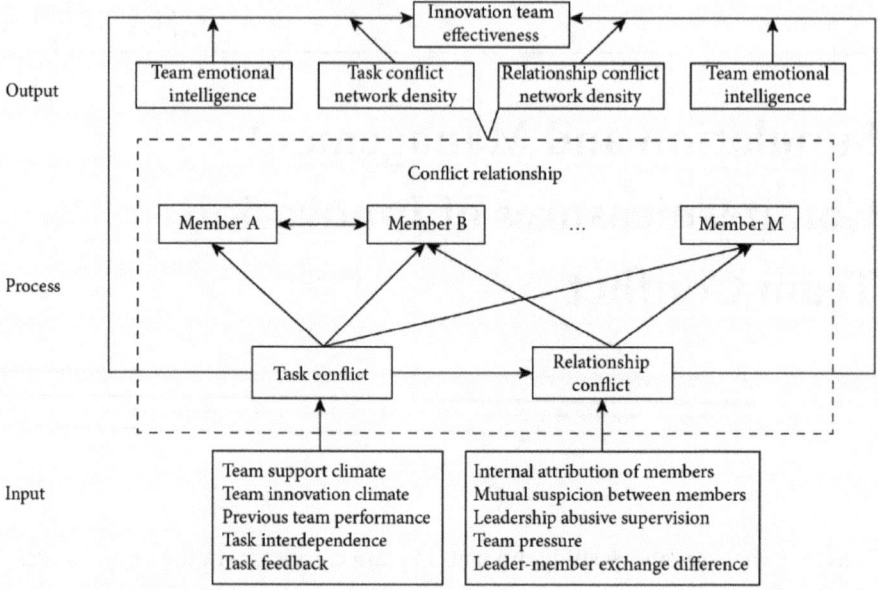

**Figure 5-1 Modified model of brittleness model of innovation team conflict**

In Figure 5-1, in the "input" stage of team operation, the main antecedent variables of task conflict are team support climate, team innovation climate, previous team performance, task interdependence and task feedback clarity. The main antecedent variables of relationship conflict are the internal attribution of members, mutual suspicion between members, abusive leadership supervision, team pressure and leader-member exchange differences. In the "process" stage of the team operation, the conflict relationship among members is mainly analyzed from three levels of "team-individual and team-individual and individual." In the "output" stage of team operation, the moderating effect of conflict network density and team emotional intelligence is considered to explore the impact of team conflict on team effectiveness in a new research context.

### 5.1.1 Simulation of Each Antecedent Variable on Team Conflict

The antecedent variables of task conflict and relationship conflict are inconsistent, so they are discussed in turn in this book.

## (1) Antecedent Variables and Task Conflict

Task conflict develops dynamically, and its level changes with time, but it will reach a stable state after developing to a certain extent, so it can be described by a retarded growth model. Let "t" be the time when the level of task conflict develops, and TC (task conflict) be the level of task conflict, then the growth rate of TC(t) within the time $[t, t + \Delta t)$ can be expressed as:

$$\frac{TC(t + \Delta t) - TC(t)}{TC(t)} \quad \text{Equation (5.1)}$$

In chapter 3, through literature review, questionnaire survey and Ridit analysis, it can be found that the top five antecedent variables leading to task conflict in innovation teams are the level of team support climate, the level of the team innovation climate, the previous level of team performance, the degree of task interdependence and the clarity of task feedback. Therefore, the following assumptions are made:

A. The inherent growth rate of task conflict level is $r_1$, and $r_1$ is constant;
B. There is a maximum limit $M_1$ on the level of task conflict;
C. The antecedent variables are independent of each other.

According to assumption A, it can be obtained:

$$\frac{TC(t + \Delta t) - TC(t)}{TC(t)} = r_1 \Delta t \quad \text{Equation (5.2)}$$

Let $\Delta t \to 0$, then:

$$dTC(t) = r_1 TC(t) dt \quad \text{Equation (5.3)}$$

According to assumption B, since $M_1$ is the maximum limit on the level of task conflict, its retardation factor is $1 - \dfrac{TC}{M_1}$, and equation (5.3) can be translated into:

$$dTC(t) = r_1 TC(t)[1 - \frac{TC(t)}{M_1}] dt \quad \text{Equation (5.4)}$$

According to assumption C and the central limit theorem, the influence degree of each antecedent variable on task conflict can be depicted by normal distribution and [0,1] random distribution. Let $\alpha_1 - \alpha_5$ be its volatility, and its values are respectively (0.2088, 0.2024, 0.1987, 0.1951, 0.1950) ( $\alpha_1 - \alpha_5$ is obtained by adding up the average Ridit value of antecedent variable in Chapter 3 and redistributing it according to the original proportion). As a result:

$$\begin{cases} dTC(t) = r_1 TC(t)[1 - \dfrac{TC(t)}{M_1}]dt + TC(t)(\alpha_1 R_1 + \alpha_2 R_2 + \alpha_3 R_3 + \alpha_4 R_4 + \alpha_5 R_5) \\ TC(0) = 0 \end{cases}$$

Equation (5.5)

In this equation, $R_1, R_2, R_3, R_4, R_5$ are the antecedent variables of task conflict respectively. Among them, $R_1$ is the level of team support climate, which is the random number that follows normal distribution of $\left[ \mu_1, \sigma_1^2 \right]$. The larger $\mu_1$ is, the better the level of team support climate. $R_2$ is the level of team innovation climate, which is the random number that follows normal distribution of $\left[ \mu_2, \sigma_2^2 \right]$. The larger $\mu_2$ is, the better the level of team innovation climate. $R_3$ is previous level of team performance and $R_3 \in [0,1]$. The closer it is to 0, the worse the previous performance level is. $R_4$ is the degree of task interdependence and $R_4 \in [0,1]$. The closer it is to 0, the lower the degree of task interdependence. $R_5$ is the clarity of task feedback and $R_5 \in [0,1]$. The closer it is to 0, the worse the clarity of task feedback. $\alpha_1, \alpha_2, \alpha_3, \alpha_4, \alpha_5$ refer to the influence degree of each antecedent variable on task conflict.

1) Each antecedent variable is fixed at 0.5

In the simulation of task conflict, the book first set five antecedent variables to be fixed at 0.5 and kept unchanged, so as to see the evolution process of the task conflict level under general circumstances. The results can be obtained by using Matlab software for simulation, as shown in Figure 5-2.

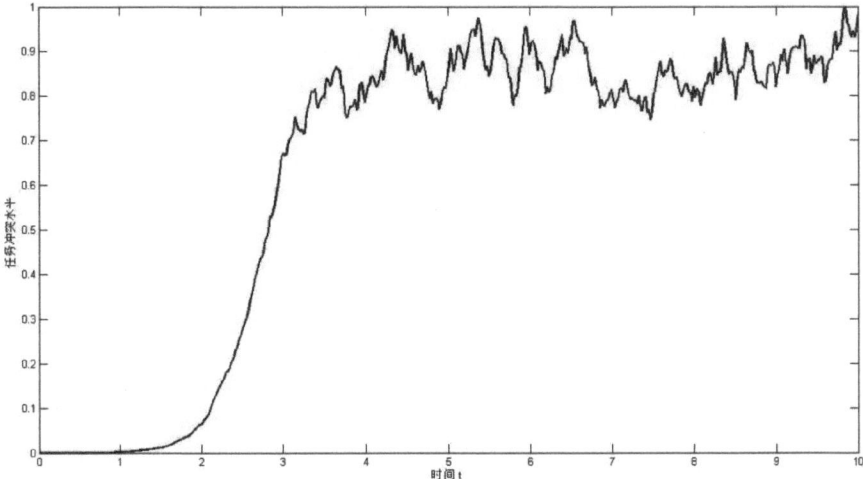

**Figure 5-2 Change of task conflict level with each antecedent variable being 0.5**

As can be seen from Figure 5-2, when the five antecedent variables are fixed at 0.5, the task conflict level shows an obvious increasing trend at the moment of $t = 3$, and the change of the task conflict level in the later stage is relatively stable with small fluctuations.

2) The impact of team support climate level on task conflict

The level of team support climate is reflected in random number $R_1$ that follows normal distribution of $\left[\mu_1, \sigma_1^2\right]$, and the values of $\mu_1$ can be different. In the simulation process of this book, $\mu_1$ is set at 0.1 and 0.9 respectively to check the impact of different levels of team support climate on task conflict, while keeping other parameters unchanged (Figure 5-3).

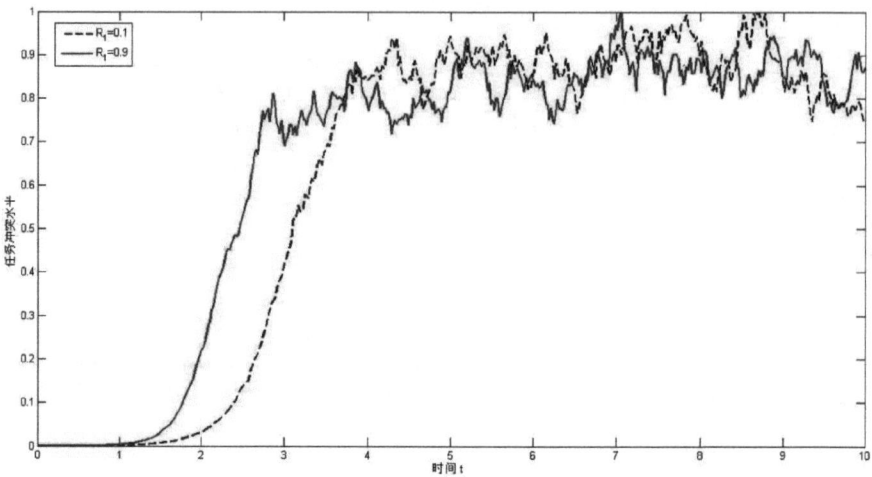

**Figure 5-3 Impact of different team support climate on task conflict level**

As can be seen from Figure 5-3, when the level of team support climate is 0.9, the task conflict can rise to a high level in a short time, and then fluctuates slightly. When the level is 0.1, the rise of task conflict level is slightly slower and takes more time, but it shows relative stability and a small fluctuation after that.

3) The impact of team innovation climate on task conflict

The level of team innovation climate is reflected in random number $R_2$ that follows normal distribution of $\left[\mu_2, \sigma_2^2\right]$, and the values of $\mu_2$ can be different. In the simulation process of this book, $\mu_2$ is set at 0.1 and 0.9 respectively to check the impact of different levels of team innovation climate on task conflict, while keeping other parameters unchanged (Figure 5-4).

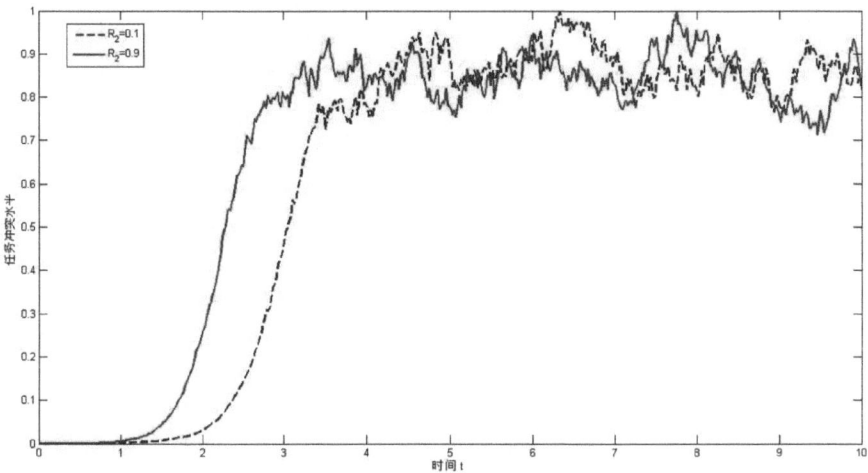

**Figure 5-4 Impact of different team innovation climate on task conflict level**

As can be seen from Figure 5-4, when the level of team innovation climate is 0.9, the task conflict can rise to a level of 0.8 in a short time, and then fluctuates slightly. When the level is 0.1, the rise of task conflict level is slightly slow and the trend is gentle, and then it also fluctuates slightly.

Research on the relationship between team climate and task conflict shows that team climate can affect the interaction process between members. If the team support climate and innovation climate are better, team members are equal in the sight of all arrangements and are encouraged to try new techniques and new methods, and there is a high degree of tolerance for mistakes and missteps; the team regards task conflict as a norm, then the members will be able to discuss issues and express opinions more openly, and the level of task conflict will continue to rise.

4) The impact of previous team performance on task conflict

$R_3$ is previous level of team performance and $R_3 \in [0,1]$. The closer it is to 0, the worse performance level is. In the simulation process of this book, $R_3$ is set at 0.1 and 0.9 respectively to check the impact of different levels of previous team performance on task conflict, while keeping other parameters unchanged (Figure 5-5).

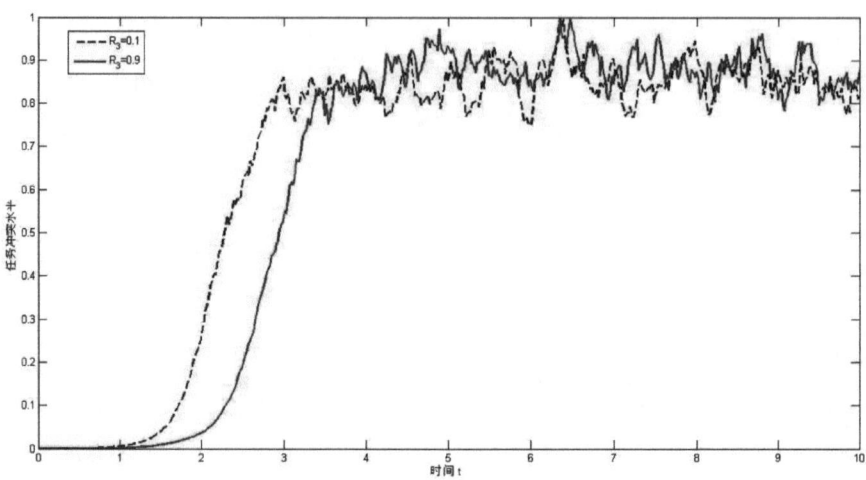

**Figure 5-5 Impact of different team performance on task conflict level**

As can be seen from Figure 5-5, when the previous level of team performance is 0.9, the rising trend of task conflict is relatively gentle. When the level is 0.1, the task conflict can rise rapidly to a high level with a steep upward trend, and then both of them become relatively stable and fluctuate slightly.

Previous performance levels affect task conflict because of the feedback effect of performance; generally speaking, enterprises with low performance have a higher probability of conflict. For example, relevant studies have found that if the previous performance level is high, the later conflict level will be decreased and the performance will be better; otherwise, there will be more conflicts resulting in worse performance. In addition, negative performance feedback is accompanied by a subsequent increase in task conflict.

5) The impact of task interdependence on task conflict

$R_4$ is task interdependence and $R_4 \in [0,1]$. The closer it is to 0, the lower the degree of interdependence. In the simulation process of this book, $R_4$ is set at 0.1 and 0.9 respectively to check the impact of different degrees of task interdependence on task conflict, while keeping other parameters unchanged (Figure 5-6).

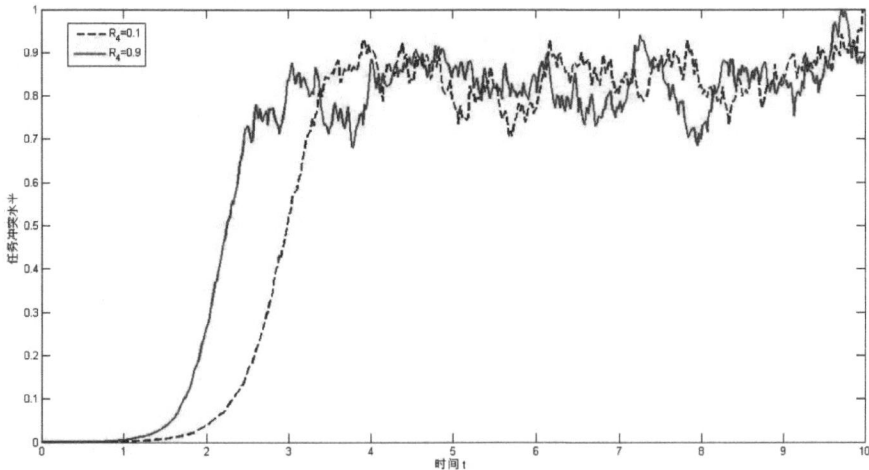

**Figure 5-6 Impact of different degrees of task interdependence on task conflict level**

As can be seen from Figure 5-6, when the degree of task interdependence is 0.9, the task conflict can rise to a high level in a short time, and then fluctuate slightly. When the degree is 0.1, the rise of task conflict level is slightly slow, and then it also fluctuates slightly.

The higher the degree of task interdependence, the greater the number and intensity of interactions between members. In teams with high task interdependence, members interact more frequently and with greater intensity, and there will be more task conflicts. That's because high task interdependence determines that members need to cooperate closely and deal with relevant task information together, which inevitably leads to task conflicts in the process of internal team interaction.

6) The impact of clarity of task feedback on task conflict

$R_5$ is the clarity of task feedback and $R_5 \in [0,1]$. The closer it is to 0, the worse the clarity of task feedback. In the simulation process of this book, $R_5$ is set at 0.1 and 0.9 respectively to check the impact of different degrees of feedback on task conflict, while keeping other parameters unchanged (Figure 5-7).

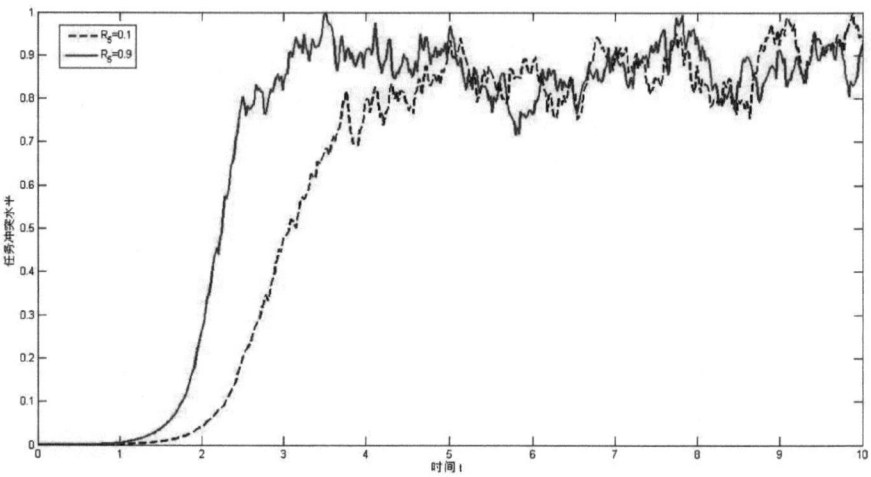

**Figure 5-7 Impact of different degrees of task feedback on task conflict level**

As can be seen from Figure 5-7, when the degree of task feedback is 0.9, the task conflict can rise to a high level in a short time, and then fluctuate slightly. When the degree is 0.1, the rise of task conflict level is slightly slow, and then it also fluctuates slightly. Relevant studies have found that clear task objectives and feedback can lead to task conflict, because they can generate positive arguments among members.

## (2) Antecedent Variables and Relationship Conflict

Relationship conflict also develops dynamically, and its level changes with time, but it will reach a stable state after developing to a certain extent, so it can be described by retarded growth model. Let "t" be the time when the level of relationship conflict develops, and RC (Relationship conflict) be the level of relationship conflict, then the growth rate of $RC(t)$ within the time $[t, t + \Delta t]$ can be expressed as:

$$\frac{RC(t + \Delta t) - RC(t)}{RC(t)} \quad \text{Equation (5.6)}$$

From chapter 3, it can be seen that the top five antecedent variables leading to relationship conflict in innovation teams are the internal attribution of members, mutual suspicion between members, leadership abusive supervision, team pressure and member exchange difference. Therefore, the following assumptions are made:

A. The inherent growth rate of relationship conflict level is $r_2$, and $r_2$ is constant;
B. There is a maximum limit $M_2$ on the level of relationship conflict;
C. The antecedent variables are independent of each other.

According to assumption a, the following can be obtained:

$$\frac{RC(t + \Delta t) - RC(t)}{RC(t)} = r_2 \Delta t \quad \text{Equation (5.7)}$$

Let $\Delta t \to 0$, then:

$$dRC(t) = r_2 RC(t)dt \quad \text{Equation (5.8)}$$

According to assumption b, since $M_2$ is the maximum limit on the level of relationship conflict, its retardation factor is $1 - \dfrac{RC}{M_2}$, and Equation (5.8) can be translated into:

$$dRC(t) = r_2 RC(t)[1 - \frac{RC(t)}{M_2}]dt \quad \text{Equation (5.9)}$$

According to assumption c and the central limit theorem, the influence of each antecedent variable on relationship conflict can be depicted by normal distribution and [0,1] random distribution. Let $\beta_1 - \beta_5$ be its volatility, and its values are respectively (0.2103, 0.2037, 0.2010, 0.1943, 0.1907) ( $\beta_1 - \beta_5$ is obtained by adding up the average Ridit value of antecedent variables in Chapter 3 and redistributing it according to the original proportion). As a result,

$$\begin{cases} dRC(t) = r_2 RC(t)[1 - \dfrac{RC(t)}{M_2}]dt + RC(t)(\beta_1 S_1 + \beta_2 S_2 + \beta_3 S_3 + \beta_4 S_4 + \beta_5 S_5) \\ RC(0) = 0 \end{cases}$$

Equation (5.10)

In this equation, $S_1, S_2, S_3, S_4, S_5$ are the antecedent variables of relationship conflict respectively. Among them, $S_1$ is internal attribution of members and $S_1 \in [0,1]$. The closer it is to 0, the less prone to internal attribution. $S_2$ is mutual suspicion among members and $S_2 \in [0,1]$. The closer it is to 0, the less suspicion among members. $S_3$ is the degree of leadership abusive supervision, which is the random number that follows normal distribution of $\left[\mu_1, \sigma_1^2\right]$. The larger $\mu_1$ is, the higher degree of abusive supervision. $S_4$ is team pressure and $S_4 \in [0,1]$. The closer it is to 0, the less pressure the team is under. $S_5$ is the leader-member exchange difference, which is the random number that follows the normal distribution of $\left[\mu_2, \sigma_2^2\right]$. The larger $\mu_2$ is, the bigger the difference between leader-member exchange. $\beta_1, \beta_2, \beta_3, \beta_4, \beta_5$ respectively show the influence degree of each antecedent variable on relationship conflict.

1) Each antecedent variable is fixed at 0.5

In the simulation of relationship conflict, the book first sets five antecedent variables to be fixed at 0.5 and kept unchanged, so as to see the evolution process of relationship conflict level under general circumstances. The results can be obtained by using Matlab software for simulation, as shown in Figure 5-8.

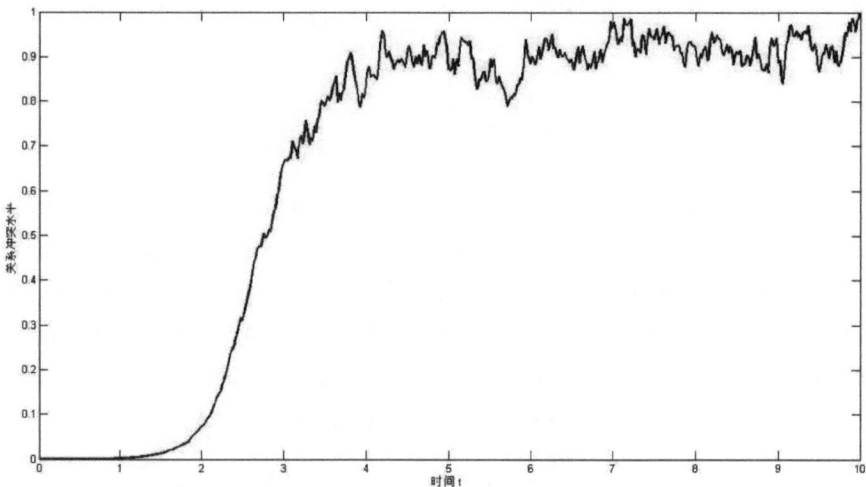

**Figure 5-8 Change of relationship conflict level with each antecedent variable being 0.5 (task conflicts are not considered)**

As can be seen from Figure 5-8, when the five antecedent variables are fixed at 0.5, the level of innovation team relationship conflict shows an obvious increasing trend in the early stage, but it shows little change and small fluctuation in the later stage.

2) Considering the impact of task conflict

According to the brittle modified model of innovation team conflict, in addition to the five factors such as internal attribution, task conflict can also affect relationship conflict. Relationship conflict plays an important mediating role between task conflict and team effectiveness, so the impact of task conflict on relationship conflict is added in the book. Equation (5.10) can be changed to:

$$\left\{ \begin{array}{l} dRC(t) = r_2 RC(t)[1 - \dfrac{RC(t)}{M_2}]dt + RC(t)(\beta_1 S_1 + \beta_2 S_2 + \beta_3 S_3 + \beta_4 S_4 + \beta_5 S_5 + \beta_6 S_6) \\ RC(0) = 0 \end{array} \right\}$$

Equation (5.11)

In this equation, $S_1, S_2, S_3, S_4, S_5$ are consistent with the definition above, while $S_6$ is the task conflict level and $S_6 \in [0,1]$. The closer it is to 0, the lower the task conflict level. $\beta_1, \beta_2, \beta_3, \beta_4, \beta_5, \beta_6$ refer to the degree of influence of each antecedent variable on relationship conflict, and its values are respectively (0.1780, 0.1724, 0.1701, 0.1645, 0.1614, 0.1536) (the value of $\beta_1 - \beta_6$ is obtained by adding up the average Ridit value of antecedent variables in Chapter 3 and redistributing it according to the original proportion).

In the process of simulation, the book first sets five antecedent variables to be fixed at 0.5 and kept unchanged, so as to see the evolution process of relationship conflict level under general circumstances. The results can be obtained by using Matlab software for simulation, as shown in Figure 5-9.

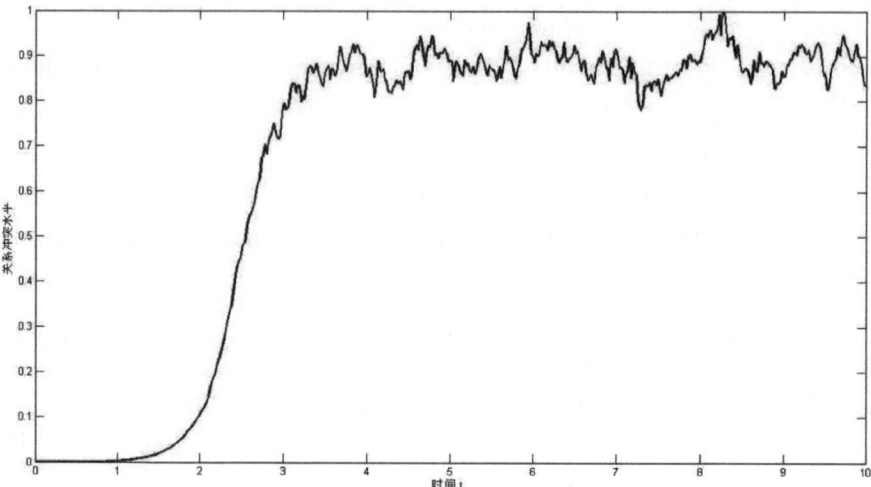

**Figure 5-9 Change of relationship conflict level with each antecedent variable being 0.5 (considering task conflicts)**

As can be seen from Figure 5-9, when the five antecedent variables and task conflict are fixed at 0.5, the level of innovation team relationship conflict shows an obvious increasing trend in the short term. At the moment of $t = 3$, the level of relationship conflict has reached 0.7, higher than the level at the same moment in Figure 5-8. In the later period, the level of relationship conflict changes little and fluctuates slightly.

3) The impact of internal attribution of members on relationship conflict
$S_1$ is the degree of member internal attribution and $S_1 \in [0,1]$. The closer it is to 0, the less prone to internal attribution. In the simulation process of this book, $S_1$ is set at 0.1 and 0.9 respectively to check the impact of different degrees of internal attribution on relationship conflict, while keeping other parameters unchanged (Figure 5-10).

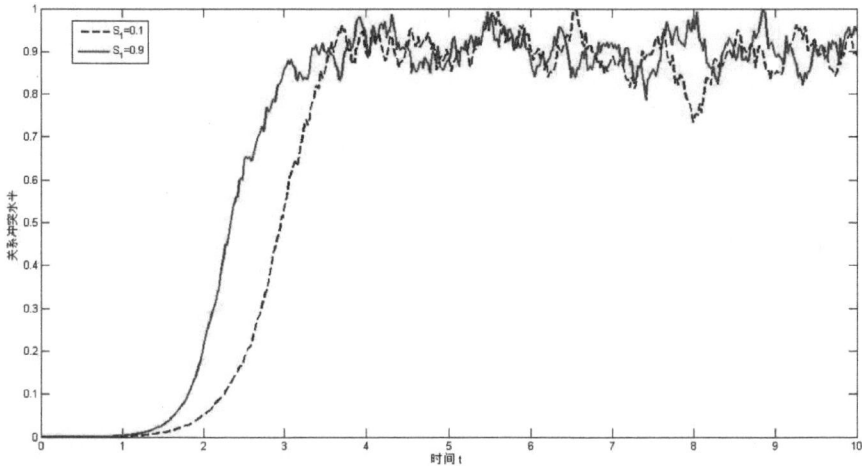

**Figure 5-10 Impact of different degrees of internal attribution on relationship conflict level**

As can be seen from Figure 5-10, when the level of internal attribution is 0.9, the relationship conflict can rise to a high level in a short time, and then fluctuates slightly. When the level is 0.1, the rise of relationship conflict level is slightly slower, and then also fluctuates slightly.

Attribution refers to the process of inferring the causes of others' or their own behavior, while internal attribution refers to the fact that the certain behavior of individuals is caused by their own unique qualities and characteristics. Existing research results show that people tend to make internal attributions when they make task conflict attributions, so task conflict is often misunderstood as relationship conflict. According to Weiner, individuals will have more emotional fluctuations when making internal attributions, while they will not generate negative emotions when making external attributions, thus they can focus more on the task itself [134]. As the relationship conflict itself is derived from the opposition of personal emotions and interpersonal friction, the higher the degree of internal attribution among members, the easier it is for members to interpret other's objections as embarrassing themselves, then the relationship conflict level of "mutual censure" will be higher.

4) The impact of mutual suspicion between members on relationship conflict

$S_2$ is the level of mutual suspicion between members and $S_2 \in [0,1]$. The closer it is to 0, the less mutual suspicion there is between members. In the simulation process of this book, $S_2$ is set at 0.1 and 0.9 respectively to check the impact of different suspicion levels on relationship conflict, while keeping the values of other parameters unchanged (Figure 5-11).

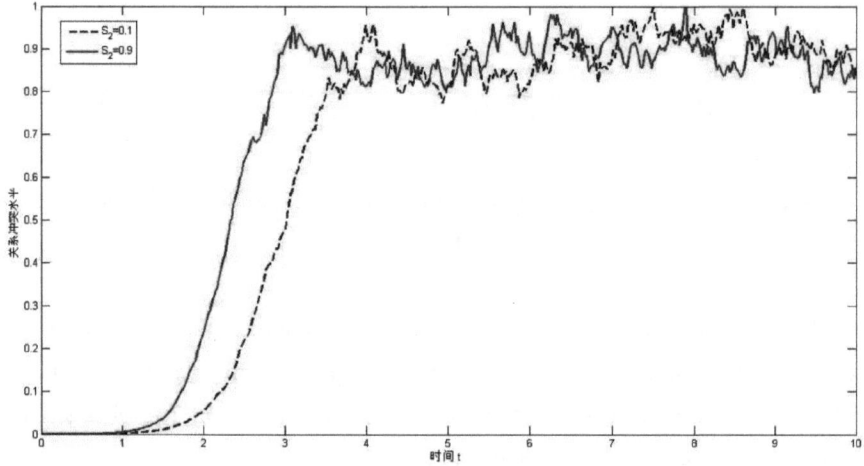

**Figure 5-11 Impact of different suspicion levels on relationship conflict level**

It can be seen from Figure 5-11 that no matter what level of suspicion between members is, it can lead to a high level of relationship conflict. When the suspicion level is 0.9, the relationship conflict level rises to a high level in a short time, and then fluctuates slightly. When the level is 0.1, the rise of relationship conflict level is slightly slower, and then it also fluctuates slightly.

5) The impact of leadership abusive supervision on relationship conflicts

$S_3$ is the level of mutual suspicion between members which follows $\left[\mu_1, \sigma_1^2\right]$, and the values of $\mu_1$ can be different. In the simulation process of this book, $\mu_1$ is set at 0.1 and 0.9 respectively to check the impact of different levels of leadership abusive supervision on relationship conflict, while keeping the values of other parameters unchanged (Figure 5-12).

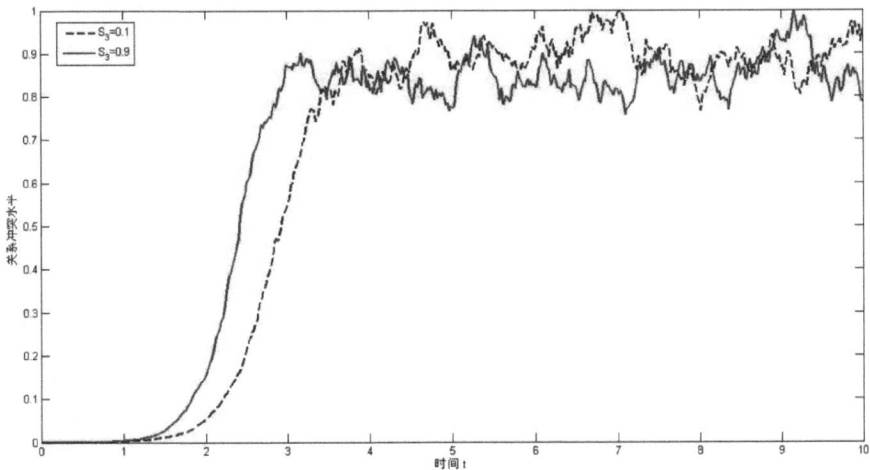

**Figure 5-12 Impact of leadership abusive supervision on relationship conflict level**

As can be seen from Figure 5-12, when the level is 0.9, the relationship conflict level rises to a high level in a short time, and then fluctuates slightly. When the level is 0.1, the rise of relationship conflict level is slightly slower, and then it also fluctuates slightly.

Abusive supervision refers to the extent to which the administrator consistently displays hostile verbal and nonverbal behavior, but excludes perceptions related to physical contact with the leader. According to social exchange theory, when employees are treated unfairly, they are likely to become dissatisfied or even angry, and then take retaliatory actions against the organization, thus intensifying internal conflicts. Thus, abusive supervision can significantly trigger relationship conflict.

6) The influence of team pressure on relationship conflict

$S_4$ is the level of team pressure and $S_4 \in [0,1]$. The closer it is to 0, the less pressure the team is under. In the simulation process of this book, $S_4$ is set at 0.1 and 0.9 respectively to check the impact of different levels of pressure on relationship conflict, while keeping the values of other parameters unchanged (Figure 5-13).

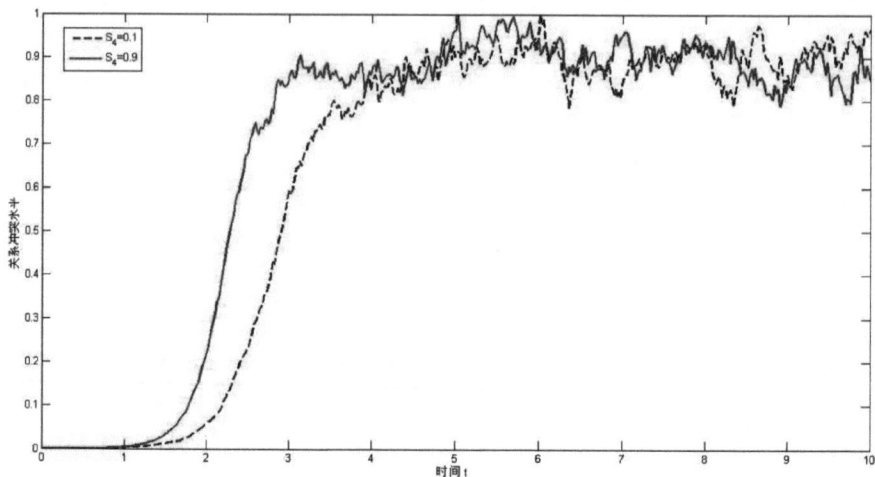

**Figure 5-13 Impact of different levels of pressure on relationship conflict level**

As can be seen from Figure 5-13, when the level is 0.9, the relationship conflict level rises to a high level in a short time, and then fluctuates slightly. When the level is 0.1, the rise of relationship conflict level is slightly slower, and then it also fluctuates slightly.

7) The impact of leader-member exchange differences on relationship conflict

$S_5$ is the leader-member exchange difference which follows $\left[ \mu_2, \sigma_2^2 \right]$, and the values of $\mu_2$ can be different. In the simulation process of this book, $\mu_2$ is set at 0.1 and 0.9 respectively to check the impact of different levels of leader-member exchange differences on relationship conflict, while keeping the values of other parameters unchanged (Figure 5-14).

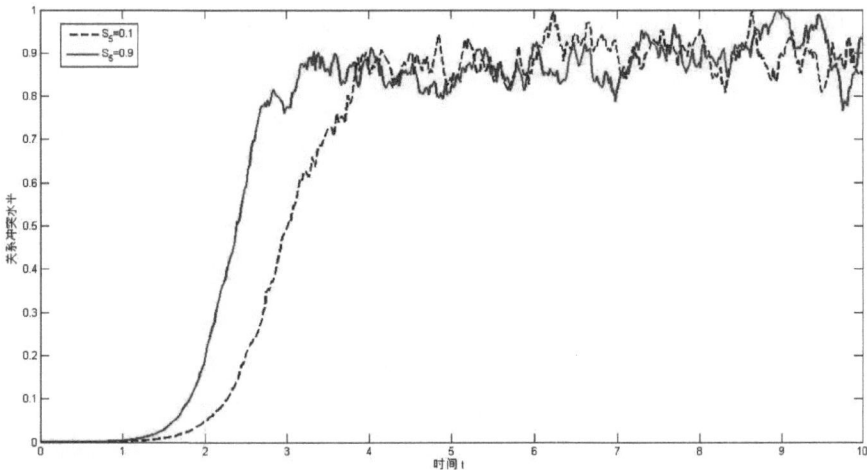

**Figure 5-14 Impact of leader-member exchange differences on relationship conflict level**

As can be seen from Figure 5-14, when the level of leader-member exchange difference is 0.9, the relationship conflict level rises to a high level in a short time, and then fluctuates slightly. When the level is 0.1, the rise of relationship conflict level is slightly slower, and then it also fluctuates slightly.

"Leader-member exchange difference" refers to the difference in the quality of leader-exchange relationship between different members of a work team. According to leader-member exchange theory, constrained by limited resources and energy, leaders will not treat their subordinates in the same way, but establish different relationships with different subordinates, that is, establish high-quality leader-member exchange relationship with some subordinates, while establish low-quality leader-member exchange relationship with others. The differences of exchange relationship between the team leader and team member will stimulate the social comparison behavior of the team member, and leader-member exchange differences will bring relationship conflicts in the team. The greater the difference, the more relationship conflicts.

8) The impact of task conflict on relationship conflict

$S_6$ is the task conflict level and $S_6 \in [0,1]$ .The closer it is to 0, the lower the level of task conflict. In the simulation process of this book, $S_6$ is set at 0.1 and 0.9 respectively to check the impact of different task conflict levels on the relationship conflict level, while keeping the values of other parameters unchanged (Figure 5-15).

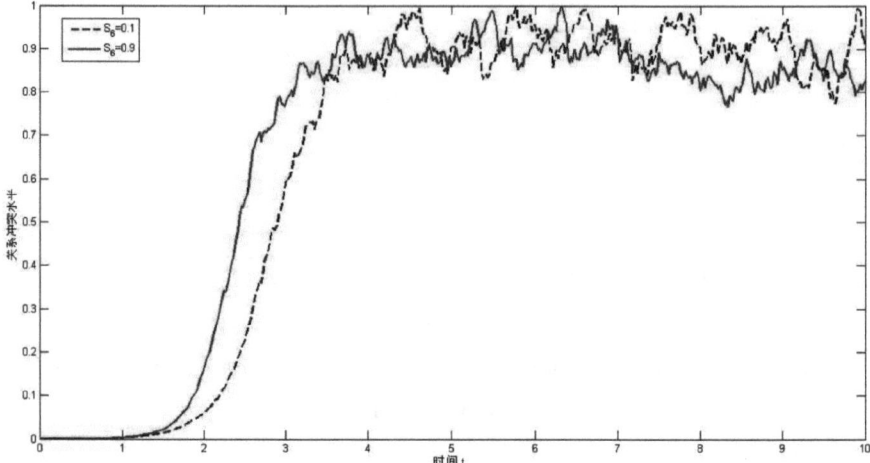

**Figure 5-15 Impact of different task conflict levels on relationship conflict level**

As can be seen from Figure 5-15, when the level of task conflict is 0.9, the relationship conflict level rises to a high level in a short time, and then fluctuates slightly. When the level is 0.1, the rise of the relationship conflict level is slightly slower, and then it also fluctuates slightly.

Existing research results show that task conflict has a great influence on relationship conflict, because task conflict can lead to relationship conflict under certain circumstances, which will affect the judgment and perception of task and program. The average correlation coefficient between the two dimensions is 0.47. Due to the high correlation, the higher the level of task conflict, the higher the level of relationship conflict.

### 5.1.2 Simulation of Team Conflict on Team Effectiveness

According to Figure 5-1, task conflict and relationship conflict are affected by different moderating variables in the process of influencing team effectiveness, so the relationship between the two types of conflict and team effectiveness is discussed separately.

## (1) Simulation of Task Conflict on Outcomes

It can be seen from Chapter 5 that task conflict has a direct negative impact on the outcomes of team effectiveness, while the influence coefficients on the other two dimensions are not significant. Therefore, this book only considers the simulation of task conflict on outcomes. In this book, through continuous attempts with Matlab software and the actual survey data obtained in Chapter 5, it can be found that there is a negative correlation between task conflict and outcomes; the functional expression can be written as follows:

$$y = ax^b + c \quad \text{Equation (5.12)}$$

where $y$ represents outcomes; $x = \dfrac{x_1 x_3}{x_2}$ ( $x_1$ is task conflict, $x_2$ is team emotional intelligence, $x_3$ is task conflict network density); $a, b, c$ are the fitting coefficients, and their values are respectively: $a = -4.477, b = 0.1761, c = 6.408$ (the values are fitted by Matlab according to the official survey data in Chapter 5).

1) Considering the moderating effect of team emotional intelligence
Team emotional intelligence (EI) is normally distributed. According to the survey data in Chapter 5, it can be concluded that its mean value and standardized variance are 0.8064 and 0.0419 respectively. This book takes the relationship between task conflict and team outcomes into account when the mean value of team emotional intelligence changes. Figure 5-16 can be obtained by simulation through Matlab software:

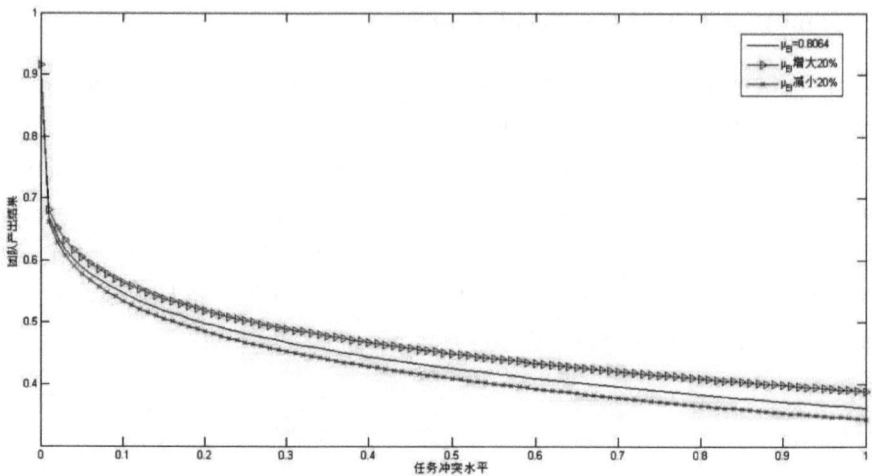

**Figure 5-16 Moderating effect of team emotional intelligence on task conflict and outcomes**

As shown in Figure 5-16, when the mean value of team emotional intelligence fluctuates, the negative correlation between task conflict and output results changes significantly: when the mean value increases by 20%, the negative effect of task conflict on outcomes weakens. When the mean value decreases by 20%, the negative effect of task conflict on outcomes is enhanced, showing that team emotional intelligence has a negative moderating effect on the relationship between task conflict and outcomes.

2) Considering the moderating effect of task conflict network density
The density of the task conflict network is in the range of [0,1]. According to the actual survey data in chapter 5, the mean value after standardization is 0.3298. Figure 5-17 can be obtained by using Matlab software for simulation.

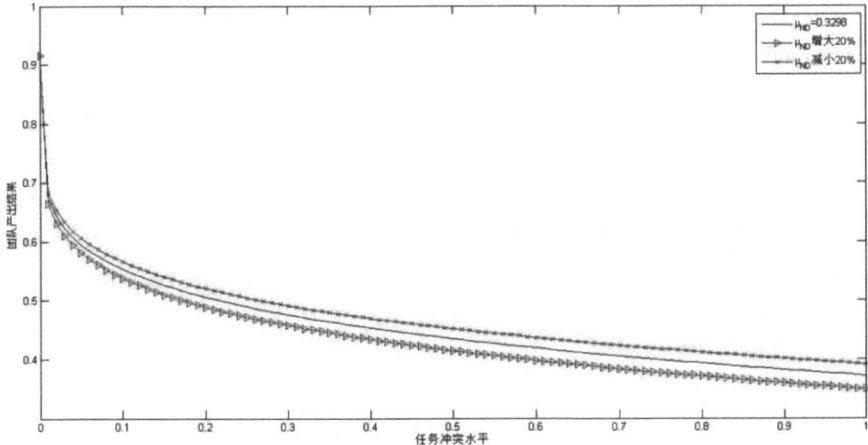

**Figure 5-17 Moderating effect of task conflict network density on task conflict and outcomes**

As shown in Figure 5-17, when the mean value of task conflict network density fluctuates, the negative correlation between task conflict and outcomes changes significantly: when the mean value increases by 20%, the negative effect of task conflict on outcomes is enhanced. When the mean value decreases by 20%, the negative effect of task conflict on outcomes weakens, showing that task conflict network density has a positive moderating effect on the relationship between task conflict and outcomes.

## (2) Simulation of Relationship Conflict on Team Effectiveness

In this book, through continuous attempts with Matlab software and the actual survey data obtained in Chapter 5, it can be found that there is a negative correlation between relationship conflict and team effectiveness, and the functional expression can be written as follows:

$$y = ax^b + c \quad \text{Equation (5.13)}$$

Where $y$ represents team effectiveness; $x = \dfrac{x_1 x_3}{x_2}$ ( $x_1$ is relationship conflict,

$x_2$ is team emotional intelligence, $x_3$ is relationship conflict network density);

$a, b, c$ are the fitting coefficient, and their values are respectively:

$a = -4.477, b = 0.1761, c = 6.408$   (the values are fitted by Matlab according to the survey data in Chapter 5).

1) Considering the moderating effect of team emotional intelligence

Team emotional intelligence (EI) is normally distributed. According to the survey data in Chapter 5, it can be concluded that its mean value and standardized variance are 0.8064 and 0.0419 respectively. Figure 5-18 can be obtained by simulation through Matlab software:

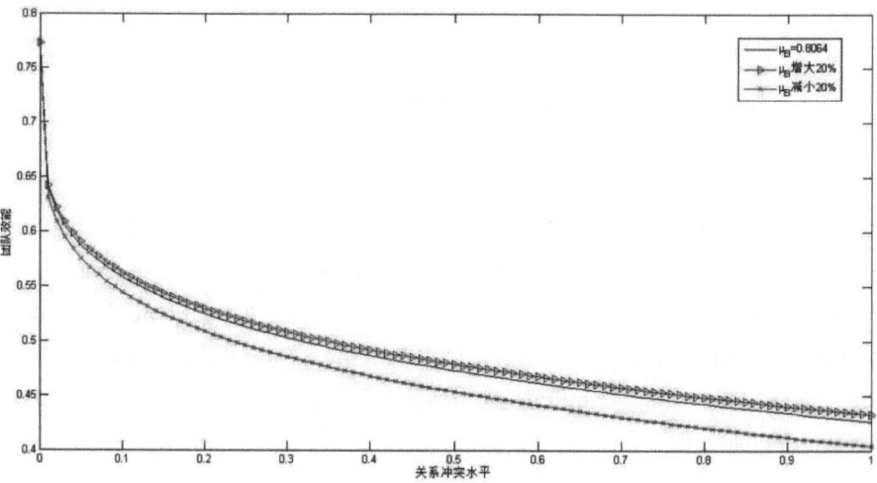

**Figure 5-18 Moderating effect of team emotional intelligence on relationship conflict and team effectiveness**

As shown in Figure 5-18, when the mean value of team emotional intelligence fluctuates, the negative correlation between relationship conflict and team effectiveness changes significantly: when the mean value increases by 20%, the negative effect of relationship conflict on team effectiveness weakens. When the mean value decreases by 20%, the negative effect of relationship conflict on team effectiveness is enhanced, showing that team emotional intelligence has a negative moderating effect on the relationship between relationship conflict and team effectiveness.

2) Considering the moderating effect of relationship conflict network density

The density of relationship conflict network is in the range of [0,1]. According to the actual survey data in chapter 5, the mean value after standardization is 0.3269. Figure 5-19 can be obtained by using Matlab software for simulation.

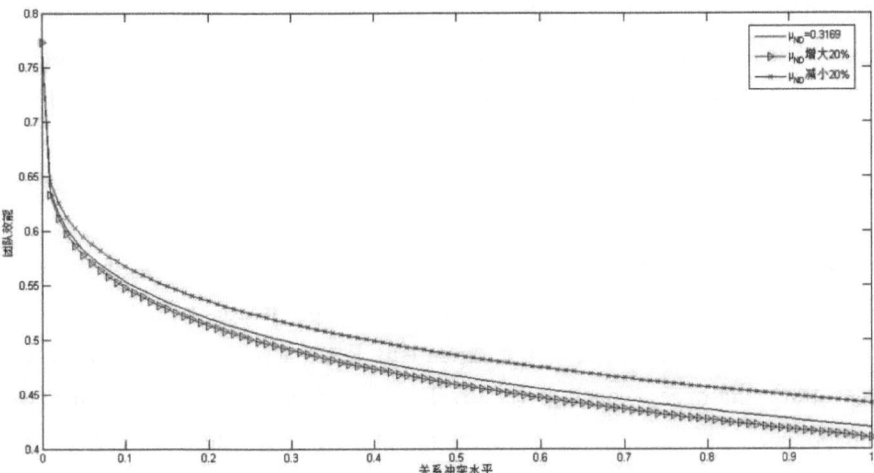

**Figure 5-19 Moderating effect of relationship conflict network density on relationship conflict and team effectiveness**

As shown in Figure 5-19, when the mean value of relationship conflict network density fluctuates, the negative correlation between relationship conflict and team effectiveness changes significantly: when the mean value increases by 20%, the negative effect of relationship conflict on team effectiveness is enhanced. When the mean value decreases by 20%, the negative effect of relationship conflict on team effectiveness is weakened, showing that relationship conflict network density has a positive moderating effect on the relationship between relationship conflict and team effectiveness.

## 5.2 Management Countermeasures of Innovation Team Conflict

In order to improve the pertinence and effectiveness of team conflict management countermeasures, this book puts forward management countermeasures from the team level and individual member level based on the above research results.

## 5.2.1 Team Level

### (1) Cultivate Appropriate Team Climate

The research in this book finds that the team climate, especially the supporting climate and innovation climate, are the main antecedent variables of task conflict. Therefore, it is of great necessity for innovation teams to create an appropriate and excellent cultural atmosphere within the team to shape common values and enhance members' sense of responsibility and cohesion, because task conflict is much less likely to turn into relationship conflict in a culture of shared cognition and cooperation, which is beneficial to the mutual understanding and cooperation among members and the improvement of team effectiveness.

On the one hand, create a team climate for the free expression of opinions. As a "soft environment" for internal innovation activities, team climate plays an important role in carrying out independent R&D activities of the team and alleviating employees' working pressure. Innovation teams should create an active, outspoken, open and inclusive working atmosphere where differences are accepted, enabling members to express their opinions freely without fear of being criticized or ridiculed, but to obtain objective and fair evaluation. In addition, the creation of a team climate also requires team members to be task-oriented. A good team climate enables team members to communicate and interact with each other around task-related issues, which contributes to offset any negative effects caused by relationship conflict, and helps members to accurately grasp the key issue and focus on the continuous improvement of new ideas related to innovation goals. The team climate can be created by encouraging members to put forward feasible plans when holding discussions or making decisions, communicating in a relaxed environment so as to encourage members to explore unknown areas and try different working methods.

On the other hand, maintain a high-trust team climate. Trust is like a "lubricant," which can not only eliminate internal friction caused by team conflict, but also promote the normal operation of the team. With a high degree of team trust, members do not have to worry about being ridiculed for their wrong views. In this way, a situation of knowledge sharing is formed, in which members can reveal their feelings. This kind of discussion helps members to form a clear understanding of each other's views and reach a consensus as soon as possible. At the same time, in the process of mutual discussion, it promotes the transformation of hidden knowledge and enables members to get to different views, which helps to improve the overall ability of members and ultimately has a positive impact on team effectiveness. As the administrator of an innovation team, he should establish a team trust mechanism, evaluate the team trust level in real-time, analyze the reasons affecting the lack of trust and continuously optimize the trust relationship between team members; at the same time, he should carefully manage the team with a high level of trust, encourage positive reflection, and avoid team-centrism and group thinking with a high trust level.

## (2) Improve the Cohesion Level of the Team

Suspicion among members is one of the main antecedent variables of relationship conflict. In order to improve harmony among members and a slowing down of bad personal relations, it is necessary to improve the level of team cohesion, because team cohesion is an important representation of internal team integration and an important factor in ensuring effective team operation.

Firstly, reinforce the team's common goal. Since members of an innovation team have their own research fields and different knowledge and skills, if the team has a common goal that is recognized by the members, they will be closely united and coordinated to achieve this goal. Secondly, strengthen the communication level of the team. Since members have different research backgrounds and ways of thinking, but they need to achieve a common team goal, the importance of team communication becomes prominent. In-depth and effective communication can encourage members to actively share knowledge and information, improve the efficiency of team work, and help members to establish common values. Team communication enables members to communicate their ideas with other members, realize perspective-taking, and reach a consensus on cognition and behavior. However, this does not mean that there will be no task conflict, because a moderate level of task conflict can promote effective analysis and communication between team members, but the members should try not to bring personal emotions into the process. In addition, members share experiences and ideas in a relaxed and open environment through informal communication, such as email, text messages and gossip. Finally, enhance members' sense of belonging to the team. In order to make members feel a sense of belonging, it is necessary to cultivate team spirit, which can be started from two aspects: one is to cultivate the spirit of cooperation among members; the second is to foster the innovation spirit of members.

### (3) Strengthen the Construction of Team Emotional Intelligence

Team emotional intelligence is the ability of a team to create shared norms to manage emotional processes, so as to build trust, group identity and team effectiveness. It plays an important role in successfully managing emotional states of members, understanding the situation and goals, improving the integration effect, and generating emotional drives for members. A series of studies have shown that team emotional intelligence is closely related to variables of team work. The research in this book also shows that different dimensions of team emotional intelligence play a negative moderating role between team conflict and team effectiveness, that is, it can mitigate the negative impact of task conflict and relationship conflict on team effectiveness. Therefore, innovation teams should attach importance to the construction of the team emotional intelligence integration mechanism.

In a team with low emotional intelligence, some emotional performances and behavior by employees with high emotional intelligence may not receive the expected recognition and support from the team, but may be laughed at and suppressed. Employees in this situation usually have only two options: be passive and show more modesty, or quit to find a team that suits them. On the contrary, in a team with a high level of emotional intelligence, even employees with low emotional intelligence can reach a certain degree of development, and can receive support, encouragement, care and understanding from the team and its members in the face of setbacks and difficulties, so they can also achieve a good performance. It can be concluded that the level of team emotional intelligence is of great significance to team building, and the team with higher team emotional intelligence is more able to attract and retain talents. Therefore, it is necessary to found a learning team, that is, to realize learning and sharing among members through mutual learning, continuous self-examination, continuous change and innovation, so as to improve the emotional intelligence of members. Secondly, it is necessary to create norms of team emotional intelligence, that is, to establish a positive and trusting team with the sense of belonging, so that members can make positive responses to bad emotions. Finally, in order to work more effectively, the team should create norms of team emotional intelligence. For example, the team should improve the harmony of interpersonal relationships through emotional connection and ideological communication among members, and form an open, tolerant and harmonious environment, emotional communication atmosphere and harmonious working atmosphere.

**(4) Promote a Change in Team Leadership Style**

Team leadership style and leader-member exchange difference have an immeasurable impact on relationship conflict. Contingency leadership theory suggests that effective leadership styles should change in different working environments, and leaders need to change their own leadership styles to improve team effectiveness. At the same time, if the leader establishes different relationships with members, the members will make social comparison. Thus, members in a low-quality leader-member exchange relationship will be jealous of members in a high-quality leader-member exchange relationship, and members in a high-quality relationship will also alienate members in low-quality relationships, leading to relationship conflicts within the team. Therefore, team leaders should pay attention to the negative effects of leader-member exchange and actively prevent and reduce potential hazards. For example, they can consider enhancing the variability of the leader-member exchange relationship by improving their own moral leadership level, so as to weaken the positive impact of leader-member exchange difference on relationship conflict.

**(5) Adopt an Appropriate Conflict Management Style**

An innovation team should advocate the modern view of conflict so that members can correctly view conflict and choose active and cooperative conflict management to effectively solve and utilize conflict.

Firstly, effective conflict management and resolution mechanisms should be set up to reduce the possibility of relationship conflict from the source. Carry out some group activities such as outings and having dinner to strengthen the private contact and communication of members, and deepen the understanding of their personalities, attitudes and motivation, so as to promote mutual trust and understanding and reduce unnecessary interpersonal friction caused by misunderstanding. Secondly, adopt a contingency approach. Based on a contingency view, different management methods should be adopted for conflicts of a different nature. Thirdly, establish various systems of conflict analysis and resolution. After the inevitable occurrence of relationship conflict, one should not try to maintain a harmonious relationship by avoiding each other, because avoidance cannot solve the problem fundamentally, but can even enlarge conflicts and give rise to a more serious problem. One should face existing relationship conflicts head-on, such as adopting third-party intervention to mediate. Fourthly, for existing task conflicts, the most important thing is to guide and encourage members to conduct in-depth communication and exchange, so that members can focus on the completion of the task, and care less about issues such as personal pride.

### 5.2.2 Individual Level

#### (1) Improve the Emotional Intelligence Level of Members

The emotional intelligence level of a team depends not only on the emotional intelligence level of the team leader, but also on the emotional intelligence level of the individual members. Therefore, the innovation team should train and improve the emotional intelligence of its members at any time, and encourage them to improve their moral level and mental models. According to Goleman, the pioneer of research on emotional intelligence, emotional intelligence is not innate and immutable, but can be developed and improved through learning. Therefore, content to improve the members' ability of emotional management should be supplemented in conducting training courses; for example, the learning of theories and cases related to emotional intelligence can make members a clear understanding of the generation, influencing mechanism and results of emotional intelligence[135]. At the same time, leaders should conduct cognitive tests of emotional intelligence sensitivity irregularly within the team to enhance the overall learning atmosphere of team emotional intelligence.

#### (2) Guide Members to Make a Correct Attribution

Just as the individual's internal attribution will induce team relationship conflict while external attribution and controllable attribution can promote individual performance, so before and during relationship conflict, the team should guide the attributional style of members, and let members pay attention to and reflect on the objective issues in discussion, so as to prevent members from shifting their attention to the internal causes of individual and other uncontrollable factors. If relationship conflict occurs, the team needs to help members make external and controllable attributions. That's because external attribution can reduce the negative emotions of members, while controllable attribution can prevent members from inferences of responsibility, so as to minimize the negative effects of relationship conflict.

**(3) Train Members to Adopt a Reasonable Conflict Management Style**

Empirical study results show that a collaborative management style of team conflict has a positive correlation with team effectiveness, because cooperative members put the common goal of the team first and tend to have open discussions with other members, and reach the key issues and solve problems directly, which is conducive to exploring viewpoints and innovating methods. However, avoidant team conflict management has a significant negative effect on team innovation performance, because avoidance is a very negative way of conflict management. It is necessary for innovation teams to solve technical and thinking dilemmas in a timely and effective manner, and avoidance behavior will affect team effectiveness for a long time. Therefore, relevant training mechanisms such as case analysis, discussion and role-playing can be adopted to train members to understand, communicate, tolerate and change those attitudes and behaviors that trigger conflicts. Through training, members can improve the communication skills of themselves or within the team, analyze the causes of team conflicts, repair conflicts and prevent new conflicts, and can learn conflict management skills.

## 5.3 Summary

The main content of this chapter is divided into two parts: one is the simulation based on the brittleness model of innovation team conflict; the other is corresponding countermeasures and suggestions based on the existing research content and results of this book, hoping to deal with and manage innovation team conflict effectively. In the brittleness simulation process of innovation team conflict, this book mainly simulates the relationship between each antecedent variable and conflict and the relationship between team conflict and team effectiveness. In terms of countermeasures, this book discusses them from the team level and individual member level: from the team level, an innovation team can cultivate an appropriate team climate, improve the level of team cohesion, strengthen the construction of team emotional intelligence, promote the transformation of team leadership style and adopt an appropriate conflict management style, etc. From the level of individual members, it can improve the emotional intelligence level of members, guide them to make correct attributions, and train them to adopt reasonable conflict management styles.

# CHAPTER 6

# Summary

In recent years, global scientific and technological innovation has entered an unprecedented period of intensive activity. A new round of scientific and technological revolution and industrial transformation is reconstructing the global innovation landscape and reshaping the global economic structure. A series of digital technologies (such as artificial intelligence, blockchain, Internet of Things, cloud computing, etc.) have been developed rapidly and been widely adopted in various fields of economy and society, promoting the rise of the digital economy; advanced manufacturing technology is accelerating the manner in which manufacturing industry becomes more intelligent. Life science, including gene editing, brain science, and regenerative medicine, breed new changes and lead the development of the biomedical industry.

Over the past 40 years of reform and opening up, China's economy has made remarkable development achievements and become the world's second-largest economy. A number of leading enterprises with international influence have been established, which have greatly promoted the catch-up of industrial technology and the adjustment of economic structure. An innovation team can quickly and efficiently complete increasingly complex innovation work involving a wide range of knowledge fields. The emergence of this model meets the needs of the times. Its creativity has always been the key to modern organizations gaining and maintaining competitiveness.

However, innovation teams do not always produce synergies such as "1+1+1>3." Compared with individual fighting alone, the internal operation process of an innovation team is more complex, and the interdependence between members is stronger. As the most common way of interaction between people, conflict cannot be avoided in the process of team operation. At the same time, the impact of conflict on team effectiveness is highly uncertain. Differences in type, level and background will result in opposite impacts between conflicts. Therefore, starting from the three stages of "input – process – output" of team operation, this paper comprehensively conducts qualitative and quantitative research to make a systematic study on the antecedents of innovation team conflict, conflict relationships among members, and the impact of team conflict on team effectiveness:

(1) The antecedent variables of team conflict were studied by constructing the conflict brittleness model of the innovation team. In the "input" stage of team operation, a complex system brittleness theory is applied to analyze the brittleness of innovation team conflict, and a four-level innovation team conflict brittleness model is constructed, which includes brittleness factors, brittleness events, relationship structure and brittleness results. The brittleness factors are classified to guide the research on the antecedents of team conflict. On this basis, we verify the applicability of the two-dimensional model of innovation team conflict (task conflict and relationship conflict) in China. Then, the antecedents of task conflict and relationship conflict are studied by literature analysis, questionnaire survey and Ridit analysis.

(2) The research model of "team-individual and team-individual and individual" is constructed. In the "process" stage of team operation, the conflict relationship among members of the innovation team is comprehensively studied from the three levels of "team-individual and team-individual and individual." At the level of "team," this book takes the whole innovation team as the research subject, constructing and analyzing the innovation team conflict network by combining the social network theory, and puts forward the implementation steps of the team conflict network; at the level of "individual and team," by adopting the classification of brittleness source of complex systems, the paper provides a method to evaluate the impact of innovation team members on the conflict network; at the level of "individual and individual," this paper takes the specific conflict relevance among members as the basis for analysis, and proposes an evaluation method of the conflict relevance of innovation team members based on the brittleness relevance of complex systems and the catastrophe progression method. Finally, the research contents of the three levels are integrated to form a "team-individual and team-individual and individual" research model of the

conflict relationship among members of the innovation team.

(3) Building a relationship model between innovation team conflict and team effectiveness. In the "output" stage of team operation, this book mainly designs new situations to study the impact of team conflict on team effectiveness; that is, according to the content of emotion theory and conflict network, to consider the moderating effect of team emotional intelligence and team conflict network density in the relationship between team conflict and team effectiveness. Through small sample testing, large-scale questionnaire survey and data analysis, a relationship model between innovation team conflict and team effectiveness is constructed.

Although the book has applied the brittleness theory of complex systems, social network theory and conflict management theory in the research process, the conflict problems of innovation teams are extremely complex. Also, limited by time, energy and research perspective, the book still falls short of efficacy in solving all the problems of innovation team conflict, and there are still many shortcomings to be rectified.

# Appendix

## Appendix A: A questionnaire on different types of conflicts in the innovation team

Dear sir / madam,

Hello! To understand the conflicts in your innovation team, I kindly invite you to answer each question carefully and truthfully, and tick ✓ in the appropriate answer ☐. This questionnaire is anonymous and handled by a specially assigned person. The answers are kept in confidentiality and used only for academic research. I appreciate your cooperation and support!

**A: Background factors: Please tick ✓ in ☐ according to your actual situation.**

1. Your gender: ☐ male    ☐ female
2. Your age: ☐ 20–29 years old    ☐ 30–39 years old    ☐ 40–49 years old
☐ ≥ 50 years old

3. Your education level: ☐ college degree or below    ☐ bachelor's degree
☐ master's degree    ☐ doctor's degree
4. Your level in the team: ☐ ordinary member of the team    ☐ the team leader
5. Your industry: ☐ universities    ☐ automobile production
☐ medicine production    ☐ software development
☐ transportation planning and design
6. size of your team: ☐ ≤ 5    ☐ 6–10    ☐ 11–15    ☐ ≥ 15
7. Your tenure in the team: ☐ ≤ 3 years    ☐ 4–6 years    ☐ 7–9 years
☐ 10–12 years    ☐ ≥ 13 years

**B: Types of innovation team conflict: Please fill in the following according to your real perception.**

| Main Contents | Degree (very low – very high) | | | | |
|---|---|---|---|---|---|
| 1. Are there big differences in the opinions of your team members? | 1 | 2 | 3 | 4 | 5 |
| 2. Do members of your team often get angry in public at work? | 1 | 2 | 3 | 4 | 5 |
| 3. Are there many occasions when there is tension among members of your team? | 1 | 2 | 3 | 4 | 5 |
| 4. Do members of your team have many conflicting opinions on how to complete the work? | 1 | 2 | 3 | 4 | 5 |
| 5. Are there many interpersonal conflicts in your team? | 1 | 2 | 3 | 4 | 5 |
| 6. Do members of your team have big controversies about team tasks? | 1 | 2 | 3 | 4 | 5 |
| 7. Are there many disputes among members of your team about how the work steps or procedures are done? | 1 | 2 | 3 | 4 | 5 |
| 8. Is there much jealousy and hostility among members of your team? | 1 | 2 | 3 | 4 | 5 |

This is the end of the questionnaire. Thank you again for your cooperation and support!

## Appendix B: A questionnaire on the causes of task conflict in the innovation team

Dear sir / madam,

Hello! To understand the reasons for the task conflict in the innovation team, I kindly invite you to fill in each question in this questionnaire carefully and honestly, and tick ✓ in the appropriate answer ☐.This questionnaire is anonymous and handled by a specially assigned person. The answers are kept in confidentiality and only for academic research use. Thank you for your cooperation and support!

**A: Background factors: Please tick ✓ in ☐ according to your actual situation.**
1. Your gender: ☐ male     ☐ female
2. Your age: ☐ 20-29 years old     ☐ 30–39 years old     ☐ 40–49 years old
☐ ≥ 50 years old
3. Your education level: ☐ college degree or below     ☐ bachelor's degree
☐ master's degree     ☐ doctor's degree
4. Your level in the team: ☐ ordinary member of the team     ☐the team leader
5. Your industry: ☐ universities     ☐ software development
☐ medicine development and production
☐ development and production of household electrical appliances
6. size of your team: ☐ ≤ 5     ☐ 6–10     ☐ 11–15     ☐ ≥ 15
7. Your tenure in the team: ☐ ≤ 3 years     ☐ 4–6 years     ☐ 7–9 years
☐ 10–12 years     ☐ ≥ 13 years

**B: Reasons for the task conflict of the innovation team: Please fill in the following questions honestly.**
Innovation team task conflict is an interactive process of opposition or inconsistency caused by different views of innovation team members on task related issues (including purpose, main decision-making, procedure and choice of best practice).

| The Initial Reason | Initiation Degree (very low – very high) | | | | |
|---|---|---|---|---|---|
| 1a. Do you think team members' personality can lead to task conflict? | 1 | 2 | 3 | 4 | 5 |
| Your reason: | | | | | |
| 1b. Do you think members' values can lead to task conflict? | 1 | 2 | 3 | 4 | 5 |
| Your reason: | | | | | |
| 2a. Do you think members' way of internal attribution can lead to task conflict? | 1 | 2 | 3 | 4 | 5 |
| Your reason: | | | | | |
| 2b. Do you think the degree of external attribution can lead to task conflict? | 1 | 2 | 3 | 4 | 5 |
| Your reason: | | | | | |
| 3.Do you think the interest request can lead to task conflict? | 1 | 2 | 3 | 4 | 5 |
| Your reason: | | | | | |
| 4.Do you think member's cognition can lead to task conflict? | 1 | 2 | 3 | 4 | 5 |
| Your reason: | | | | | |
| 5. Do you think the visions of the members can lead to task conflict? | 1 | 2 | 3 | 4 | 5 |
| Your reason: | | | | | |
| 6. Do you think the motivation of the members can lead to task conflict? | 1 | 2 | 3 | 4 | 5 |
| Your reason: | | | | | |
| 7.Do you think the emotions of the members can lead to task conflict? | 1 | 2 | 3 | 4 | 5 |
| Your reason: | | | | | |
| 8. Do you think the preference of the members can lead to task conflict? | 1 | 2 | 3 | 4 | 5 |
| Your reason: | | | | | |
| 9. Do you think the demand of the members can lead to task conflict? | 1 | 2 | 3 | 4 | 5 |
| Your reason: | | | | | |
| 10. Do you think the skill level of the members can lead to task conflict? | 1 | 2 | 3 | 4 | 5 |
| Your reason: | | | | | |
| 11. Do you think the mind-set of the members can lead to task conflict? | 1 | 2 | 3 | 4 | 5 |
| Your reason: | | | | | |
| 12. Do you think the ideological system can lead to task conflict? | 1 | 2 | 3 | 4 | 5 |
| Your reason: | | | | | |

| 13. Do you think the behavior mode of the members can lead to task conflict? | 1 | 2 | 3 | 4 | 5 |
|---|---|---|---|---|---|
| Your reason: | | | | | |
| 14. Do you think the differences of the roles can lead to task conflict? | 1 | 2 | 3 | 4 | 5 |
| Your reason: | | | | | |
| 15. Do you think the member's social experience can lead to task conflict? | 1 | 2 | 3 | 4 | 5 |
| Your reason: | | | | | |
| 16. Do you think the differences in the status among members can lead to task conflict? | 1 | 2 | 3 | 4 | 5 |
| Your reason: | | | | | |
| 17. Do you think the work pressure of the members can lead to task conflict? | 1 | 2 | 3 | 4 | 5 |
| Your reason: | | | | | |
| 18. Do you think the levels of members' engagement can lead to task conflict? | 1 | 2 | 3 | 4 | 5 |
| Your reason: | | | | | |
| 19. Do you think the interactive behaviors of the members can lead to task conflict? | 1 | 2 | 3 | 4 | 5 |
| Your reason: | | | | | |
| 20. Do you think the perceptions of performance can lead to task conflict? | 1 | 2 | 3 | 4 | 5 |
| Your reason: | | | | | |
| 21. Do you think the similarities in the goals of members can lead to task conflict? | 1 | 2 | 3 | 4 | 5 |
| Your reason: | | | | | |
| 22. Do you think members' degree of recognition can lead to task conflict? | 1 | 2 | 3 | 4 | 5 |
| Your reason: | | | | | |
| 23a. Do you think routine task can lead to task conflict? | 1 | 2 | 3 | 4 | 5 |
| Your reason: | | | | | |
| 23b. Do you think unconventional task can lead to task conflict? | 1 | 2 | 3 | 4 | 5 |
| Your reason: | | | | | |
| 24. Do you think the uncertainty in the task can lead to task conflict? | 1 | 2 | 3 | 4 | 5 |
| Your reason: | | | | | |
| 25. Do you think the degree of codependency can lead to task conflict? | 1 | 2 | 3 | 4 | 5 |
| Your reason: | | | | | |
| 26. Do you think the difficulty of the tasks can lead to task conflict? | 1 | 2 | 3 | 4 | 5 |

| | | | | | |
|---|---|---|---|---|---|
| Your reason: | | | | | |
| 27. Do you think the feedback clarity of tasks can lead to task conflict? | 1 | 2 | 3 | 4 | 5 |
| Your reason: | | | | | |
| 28. Do you think distribution of responsibilities can lead to task conflict? | 1 | 2 | 3 | 4 | 5 |
| Your reason: | | | | | |
| 29. Do you think the size of the team can lead to task conflict? | 1 | 2 | 3 | 4 | 5 |
| Your reason: | | | | | |
| 30. Do you think the goal of the team can lead to task conflict? | 1 | 2 | 3 | 4 | 5 |
| Your reason: | | | | | |
| 31. Do you think the resource of the team can lead to task conflict? | 1 | 2 | 3 | 4 | 5 |
| Your reason: | | | | | |
| 32. Do you think the previous team performance can lead to task conflict? | 1 | 2 | 3 | 4 | 5 |
| Your reason: | | | | | |
| 33. Do you think the organizational structure can lead to task conflict? | 1 | 2 | 3 | 4 | 5 |
| Your reason: | | | | | |
| 34. Do you think the power politics of the team can lead to task conflict? | 1 | 2 | 3 | 4 | 5 |
| Your reason: | | | | | |
| 35. Do you think team management mechanism can lead to task conflict? | 1 | 2 | 3 | 4 | 5 |
| Your reason: | | | | | |
| 36. Do you think the communication techniques can lead to task conflict? | 1 | 2 | 3 | 4 | 5 |
| Your reason: | | | | | |
| 37. Do you think the diversity of team information can lead to task conflict? | 1 | 2 | 3 | 4 | 5 |
| Your reason: | | | | | |
| 38. Do you think the degree of information asymmetry. | 1 | 2 | 3 | 4 | 5 |
| Your reason: | | | | | |
| 39. Do you think the salary level of the team can lead to task conflict? | 1 | 2 | 3 | 4 | 5 |
| Your reason: | | | | | |
| 40. Do you think the construction level of common vision can lead to task conflict? | 1 | 2 | 3 | 4 | 5 |
| Your reason: | | | | | |

| | | | | | |
|---|---|---|---|---|---|
| 41. Do you think the level of team pressure can lead to task conflict? | 1 | 2 | 3 | 4 | 5 |
| Your reason: | | | | | |
| 42. Do you think the distribution characteristics of the team can lead to task conflict? | 1 | 2 | 3 | 4 | 5 |
| Your reason: | | | | | |
| 43. Do you think the way of interaction in the team can lead to task conflict? | 1 | 2 | 3 | 4 | 5 |
| Your reason: | | | | | |
| 44. Do you think the synergy level of the team can lead to task conflict? | 1 | 2 | 3 | 4 | 5 |
| Your reason: | | | | | |
| 45. Do you think the cohesion level of the team can lead to task conflict? | 1 | 2 | 3 | 4 | 5 |
| Your reason: | | | | | |
| 46. Do you think the emotional intelligence of the team can lead to task conflict? | 1 | 2 | 3 | 4 | 5 |
| Your reason: | | | | | |
| 47. Do you think the team fault zone can lead to task conflict? | 1 | 2 | 3 | 4 | 5 |
| Your reason: | | | | | |
| 48a. Do you think the previous developmental period of the team can lead to task conflict? | 1 | 2 | 3 | 4 | 5 |
| Your reason: | | | | | |
| 48b. Do you think the later stage of development can lead to task conflict? | 1 | 2 | 3 | 4 | 5 |
| Your reason: | | | | | |
| 49a. Do you think the innovation atmosphere in the team can lead to task conflict? | 1 | 2 | 3 | 4 | 5 |
| Your reason: | | | | | |
| 49b. Do you think the equal atmosphere in the team can lead to task conflict? | 1 | 2 | 3 | 4 | 5 |
| Your reason: | | | | | |
| 49c. Do you think the supportive atmosphere of the team can lead to task conflict? | 1 | 2 | 3 | 4 | 5 |
| Your reason: | | | | | |
| 49d. Do you think the interpersonal atmosphere of the team can lead to task conflict? | 1 | 2 | 3 | 4 | 5 |
| Your reason: | | | | | |
| 49e. Do you think the sense of identity can lead to task conflict? | 1 | 2 | 3 | 4 | 5 |
| Your reason: | | | | | |
| 50a. Do you think handling the team conflict by fighting can lead to task conflict? | 1 | 2 | 3 | 4 | 5 |

| Your reason: | | | | | |
|---|---|---|---|---|---|
| 50b. Do you think handling team conflict by cooperating can lead to task conflict? | 1 | 2 | 3 | 4 | 5 |
| Your reason: | | | | | |
| 50c. Do you think handling team conflict by avoidance can lead to task conflict? | 1 | 2 | 3 | 4 | 5 |
| Your reason: | | | | | |
| 50d. Do you think handling team conflict by accommodative methods can lead to task conflict? | 1 | 2 | 3 | 4 | 5 |
| Your reason: | | | | | |
| 50e. Do you think handling team conflict by a compromise can lead to task conflict? | 1 | 2 | 3 | 4 | 5 |
| Your reason: | | | | | |
| 51a. Do you think the joint decision level of behavioral integration can lead to task conflict? | 1 | 2 | 3 | 4 | 5 |
| Your reason: | | | | | |
| 51b. Do you think the open communication integrating the team behavior can lead to task conflict? | 1 | 2 | 3 | 4 | 5 |
| Your reason: | | | | | |
| 51c. Do you think the team cooperation level of team behavior integration can lead to task conflict? | 1 | 2 | 3 | 4 | 5 |
| Your reason: | | | | | |
| 52a. Do you think the open conflict specification adopted by the team can lead to task conflict? | 1 | 2 | 3 | 4 | 5 |
| Your reason: | | | | | |
| 52b. Do you think the team's adoption of conflict avoidance norms can lead to task conflict? | 1 | 2 | 3 | 4 | 5 |
| Your reason: | | | | | |
| 53a. Do you think a centralized team approach can lead to task conflict? | 1 | 2 | 3 | 4 | 5 |
| Your reason: | | | | | |
| 53b. Do you think the decentralization of the team can lead to task conflict? | 1 | 2 | 3 | 4 | 5 |
| Your reason: | | | | | |
| 54a. Do you think the cognitive trust level of the team can lead to task conflict? | 1 | 2 | 3 | 4 | 5 |
| Your reason: | | | | | |
| 54b. Do you think the team's emotional trust level can lead to task conflict? | 1 | 2 | 3 | 4 | 5 |
| Your reason: | | | | | |
| 55a. Do you think the level of social capital within the team can lead to task conflict? | 1 | 2 | 3 | 4 | 5 |
| Your reason: | | | | | |

| | | | | | |
|---|---|---|---|---|---|
| 55b. Do you think the level of social capital outside the team can lead to task conflict? | 1 | 2 | 3 | 4 | 5 |
| Your reason: | | | | | |
| 56a. Do you think the characteristics of team leadership can lead to task conflict? | 1 | 2 | 3 | 4 | 5 |
| Your reason: | | | | | |
| 56b. Do you think the leadership style of team leaders can lead to task conflict? | 1 | 2 | 3 | 4 | 5 |
| Your reason: | | | | | |
| 57a. Do you think a heterogenous team can lead to task conflict? | 1 | 2 | 3 | 4 | 5 |
| Your reason: | | | | | |
| 57b. Do you think the deep heterogeneity of the team can lead to task conflict? | 1 | 2 | 3 | 4 | 5 |
| Your reason: | | | | | |
| 57c. Do you think team time focused on heterogeneous performance can lead to task conflict? | 1 | 2 | 3 | 4 | 5 |
| Your reason: | | | | | |
| 58. Do you think the external cultural context can lead to task conflict? | 1 | 2 | 3 | 4 | 5 |
| Your reason: | | | | | |
| 59. Do you think the changes of the external environment of the team can lead to task conflict? | 1 | 2 | 3 | 4 | 5 |
| Your reason: | | | | | |
| 60. Do you think the supportive external environment of the team can lead to task conflict? | 1 | 2 | 3 | 4 | 5 |
| Your reason: | | | | | |
| 61. Do you think threat situations outside the team can lead to task conflict? | 1 | 2 | 3 | 4 | 5 |
| Your reason: | | | | | |
| 62. Do you think the complexity of the outside environment can lead to task conflict? | 1 | 2 | 3 | 4 | 5 |
| Your reason: | | | | | |

What other factors do you think will cause the task conflict of the innovation team:

## C: Interpretation of partial antecedent variables

- **Similarity of the goal** – similarity of the goal indicates the shared responsibility that is perceived by team members and the degree of unity of purpose.

- **Sense of identity** – the process in which team members define themselves and ultimately belong to the team. Members are consistent with the team in behavior and concept.

- **Information asymmetry** – information is unevenly and asymmetrically distributed among corresponding economic individuals, that is, some people have more information about certain things than others.

- **Team collaboration** – means that all members who trust and depend on each other actively give full play to the potential of each member, work together and strive together to achieve common goals and tasks according to certain rules.

- **Team cohesion** – a dynamic process in which team members work together in the team to maintain the relative stability of the team with the external performance of completing team tasks and the internal purpose of realizing their own value.

- **Emotional intelligence** – Druskat & Wolff (1999) defined team emotional intelligence as the ability of a group to manage its emotional process norms formed in a certain way. The group uses this norm to cultivate the sense of trust, group identity and group efficacy among group members; Wong & Law conducted research in the context of Chinese culture and proposed that group emotional intelligence refers to the ability of group members to perceive, regulate and use group emotions.

- **Team fault zone** – reflects the diversified structure of team members. Members are divided into several subgroups based on multiple similar characteristics. The difference or boundary between these subgroups is the team fault zone, such as the boundary between subgroups formed by the similarity of age, hometown, personality and other characteristics.

- **Team atmosphere** – refers to each organization members' direct or indirect perception of the environment in a specific situation.

- **Conflict management mode** – refers to the tendentious behavior and performance taken by both sides of the conflict when the conflict occurs. Thomas & Rahim (1992) explored five types of conflict handling from the two dimensions of positive or negative and cooperation or non-cooperation, including resistance, cooperation, avoidance, accommodation and compromise. It is a more classic model.

- **Behavior integration** – is the interaction of team members in thought and action. It is a behavioral process of actively sharing information, decision-making and resources. It can be divided into three dimensions: joint decision-making, open communication and team cooperation.

- **Conflict norms** – Jehn defines conflict norms as the normal model that controls how members understand and view conflict and communicate with each other. It is the standard that members of the team use to correct their behavior. When the group accepts conflict as the normal model, members can more openly discuss problems and express their opinions on conflicts, that is, conflict tolerance norms.

- **Power distribution model** – refers to the average degree of power distribution, such as the degree of centralization and decentralization.

- **Team trust** – team trust can be divided into two dimensions: team cognitive trust and team emotional trust. Team cognitive trust is the trust of the trustee based on the trustor's ability and responsibility; Team emotional trust refers to the trust established by emotional ties between the trustor and the trustee in the team, which is reflected in their mutual attention and care.

- **Team social capital** – team external social capital refers to the contact network and resources between team members and the outside, especially the team leaders; Team internal social capital refers to the ability of members to exchange resources through the team internal interpersonal network, emphasizing the integration of trust, norms and common vision on the behaviors of team members.

- **Leadership traits and leadership style** – Ghiselli (1963) proposed eight personality characteristics and five incentive characteristics on leadership traits. The eight personality characteristics are intelligence, innovation, sharpness, self-confidence, decisiveness, adaptability, gender and maturity. Early leadership trait theories believed that some traits could provide the possibility of leadership success. Scholars have found that there is a close relationship between leadership behavior and the leadership efficiency in the process of leadership. A more representative is the "management grid theory" proposed by Blake & Mouton (1964). The ordinate represents the leadership's concern for the people, and the abscissa represents the leadership's concern for production. It is divided into nine equal parts according to the degree, so as to form a grid, clustering into five typical leadership styles.

- **Team heterogeneity** – the characteristic difference of team members in gender, age, educational background, values and personality is team heterogeneity. With the deepening of research, the views of surface heterogeneity and deep heterogeneity are gradually put forward. The former refers to the characteristics that are lowerly related to the team task to be completed, such as gender and age, which are more connected with the members' social relationship than the objective task goal; the latter is directly related to the task to be completed, such as education level, team tenure, professional background, etc., which tends to reflect the differences of experience and views related to the task. Team time attention heterogeneity refers to focusing on one aspect of team members' time cognition within the scope of team heterogeneity research, that is, the degree of difference in time attention, which belongs to the category of deep team heterogeneity.

This is the end of the questionnaire. Thank you again for your cooperation and support!

## Appendix C: A questionnaire on causes of conflict in the innovation team relationship

Dear sir / madam,

Hello! To understand the reasons for the relationship conflict in the innovation team, I kindly invite you to fill in each question in this questionnaire carefully and honestly, and tick ✓ in the appropriate answer □. This questionnaire is anonymous and handled by a specially assigned person. The answers are kept in confidentiality and only for academic research use. Thank you for your cooperation and support!

### A: Background factors: Please tick ✓ in □ according to your actual situation.

1. Your gender: □ male      □ female
2. Your age: □ 20–29 years old      □ 30–39 years old      □ 40–49 years old
□ ≥ 50 years old
3. Your education level: □ college degree or below      □ bachelor's degree
□ master's degree      □ doctor's degree
4. Your level in the team: □ ordinary member of the team      □ the team leader
5. Your industry: □ universities      □ software development
□ medicine development and production
□ development and production of household electrical appliances
6. Size of your team: □ ≤ 5      □ 6–10      □ 11–15      □ ≥ 15
7. Your tenure in the team: □ ≤ 3 years      □ 4–6 years      □7–9 years
□ 10–12 years      □ ≥ 13 years

### B: Reasons for conflict in innovation team relations: Please fill in the following questions honestly.

Innovation team relationship conflict is an interactive process of opposition or inconsistency among members in the innovation team due to emotional opposition and interpersonal friction.

| The Initial Reason | Degree (very low – very high) | | | | |
|---|---|---|---|---|---|
| 1a. Do you think the different personalities of team members can lead to relationship conflict? | 1 | 2 | 3 | 4 | 5 |
| Your reason: | | | | | |
| 1b. Do you think members' different values can lead to relationship conflict? | 1 | 2 | 3 | 4 | 5 |
| Your reason: | | | | | |
| 2a. Do you think members' internal attribution can lead to relationship conflict? | 1 | 2 | 3 | 4 | 5 |
| Your reason: | | | | | |
| 2b. Do you think the external attribution of members can lead to relationship conflict? | 1 | 2 | 3 | 4 | 5 |
| Your reason: | | | | | |
| 3. Do you think members' interest requests can lead to relationship conflicts? | 1 | 2 | 3 | 4 | 5 |
| Your reason: | | | | | |
| 4. Do you think members' awareness can lead to relationship conflict? | 1 | 2 | 3 | 4 | 5 |
| Your reason: | | | | | |
| 5. Do you think members' cognition can lead to relationship conflict? | 1 | 2 | 3 | 4 | 5 |
| Your reason: | | | | | |
| 6. Do you think members' vision can lead to relationship conflict? | 1 | 2 | 3 | 4 | 5 |
| Your reason: | | | | | |
| 7. Do you think different motives of members can lead to relationship conflict? | 1 | 2 | 3 | 4 | 5 |
| Your reason: | | | | | |
| 8. Do you think members' emotions can lead to relationship conflict? | 1 | 2 | 3 | 4 | 5 |
| Your reason: | | | | | |
| 9. Do you think members' preferences can lead to relationship conflict? | 1 | 2 | 3 | 4 | 5 |
| Your reason: | | | | | |
| 10. Do you think members' demands can lead to relationship conflict? | 1 | 2 | 3 | 4 | 5 |
| Your reason: | | | | | |
| 11. Do you think members' skill level can lead to relationship conflict? | 1 | 2 | 3 | 4 | 5 |
| Your reason: | | | | | |
| 12. Do you think members' fear can lead to relationship conflict? | 1 | 2 | 3 | 4 | 5 |
| Your reason: | | | | | |

| | | | | | |
|---|---|---|---|---|---|
| 13. Do you think members' sentiments can lead to relationship conflict? | 1 | 2 | 3 | 4 | 5 |
| Your reason: | | | | | |
| 14. Do you think members' misunderstanding of others can lead to relationship conflict? | 1 | 2 | 3 | 4 | 5 |
| Your reason: | | | | | |
| 15. Do you think members' hostility to others can lead to relationship conflict? | 1 | 2 | 3 | 4 | 5 |
| Your reason: | | | | | |
| 16. Do you think the competition between members can lead to relationship conflict? | 1 | 2 | 3 | 4 | 5 |
| Your reason: | | | | | |
| 17. Do you think the attitudes of members can lead to relationship conflict? | 1 | 2 | 3 | 4 | 5 |
| Your reason: | | | | | |
| 18. Do you think members' recognition can lead to relationship conflict? | 1 | 2 | 3 | 4 | 5 |
| Your reason: | | | | | |
| 19. Do you think members' thinking mode can lead to relationship conflict答 | 1 | 2 | 3 | 4 | 5 |
| Your reason: | | | | | |
| 20. Do you think members' behavior mode can lead to relationship conflict? | 1 | 2 | 3 | 4 | 5 |
| Your reason: | | | | | |
| 21. Do you think members' thinking system can lead to relationship conflict? | 1 | 2 | 3 | 4 | 5 |
| Your reason: | | | | | |
| 22. Do you think the different roles played by members can lead to relationship conflict? | 1 | 2 | 3 | 4 | 5 |
| Your reason: | | | | | |
| 23. Do you think members social experience can lead to relationship conflict? | 1 | 2 | 3 | 4 | 5 |
| Your reason: | | | | | |
| 24. Do you think members' difference status can lead to relationship conflict? | 1 | 2 | 3 | 4 | 5 |
| Your reason: | | | | | |
| 25. Do you think members' interpersonal relations can lead to relationship conflict? | 1 | 2 | 3 | 4 | 5 |
| Your reason: | | | | | |
| 26. Do you think mutual suspicion among members can lead to relationship conflict? | 1 | 2 | 3 | 4 | 5 |
| Your reason: | | | | | |

| | | | | | |
|---|---|---|---|---|---|
| 27. Do you think the members' perception of equality can lead to relationship conflict? | 1 | 2 | 3 | 4 | 5 |
| Your reason: | | | | | |
| 28. Do you think members' perception of performance can lead to relationship conflict? | 1 | 2 | 3 | 4 | 5 |
| Your reason: | | | | | |
| 29. Do you think members' similarity of individual goals can lead to relationship conflict? | 1 | 2 | 3 | 4 | 5 |
| Your reason: | | | | | |
| 30. Do you think members' degree of engagement in organizational goal can lead to relationship conflict? | 1 | 2 | 3 | 4 | 5 |
| Your reason: | | | | | |
| 31a. Do you think routine tasks can lead to relationship conflict? | 1 | 2 | 3 | 4 | 5 |
| Your reason: | | | | | |
| 31b. Do you think unconventional tasks can lead to relationship conflict? | 1 | 2 | 3 | 4 | 5 |
| Your reason: | | | | | |
| 32. Do you think how difficult the task is can lead to relationship conflict? | 1 | 2 | 3 | 4 | 5 |
| Your reason: | | | | | |
| 33. Do you think the uncertainty of tasks can lead to relationship conflict? | 1 | 2 | 3 | 4 | 5 |
| Your reason: | | | | | |
| 34. Do you think the degree of interdependence of tasks can lead to relationship conflict? | 1 | 2 | 3 | 4 | 5 |
| Your reason: | | | | | |
| 35. Do you think the clarity of feed backs can lead to relationship conflict? | 1 | 2 | 3 | 4 | 5 |
| Your reason: | | | | | |
| 36.Do you think the size of the team can lead to relationship conflict? | 1 | 2 | 3 | 4 | 5 |
| Your reason: | | | | | |
| 37.Do you think the team establishment time can lead to relationship conflict? | 1 | 2 | 3 | 4 | 5 |
| Your reason: | | | | | |
| 38. Do you think the resources of the team can lead to relationship conflict? | 1 | 2 | 3 | 4 | 5 |
| Your reason: | | | | | |
| 39. Do you think the previous performance of the team can lead to relationship conflict? | 1 | 2 | 3 | 4 | 5 |
| Your reason: | | | | | |
| 40. Do you think the organizational structure of the team can lead to relationship conflict? | 1 | 2 | 3 | 4 | 5 |

| Your reason: | | | | | |
|---|---|---|---|---|---|
| 41.Do you think the power politics of the team can lead to relationship conflict? | 1 | 2 | 3 | 4 | 5 |
| Your reason: | | | | | |
| 42. Do you think team management mechanism can lead to relationship conflict? | 1 | 2 | 3 | 4 | 5 |
| Your reason: | | | | | |
| 43. Do you think the communication skill used in the team can lead to relationship conflict? | 1 | 2 | 3 | 4 | 5 |
| Your reason: | | | | | |
| 44. Do you think the information asymmetry can lead to relationship conflict? | 1 | 2 | 3 | 4 | 5 |
| Your reason: | | | | | |
| 45.Do you think the salary level of the team can lead to relationship conflict? | 1 | 2 | 3 | 4 | 5 |
| Your reason: | | | | | |
| 46. Do you think the construction of common vision can lead to relationship conflict? | 1 | 2 | 3 | 4 | 5 |
| Your reason: | | | | | |
| 47. Do you think the pressure in the team can lead to relationship conflict? | 1 | 2 | 3 | 4 | 5 |
| Your reason: | | | | | |
| 48. Do you think the distribution characteristics of the team can lead to relationship conflict? | 1 | 2 | 3 | 4 | 5 |
| Your reason: | | | | | |
| 49. Do you think the ways the team members interact can lead to relationship conflict? | 1 | 2 | 3 | 4 | 5 |
| Your reason: | | | | | |
| 50. Do you think the synergy level of the team can lead to relationship conflict? | 1 | 2 | 3 | 4 | 5 |
| Your reason: | | | | | |
| 51. Do you think the emotional intelligence of the team can lead to relationship conflict? | 1 | 2 | 3 | 4 | 5 |
| Your reason: | | | | | |
| 52. Do you think the unity of the team can lead to relationship conflict? | 1 | 2 | 3 | 4 | 5 |
| Your reason: | | | | | |
| 53. Do you think the social network group centrality of the team can lead to relationship conflict? | 1 | 2 | 3 | 4 | 5 |
| Your reason: | | | | | |
| 54. Do you think the exchange differences of the team leader and members can lead to relationship conflict? | 1 | 2 | 3 | 4 | 5 |
| Your reason: | | | | | |

| | | | | | |
|---|---|---|---|---|---|
| 55. Do you think the task conflict in the team can lead to relationship conflict? | 1 | 2 | 3 | 4 | 5 |
| Your reason: | | | | | |
| 56. Do you think the emotional trust in the team can lead to relationship conflict? | 1 | 2 | 3 | 4 | 5 |
| Your reason: | | | | | |
| 57. Do you think the team fault zone can lead to relationship conflict? | 1 | 2 | 3 | 4 | 5 |
| Your reason: | | | | | |
| 58. Do you think the construction of team shared values can lead to relationship conflict? | 1 | 2 | 3 | 4 | 5 |
| Your reason: | | | | | |
| 59a. Do you think the previous developmental period of the team can lead to relationship conflict? | 1 | 2 | 3 | 4 | 5 |
| Your reason: | | | | | |
| 59b. Do you think the later stage of development of the team can lead to relationship conflict? | 1 | 2 | 3 | 4 | 5 |
| Your reason: | | | | | |
| 60a. Do you think the innovation atmosphere of the team can lead to relationship conflict? | 1 | 2 | 3 | 4 | 5 |
| Your reason: | | | | | |
| 60b. Do you think the equal atmosphere of the team can lead to relationship conflict? | 1 | 2 | 3 | 4 | 5 |
| Your reason: | | | | | |
| 60c. Do you think the supportive atmosphere of the team can lead to relationship conflict? | 1 | 2 | 3 | 4 | 5 |
| Your reason: | | | | | |
| 60d. Do you think the interpersonal relationship atmosphere of the team can lead to relationship conflict? | 1 | 2 | 3 | 4 | 5 |
| Your reason: | | | | | |
| 60e. Do you think the sense of identity can lead to relationship conflict? | 1 | 2 | 3 | 4 | 5 |
| Your reason: | | | | | |
| 61a. Do you think the joint decision level of behavioral integration can lead to relationship conflict? | 1 | 2 | 3 | 4 | 5 |
| Your reason: | | | | | |
| 61b. Do you think the open communication of behavioral integration can lead to relationship conflict? | 1 | 2 | 3 | 4 | 5 |
| Your reason: | | | | | |
| 61c. Do you think team cooperation level of team behavior integration can lead to relationship conflict? | 1 | 2 | 3 | 4 | 5 |

| Your reason: | | | | | |
|---|---|---|---|---|---|
| 62a. Do you think the team's adoption of an open conflict specification can lead to relationship conflict? | 1 | 2 | 3 | 4 | 5 |
| Your reason: | | | | | |
| 62b. Do you think the team's adoption of avoidance of conflict can lead to relationship conflict? | 1 | 2 | 3 | 4 | 5 |
| Your reason: | | | | | |
| 63a. Do you think the team's adoption of a centralized approach can lead to relationship conflict? | 1 | 2 | 3 | 4 | 5 |
| Your reason: | | | | | |
| 63b. Do you think the team's adoption of a decentralized approach can lead to relationship conflict? | 1 | 2 | 3 | 4 | 5 |
| Your reason: | | | | | |
| 64a. Do you think the team's dealing with conflict by fighting can lead to relationship conflict? | 1 | 2 | 3 | 4 | 5 |
| Your reason: | | | | | |
| 64b. Do you think the adoption of conflict cooperation approach in the team can lead to relationship conflict? | 1 | 2 | 3 | 4 | 5 |
| Your reason: | | | | | |
| 64c. Do you think the adoption of avoidance in dealing with conflict can lead to relationship conflict? | 1 | 2 | 3 | 4 | 5 |
| Your reason: | | | | | |
| 64d. Do you think dealing with conflict by accommodating can lead to relationship conflict? | 1 | 2 | 3 | 4 | 5 |
| Your reason: | | | | | |
| 64e. Do you think dealing with conflict by compromise can lead to relationship conflict? | 1 | 2 | 3 | 4 | 5 |
| Your reason: | | | | | |
| 65a. Do you think a surface heterogenous team can lead to relationship conflict? | 1 | 2 | 3 | 4 | 5 |
| Your reason: | | | | | |
| 65b. Do you think the deep heterogeneity of the team can lead to task conflict? | 1 | 2 | 3 | 4 | 5 |
| Your reason: | | | | | |
| 65c. Do you think team time focus heterogeneity can lead to relationship conflict? | 1 | 2 | 3 | 4 | 5 |
| Your reason: | | | | | |
| 66a. Do you think internal social capital level of the team can lead to relationship conflict? | 1 | 2 | 3 | 4 | 5 |
| Your reason: | | | | | |
| 66b. Do you think the external social capital level of the team can lead to relationship conflict? | 1 | 2 | 3 | 4 | 5 |

| Your reason: | | | | | |
|---|---|---|---|---|---|
| 67a. Do you think the characteristics of the team leadership can lead to relationship conflict? | 1 | 2 | 3 | 4 | 5 |
| Your reason: | | | | | |
| 67b. Do you think the leadership style of the team leadership can lead to relationship conflict? | 1 | 2 | 3 | 4 | 5 |
| Your reason: | | | | | |
| 67b.Do you think the abusive supervision of the team can lead to relationship conflict? | 1 | 2 | 3 | 4 | 5 |
| Your reason: | | | | | |
| 68. Do you think the external cultural situation can lead to relationship conflict? | 1 | 2 | 3 | 4 | 5 |
| Your reason: | | | | | |
| 69. Do you think the external support of the team can lead to relationship conflict? | 1 | 2 | 3 | 4 | 5 |
| Your reason: | | | | | |
| 70. Do you think the external threat situation can lead to relationship conflict? | 1 | 2 | 3 | 4 | 5 |
| Your reason: | | | | | |
| 71. Do you think the complexity of the external environment can lead to relationship conflict? | 1 | 2 | 3 | 4 | 5 |
| Your reason: | | | | | |

What other factors do you think can lead to relationship conflict in the innovation team?_____

_____

## C: Interpretation of partial antecedent variables

Social network centrality – social network centrality is an indicator of the structural position of an individual in the network. It is often used to evaluate whether a person is important or not and measure the status superiority or privilege of his position and social reputation. The evaluation of network centrality is not about the importance of individuals, but the degree of centralization of the whole network, that is, whether the interaction within the organization is distributed among all members or concentrated among a few people.

Leader-member exchange difference – is concept on the team level, which refers to the difference in the quality of leader exchange relationship between different members in a work team. LMX theory holds that, constrained by limited resources and energy, leaders will not treat subordinate members in the same way, but establish differential relations with different subordinates, that is, establish high-quality leader-member exchange relations with some subordinates and low-quality leader-member exchange relations with other subordinates.

This is the end of the questionnaire. Thank you again for your cooperation and support!

## Appendix D: A questionnaire on financial services team conflict

Dear sir / madam,

Hello! To understand the reasons for the conflict in your innovation team, I kindly invite you to fill in each question in this questionnaire carefully and honestly, and tick ✓ in the appropriate answer □. This questionnaire is anonymous and handled by a specially assigned person. The answers are kept in confidentiality and only for academic research use. Thank you for your cooperation and support!

**A: Background factors: Please tick ✓ in □ according to your actual situation.**

1. Your gender: □ male      □ female
2. Your age: □ 20–29 years old      □ 30–39 years old      □ 40–49 years old
□ ≥ 50 years old
3. Your education level: □ college degree or below      □ bachelor's degree
□ master's degree      □ doctor's degree
4. Your tenure in the team: □ ≤ 3 years      □ 4–6 years      □ 7–9 years
□ 10–12 years      □ ≥ 13 years

**B: The conflict level in the innovation team: Please fill in the following questions according to your real perception.**

| Main Contents | Degree (very low – very high) | | | | |
|---|---|---|---|---|---|
| 1. Are there big differences in the views of members of your team? | 1 | 2 | 3 | 4 | 5 |
| 2. Do members of your team have many different opinions on how to complete the work? | 1 | 2 | 3 | 4 | 5 |
| 3. Do members of your team have a deep degree of debate about team tasks? | 1 | 2 | 3 | 4 | 5 |
| 4. Are there many disputes among members of your team about how to complete the work steps or procedures? | 1 | 2 | 3 | 4 | 5 |
| 5. Do members of your team often get angry in public at work? | 1 | 2 | 3 | 4 | 5 |
| 6. Are there many occasions when there are tensions among members of your team? | 1 | 2 | 3 | 4 | 5 |
| 7. Are there many interpersonal conflicts in your team? | 1 | 2 | 3 | 4 | 5 |
| 8. Is there much jealousy and hostility among members of your team? | 1 | 2 | 3 | 4 | 5 |

This is the end of the questionnaire. Thank you again for your cooperation and support!

## Appendix E: A questionnaire on financial services team conflict (small sample test)

Dear sir / madam,

Hello! To understand the reasons for the conflict in your innovation team, I kindly invite you to fill in each question in this questionnaire carefully and honestly, and tick ✓ in the appropriate answer ☐. This questionnaire is anonymous and handled by a specially assigned person. The answers are kept in confidentiality and only for academic research use. Thank you for your cooperation and support!

**A. Task conflict network: Please fill in the following content according to your actual situation, and the name of the member is filled in horizontally. If there is no qualified member, it cannot be filled in; If yes, you can fill in one or more.**

Who do you often have to exchange your opinions with to complete the task?
_____

Who do you often disagree with?_____

_____

Who do you often make different decisions with when making decisions?__

_____

**B. Relationship conflict network:** Please fill in the following content according to your actual situation, and the name of the member is filled in horizontally. If there is no qualified member, it cannot be filled in; If yes, you can fill in one or more.

Who are you often angry or dissatisfied with in the team?_____
Who do you often feel tense with in the team?_____
Who do you often have friction with in the team?_____

There are 28 members in your team (for sensitivity, the list will be omitted here. In the actual investigation process, the list of 28 members will be attached).

This is the end of the questionnaire. Thank you again for your cooperation and support!

## Appendix F: A questionnaire on the relationship between innovation team conflict and team effectiveness (small sample test)

Dear sir / madam,

Hello! To understand the innovation team conflict and team effectiveness, I kindly invite you to fill in each question in this questionnaire carefully and honestly, and tick ✓ in the appropriate answer □. This questionnaire is anonymous and handled by a specially assigned person. The answers are kept in confidentiality and only for academic research use. Thank you for your cooperation and support!

**A: Background factors: Please tick ✓ in □ according to your actual situation.**

1. Your gender: □ male     □ female
2. Your age: □ 20–29 years old     □ 30–39 years old     □ 40–49 years old
□ ≥ 50 years old
3. Your education level: □ college degree or below     □ bachelor's degree
□ master's degree     □ doctor's degree
4. Size of your team: □ ≤ 5     □ 6–10     □ 11–15     □ ≥ 15
5. Your tenure in the team: □ ≤ 3 years     □ 4–6 years     □ 7–9 years
□10–12 years     □ ≥ 13 years

**B: Innovation Team Conflict: Please fill in the following according to your real perception.**

| Main Contents | Degree (very low – very high) | | | | |
|---|---|---|---|---|---|
| 1. Are there deep differences in the views of members of your team? | 1 | 2 | 3 | 4 | 5 |
| 2. Do members of your team have many different opinions on how to complete the work? | 1 | 2 | 3 | 4 | 5 |
| 3. Do members of your team have a deep degree of debate about team tasks? | 1 | 2 | 3 | 4 | 5 |
| 4. Are there many disputes among members of your team about how to complete the work steps or procedures? | 1 | 2 | 3 | 4 | 5 |

| 5. Do members of your team often get angry in public at work? | 1 | 2 | 3 | 4 | 5 |
|---|---|---|---|---|---|
| 6. Are there many tensions among members of your team? | 1 | 2 | 3 | 4 | 5 |
| 7. Are there many interpersonal conflicts in your team? | 1 | 2 | 3 | 4 | 5 |
| 8. Is there much jealousy and hostility among members of your team? | 1 | 2 | 3 | 4 | 5 |

**C: Innovation team emotional intelligence: Please fill in the following questions according to your true perception.**

| Main Contents | Degree of consent (very disagree – very agree) | | | | |
|---|---|---|---|---|---|
| 1. Team members always understand others' emotions | 1 | 2 | 3 | 4 | 5 |
| 2. Team members understand the mainstream atmosphere in the team | 1 | 2 | 3 | 4 | 5 |
| 3. Members can understand the signals sent by team emotions | 1 | 2 | 3 | 4 | 5 |
| 4. When there is tension in the team, members will admit and talk about it | 1 | 2 | 3 | 4 | 5 |
| 5. There are specific words or phrases in the team to identify the emotions in the team | 1 | 2 | 3 | 4 | 5 |
| 6. The team pays attention to the emotional feelings of each member and shares them with each other | 1 | 2 | 3 | 4 | 5 |
| 7. The team can clearly and timely feel the overall mood of members in the team | 1 | 2 | 3 | 4 | 5 |
| 8. The team is good at grasping the overall mood and raising and solving problems in an appropriate emotional atmosphere | 1 | 2 | 3 | 4 | 5 |
| 9. When the overall mood is bad, the team can always find and adjust in time | 1 | 2 | 3 | 4 | 5 |
| 10. The team can often create a positive overall mood | 1 | 2 | 3 | 4 | 5 |
| 11. The team can guide members to show the emotions needed by the team | 1 | 2 | 3 | 4 | 5 |
| 12. When a member's mood is inconsistent with the team, the team can make it consistent with the team in various ways | 1 | 2 | 3 | 4 | 5 |
| 13. The influence of the emotional interaction between team members | 1 | 2 | 3 | 4 | 5 |

**D: Innovation team effectiveness: Please fill in the following questions according to your true perception.**

| Main Contents | Degree of agreement (very disagree – very agree) | | | | |
|---|---|---|---|---|---|
| 1. The achievement of team goals is in good condition | 1 | 2 | 3 | 4 | 5 |
| 2. The schedule of the team is good | 1 | 2 | 3 | 4 | 5 |
| 3. A good use of team resources | 1 | 2 | 3 | 4 | 5 |
| 4. The team provides high-quality products or services | 1 | 2 | 3 | 4 | 5 |
| 5. I am very satisfied with working in the team | 1 | 2 | 3 | 4 | 5 |
| 6. Working in this team often gives me a pleasant feeling | 1 | 2 | 3 | 4 | 5 |
| 7. I can learn and grow in this team | 1 | 2 | 3 | 4 | 5 |
| 8. I am willing to sacrifice my personal interests for the success of the team | 1 | 2 | 3 | 4 | 5 |
| 9. I think I have the obligation to support the team and carry out the team mission | 1 | 2 | 3 | 4 | 5 |
| 10. I am willing to continue to work in this team | 1 | 2 | 3 | 4 | 5 |

**E: Innovation team conflict network:** Please fill in the following content according to your actual situation, and the name of the member is filled in horizontally. If there is no qualified member, it cannot be filled in; If yes, you can fill in one or more.

**Task conflict network:**

Who do you often have to discuss your views on the task in order to complete the task? _____

Who do you often disagree with? _____

Who do you often have difference decisions with when decision making?___

_____

**Relationship Conflict Network:**

Who are you often angry or dissatisfied with in the team?_____

Who do you often feel tense with in the team?_____

Who do you often have friction with in the team?_____

There is a total of (    ) members in your team (for sensitivity, the list will be omitted here. In the actual investigation process, the list of members will be attached).

This is the end of the questionnaire. Thank you again for your cooperation and support!

## Appendix G: A questionnaire on the relationship between innovation team conflict and team effectiveness (formal survey)

Dear sir / madam,

Hello! To understand the innovation team conflict and team effectiveness, I kindly invite you to fill in each question in this questionnaire carefully and honestly, and tick ✓ in the appropriate answer ☐. This questionnaire is anonymous and handled by a specially assigned person. The answers are kept in confidentiality and only for academic research use. Thank you for your cooperation and support!

**A: Background factors: Please tick ✓ in ☐ according to your actual situation.**

1. Your gender: ☐ male      ☐ female
2. Your age: ☐ 20–29 years old      ☐ 30–39 years old      ☐ 40–49 years old
☐ ≥ 50 years old
3. Your education level: ☐ college degree or below      ☐ bachelor's degree
☐ master's degree      ☐ doctor's degree
4. Size of your team: ☐ ≤ 5      ☐ 6–10      ☐ 11–15      ☐ ≥ 15
5. Your tenure in the team: ☐ ≤ 3 years      ☐ 4–6 years      ☐ 7–9 years
☐ 10–12 years      ☐ ≥ 13 years

**B: Innovation Team Conflict: Please fill in the following according to your real perception.**

| Main Contents | Degree (very low – very high) | | | | |
|---|---|---|---|---|---|
| 1. Are there big differences in the views of members of your team? | 1 | 2 | 3 | 4 | 5 |
| 2. Do members of your team have many different opinions on how to complete the work? | 1 | 2 | 3 | 4 | 5 |
| 3. Do members of your team have a deep degree of debate about team tasks? | 1 | 2 | 3 | 4 | 5 |
| 4. Are there many disputes among members of your team about how to complete the work steps or procedures? | 1 | 2 | 3 | 4 | 5 |

| 5. Do members of your team often get angry in public at work? | 1 | 2 | 3 | 4 | 5 |
| 6. Are there many tensions among members of your team? | 1 | 2 | 3 | 4 | 5 |
| 7. Are there many interpersonal conflicts in your team? | 1 | 2 | 3 | 4 | 5 |
| 8. Is there much jealousy and hostility among members of your team? | 1 | 2 | 3 | 4 | 5 |

**C: Innovation team emotional intelligence: Please fill in the following questions according to your actual perception.**

| Main Contents | Degree of consent (very disagree – very agree) | | | | |
|---|---|---|---|---|---|
| 1. Team members always understand each other's emotions | 1 | 2 | 3 | 4 | 5 |
| 2. Team members understand the mainstream atmosphere in the team | 1 | 2 | 3 | 4 | 5 |
| 3. Members can understand the signals sent by team emotions | 1 | 2 | 3 | 4 | 5 |
| 4. When there is tension in the team, members will admit and talk about it | 1 | 2 | 3 | 4 | 5 |
| 5. The team pays attention to the emotional feelings of each member and shares them with each other | 1 | 2 | 3 | 4 | 5 |
| 6. The team can clearly and timely feel the overall mood of members in the team | 1 | 2 | 3 | 4 | 5 |
| 7. The team is good at grasping the overall mood and raising and solving problems in an appropriate emotional atmosphere | 1 | 2 | 3 | 4 | 5 |
| 8. When the overall mood is bad, the team can always find and adjust in time | 1 | 2 | 3 | 4 | 5 |
| 9. The team can often create a positive overall mood | 1 | 2 | 3 | 4 | 5 |
| 10. The team can guide members to show the emotions needed by the team | 1 | 2 | 3 | 4 | 5 |
| 11. When a member's mood is inconsistent with the team, the team can make it consistent with the team in various ways | 1 | 2 | 3 | 4 | 5 |

**D: Innovation team effectiveness: Please fill in the following questions according to your true perception.**

| Main Contents | Degree of consent (very disagree – very agree) | | | | |
|---|---|---|---|---|---|
| 1. Team goals are well achieved | 1 | 2 | 3 | 4 | 5 |
| 2. The schedule of the team is good | 1 | 2 | 3 | 4 | 5 |
| 3. A good use of team resources | 1 | 2 | 3 | 4 | 5 |
| 4. The team provides high-quality products or services | 1 | 2 | 3 | 4 | 5 |
| 5. I am very satisfied with working in the team | 1 | 2 | 3 | 4 | 5 |
| 6. Working in this team often gives me a pleasant feeling | 1 | 2 | 3 | 4 | 5 |
| 7. I can learn and grow in this team | 1 | 2 | 3 | 4 | 5 |
| 8. I am willing to sacrifice my personal interests for the success of the team | 1 | 2 | 3 | 4 | 5 |
| 9. I think I have the obligation to support the team and carry out the team mission | 1 | 2 | 3 | 4 | 5 |
| 10. I am willing to continue to work in this team | 1 | 2 | 3 | 4 | 5 |

**E: Innovation team conflict network:** Please fill in the following content according to your actual situation, and the name of the member is filled in horizontally. If there is no qualified member, it cannot be filled in; If yes, you can fill in one or more.

**Task conflict network:**

Who do you often have to discuss your views on the task in order to complete the task? _____

_____

Who do you often disagree with?_____

_____

Who do you often make different decisions with when making decisions?___

_____

**Relationship conflict network:**

Who are you often angry or dissatisfied with in the team?_____

_____

Who do you often feel tense with in the team?_____

_____

Who do you often have friction with in the team?_____

_____

There is a total of (    ) members in your team (for sensitivity, the list will be omitted here. In the actual investigation process, the list of members will be attached).

This is the end of the questionnaire. Thank you again for your cooperation and support!

# References

[1] Zhou Ruichao, Tan Mingfang. "How to Deal with the Conflict in a Group of Scientific Research & Originality." *Journal of Nanning Teachers College* 22, no. 3 (2005): 66–68.

[2] Lin Li, Wang Zhenwei. "Discussion on Internal Conflict Management Strategy of Innovation Team." *Journal of Ningxia University (Humanities & Social Sciences Edition)* 31, no. 5 (2009): 142–144.

[3] Gao Xiaoqing. "Research on Enterprise Innovation Team." Master's thesis, Shanxi University, 2008.

[4] Men Yazhen. "The Effect of Trust, Conflict and Performance in Innovate Team: Empirical Study Based on Innovate Teams in Zhejiang." Master's thesis, Zhejiang Gongshang University, 2010.

[5] Han Fei, Guo Lifang. "Theory of Conflict and Performance Relationship in Enterprise Technology Innovation Team." *Science and Technology Management Research* 2, (2014): 71–74.

[6] Yin Huibin. "Fuzzy Synthetic Evaluation of the Inner Knowledge Conflict Level of Radical Innovation Team." *Soft Science* 27, no. 11 (2013): 81–84.

[7] Jehn K A. "A Multimethod Examination of the Benefits and Determents of Intragroup Conflict." *Administrative Science Quarterly* 40, (1995): 256–282.

[8] Rahim M A. "Toward a Theory of Managing Organizational Conflict." *The International Journal of Conflict Management* 13, (2002): 206–235.

[9] De Dreu C K W and Gelfand M J. *Conflict in the Workplace: Sources, Functions and Dynamics Across Multiple Levels of Analysis.* New York: Lawrence Erlbaum, 2008.

[10] Wang Jie. "The Research on the Mechanisms of Team Task Conflict on Task Performance." Doctor's thesis, Zhejiang University, 2009.

[11] Xie Fengtao. "The Study on Relationship of Team Climate and Effectiveness: Team Conflict as a Medium Variable." Master's thesis, Shandong University, 2012

[12] Pinkley R L. "Dimensions of Conflict Frame: Disputant Interpretations of Conflict." *Journal of Applied Psychology* 75, (1990): 117–126.

[13] Amason A C. "Distinguishing the Effects of Functional and Dysfunctional Conflict on Strategic Decision-Making: Resolving A Paradox for Top Management Teams." *Academy of Management Journal* 39, (1996): 123–148.

[14] De Dreu, Van Vianen. "Managing Relationship Conflict and the Effectiveness of Organizational Teams." *Journal of Organizational Behavior* 22, (2001): 309–328.

[15] Amason A C, Sapienza H J. "The Effect of Top Management Team Size and Interaction Norms on Cognitive Conflict and Affective Conflict." *Journal of Management* 23, no. 4 (1997): 459–516.

[16] Jehn K A, Mannin E A. "The Dynamic Nature of Conflict: A Longitudinal Study of Intra-Group Conflict and Group Performance." *Academy of Managemen* 11, (2001): 231–254.

[17] Zeng Deming, Zhou Qing. "The Flexible Mechanism of High-Tech Enterprise R&D Team Conflict Management." *Management Review* 17, no. 2 (2005): 22–26.

[18] Simons T L, Peterson R S. "Task Conflict and Relationship Conflict in Top Management Teams: The Pivotal Role of Intragroup Trust." *Journal of Applied Psychology* 85, (2000): 102–111.

[19] De Dreu C K, Weingart L R. "Task Versus Relationship Conflict, Team Performance and Team Member Satisfaction: A Meta-Analysis." *Journal of Applied Psychology* 88, no. 4 (2003): 741–749.

[20] Lang C G, Xi Y M. "Impact of Team Conflict on Team Decision Quality and Satisfaction: An Empirical Research in China." *Frontiers of Business Research in China* 2, no. 1 (2008): 1–14.

[21] Tjosvold D. "The Conflict-Positive Organization: It Depends Upon Us." *Journal of Organizational Behavior* 29, (2008): 19–28.

[22] Ross R S. *Small groups in organizational settings.* Engle-wood Cliffs, NJ: Prentice Hall, 1989.

[23] Zhang Xinan, He Hui, Gu Feng. "The Effects of Paternalistic Leading on Team's Achievements: The Mediating Role of Approaches to the Management of Team's Conflicts." *Journal of Management World*, no.3 (2009): 121–133.

[24] Mooney A C, Holahan P J. "Don't Take it Personally: Exploring Cognitive Conflict as A Mediator of Affective Conflict." *Journal of Management Studies* 44, no. 5 (2007): 733-758.

[25] Bsino H. *Managing Conflict.* Beverly Hills: Sage Publications, 1988: 45–112.

[26] Forsyth D R. *Group Dynamics.* Pacific Grove, CAZ; Brooks, 1990: 56–96.

[27] Steven L. McShane, Mary Ann Von Glinow. *Organizational Behavior.* Translated by Tang Chaoying. Beijing: China Renmin University Press, 2008.

[28] Cronin M A, Weingart L R. "Representational Gaps, Information Processing and Conflict in Functionally Diverse Teams." *Academy of Management Review* 32, no. 3 (2007): 761–773.

[29] Bodtker A M, Jameson K J. "Emotion in Conflict Formation and Its Transformation: Application to Organizational Conflict Management." *International Journal of Conflict Management* 12, (2001): 259–275.

[30] Olson B J, Parayitam S. "Strategic Making: The Effects of Cognitive Diversity, Conflict and Trust on Decision Outcomes." *Journal of Management* 33, no. 2 (2007): 196–222.

[31] Jehn K A, Northcraft G B, Neale M A. "Why Differences Make a Difference: A Field Study of Diversity, Conflict and Performance in Workgroups." *Administrative Science Quarterly* 44, no. 4 (1999): 741–763.

[32] Lu Hongxu. "Study on How Team Conflict Affects Team Performance: Perspective Based on Trust." Master's thesis, Zhejiang University of Technology, 2011.

[33] Mooney A C, Holahan P J. "Don't Take it Personally: Exploring Cognitive Conflict as A Mediator of Affective Conflict." *Journal of Management Studies* 44, no. 5 (2007): 733–758.

[34] Wu Xin, Wu Zhiming. "Research Status and Development Trend of Influencing Factors of Team Effectiveness Abroad." *Foreign Economies & Management* 27, no. 1 (2005): 47–50.

[35] Li Guangju. "Comparative Analysis of Influencing Factors of Scientific Research Team Size." *Theory Research* 14, (2010): 61–62.

[36] Greening D W, Johnson R A. "Do Managers and Strategies Matter? A Study in Crisis." *Journal of Management Studies* 33, (1996): 25–31.

[37] Lau D C, Murnighan J K. "Interactions Within Groups and Subgroups: The Effects of Demographic Faultlines." *Academy of Management Journal* 48, no. 4 (2005): 645–659.

[38] Harrison D A, Price K H. "Time, Teams and Task Performance: Changing Effects of Surface and Deep-Level Diversity on Group Functioning." *Academy of Management Journal* 45, no. 5 (2002): 1029–1045.

[39] Peterson R S, Behfar K J. "The Dynamic Relationship between Performance Feedback, Trust, And Conflict in Groups: A Longitudinal Study." *Organizational Behavior& Human Decision Processes* 92, no.1/2 (2003): 102.

[40] Michalisin M D, Karau S J. "Top Management Team Cohesion and Superior Industry Returns: An Empirical Study of the Resource-Based View." *Group& Organization Management* 29, no. 1 (2004): 125–140.

[41] Jehn K A. "Intragroup Conflict in Organizations: A Contingency Perspective on the Conflict-Outcome Relationship." *Research in Organizational Behavior* 25, (2003): 187–242.

[42] Kriedler William. *Creative Conflict Resolution: More Than 200 Activities for Keeping Peace in the Classroom k-6*. Glenview, 1984: 15–89.

[43] Eisenhardt K M, Kahwajy J L. "Conflict and Strategic Choice: Low Top Management Team Disagree." *California Management Review* 39, no. 2 (1997): 42–62.

[44] Sessa V I, Susan E J. "Diversity in Decision-Making Teams: All Differences Are Not

Created Equal." In *Diversity in Organizations: New Perspectives for A Changing Workplace*, Martin M C, Stuart O (Eds.), 1995: 133-156.

[45] Chen Jia. "The Research of Top Management Team's Operating to Enterprise's Performance." Master's thesis, Hunan University, 2004.

[46] Jehn K A, Jennifer A C. "The Influence of Proportional and Perceptual Conflict Composition on Team Performance." *The International Journal of Conflict Management* 11, no. 1 (2000): 56–73.

[47] Langfred C W. "The Downside of Self-Management: A Longitudinal Study of the Effects of Conflict on Trust, Autonomy and Task Interdependence in Self-Managing Teams." *Academy of Management Journal* 50, (2007): 885–900.

[48] Mortensen M, Hinds P J. "Conflict and Shared Identity in Geographically Distributed Teams." *International Journal of Conflict Management*, no. 12 (2001): 212–239.

[49] Camevale P J, Probst T M. "Social Values and Social Conflict in Creative Problem Solving and Categorization." *Journal of Personality and Social Psychology* 74, (1998): 1300–1309.

[50] Friedman R A, Tidd S T. "What Goes Around Comes Around: The Impact of Personal Conflict Styles on Work Conflict and Stress." *International Journal of Conflict Management* 11, (2000): 32–55.

[51] Sonnentag S, Unger D. "Workplace Conflict and Employee Well-Being: The Moderating Role of Detachment from Work During Off-Job Time." *International Journal of Conflict Management* 24, no.2 (2013): 166–183.

[52] Carnevale P J, Probst T M. "Social Values and Social Conflict in Creative Problem Solving and Categorization." *Journal of Personality and Social Psychology* 74, (1998): 1300–1309.

[53] Wang Guofeng, Li Mao. "Research on Conflict, Cohesion and Decision Quality in Top Management Team." *Nankai Business Review* 10, no. 5 (2007): 89–93.

[54] Amason A C, Sapienza H J. "The Effects of Top Management Team Size and Interaction Norms on Cognitive and Affective Conflict." *Journal of Management*, no. 23 (1997): 495–516.

[55] Kurtzberg T R. "Creative Styles and Teamwork: Effects of Coordination and Conflict on Group Outcomes." ProQuest Information&Learning,2000.

[56] Levine J M, Resnick L B. "Social Foundations of Cognition." *Annual Review of Psychology* 44, no. 1 (1993): 585–612.

[57] Parayitam S, Dooley R S. "Is Too Much Cognitive Conflict in Strategic Decision-Making Teams Too Bad?" *International Journal of Conflict Management* 22, no. 4 (2011): 342–357.

[58] Shah P P, Jehn K A. "Do Friends Perform Better Than Acquaintances? The Interaction of Friendship, Conflict and Task." *Group Decision and Negotiation* 2, no.

2 (1993): 149–165.

[59] De Dreu C K W. "When Too Little or Too Much Hurts: Evidence for A Curvilinear Relationship between Task Conflict and Innovation in Teams." *Journal of Management* 32, (2006): 83–107.

[60] Kurtzberg T R, Mueller J S. "The Influence of Daily Conflict on Perceptions of Creativity: A Longitudinal Study." *International Journal of Conflict Mangement* 16, no. 4 (2005): 335–353.

[61] Blake R R, Mouton J S. *The Managerial Grid*. Houston, Texas: Gulf Publishing Co., 1964.

[62] Singh A, Vlates D A. "Using Conflict Management for Better Decision Making." *Journal of Management Engrg* 7, no. 1 (1991): 70–82.

[63] Chen Zhenjiao. "Exploring the Underlying Mediating Processes between Intragroup Conflict and Team Outcomes: A Social Information Processing Perspective." Master's thesis, University of Science and Technology of China, 2009.

[64] Thomas K W. *Conflict and Conflict Management//M D Dunnette. Handbook of Industrial and Organizational Psychology*. Chicago: Rand McNally Publishing, 1976: 889–935.

[65] Gardner A M. "Diagnosing Conflict: What Do We Know?" *From Reaction to Conflict Prevention: Opportunities for the UN System*, 15 (2002): 23-43.

[66] Chang Zheng et al. *International politics*. Beijing: China Renmin University Press, 1995.

[67] Liu Junbo. "Theory and Practice of Conflict Management--The Korean Nuclear Issue and China's Policy Choice." Master's thesis, China Foreign Affairs University, 2006.

[68] Wei Changwei. "Study on the Roles of Government Plays as a Third Party in the Process of Intervening Public Conflict." Doctor's thesis, Nankai University, 2013.

[69] Joseph Schumpeter. *The Theory of Economic Development*. Translated by He Wei et al. The Commercial Press, 1997.

[70] Peter F. Drucker. *Innovation and Entrepreneurship*. Translated by Zhang Wei. Shanghai: Shanghai People's Publishing House, 2002.

[71] Hackman J R. "Employee Reaction to Job Characteristics." *Journal of Applied Psychology Monograph*, no. 55 (1971): 259–286.

[72] Auynag S Y. *Foundations of Complex System Theories in Economics, Evolutionary Biology and Statistical Physics*. Cambridge: Cambridge University Press, 1998.

[73] Jin Hongzhang, Wei Qi. *Brittleness Theory and Application of Complex Systems*. Xi'an: Northwestern Polytechnical University Press Co. Ltd, 2010.

[74] Wu Hongmei. "Brittleness Theory of Complex System and Its Application on Coal Mine Accident System." Doctor's thesis, Harbin Engineering University, 2008.

[75] Lin Deming. "Adaptive Agent Digraph and Its Application on Brittleness Analysis

of Complex System." Doctor's thesis, Harbin: Harbin Engineering University, 2007.

[76] Yan Limei, Jin Hongzhang. "Brittleness and the Brittle Source of System." *Journal of Harbin Engineering University* 27, no. 2 (2006): 223–226.

[77] Rahim A M. "Empirical Studies on Managing Conflict." *International Journal of Conflict Management* 11, no. 1 (2000): 37–60.

[78] Pondy L R. "Organizational Conflict: Concepts and Models." *Administrative Science Quarterly* 12, no. 2 (1967): 296–320.

[79] Ury W. *The Third Side: Why We Fight and How We Can Stop.* New York: Penguin Books, 2000.

[80] Deutsch M. *The Resolution of Conflict: Constructive and Destructive Process.* New Haven: Yale University Press, 1973.

[81] Reimann C. "Assessing the State-of-the-art in Conflict Transformation-Reflections from A Theoretical Perspective." *Berghor Research Center for Constructive Conflict Management,* (2005): 9–13.

[82] Mitchell J C. *Social Networks in Urban Situations.* Manchester: Manchester University Press, 1969.

[83] Wellman B. *Structural Analysis from Method and Metaphor to Theory and Substance in Social Structures: A Network Approach.* Cambridge: Cambridge University Press, 1988.

[84] Liu Jun. *Lectures on Whole Network Approach—A Practical Guide to UCINET.* Shanghai: Truth & Wisdom Press, 2009.

[85] Liu Jun. *An Introduction to Social Network Analysis.* Beijing: Social Sciences Academic Press (China), 2004.

[86] Zhao Yanqiu. "Research on the Influence of Organizational Internal Social Network Structure on Organizational Learning Capability—Based on A Business Bank." Master's thesis, Nanchang University, 2012.

[87] Scott J, Carrington P J. *The SAGE Handbook of Social Network Analysis.* London: SAGE Publications, 2011.

[88] Freeman L C. "Centrality in Social Networks: Conceptual Clarification." *Social Networks* 1, (1979): 215–239.

[89] Newman M E J. "The Structure and Function of Complex Networks." *SIAM Review* 45, (2003): 167–256.

[90] Krackhardt D. "Informal Networks and Organizational Crisis: An Experimental Simulation." *Social Psychological Quarterly* 51, no. 2 (1988): 123–140.

[91] Cheng Zhaoqian, Zhang De. "Intra-group Conflict from A Process Perspective." *Technoeconomics & Management Research* 4, (2006): 17–19.

[92] Turner J C, Hogg M A. *Rediscovering the Social Group: A Self-Categorization Theory.* Basil Blackwell, 1987.

[93] Brown S,L. Competing on the Edge: Strategy As Structured Chaos. Boston: Harvard

Business School Press, 1998.

[94] Jin Hongzhang, Li Qi. "Analyzing Brittleness Factors of Complex Systems." *Journal of Harbin Engineering University* 26, no. 6 (2005): 739–743.

[95] Wei Qi. "Brittleness Theory of Complex System and its Application to Crisis Analysis." Master's thesis, Harbin Engineering University, 2004.

[96] Liu Wenxing, Liao Jianqiao. "Inner Mechanisms between Abusive Supervision and Employee Creativity." *Industrial Engineering and Management* 17, no. 5 (2012): 112–118.

[97] Bisseling D, Sobral F. "A Cross-Cultural Comparison of Intragroup Conflict in the Netherlands and Brazil." *International Journal of Conflict Management* 22, no. 2 (2011): 151–169.

[98] Chen Xiaoping. *Managing Across Cultures*. Beijing: Tsinghua University, 2005.

[99] Yang J X, Mossholder K W. "Decoupling Task and Relationship Conflict: The Role of Intragroup Emotional Processing." *Journal of Organizational Behavior* 25, no. 5 (2004): 589–605.

[100] Hair Jr J F. Anderson R E. Tatham R L. *Multivariate Data Analysis with Readings*. Macmillan Publishing Co., Inc., 1986.

[101] Xue Jing, Ren Ziping. "A Case Study—from the Angle of Social Net—of the Relationship between the Resources of Personal External Relations and the Behavior of Innovation." *Journal of Management World* 5, (2006): 150–151.

[102] Wei Jiang. "On the Mechanism of the Impact of Relational Embeddedness on Firm's Technological Innovation: The Mediation and Moderation Effects of Organizational Learning Capability." *Journal of Zhejiang University (Humanities and Social Sciences)* 40, no. 6 (2010): 168–180.

[103] Labianca G, Brass D J. "Social Networks and Perceptions of Intragroup Conflict: The Role of Negative Relationships and Third Parties." *Academy of Management Journal* 41, (1998): 55–67.

[104] Rene Thom. *Ideas and Applications of Mutationism*. Translated by Zhou Zhongliang, Shanghai: Shanghai Translation Publishing House, 1989.

[105] Wen Zhonglin, Zhang Lei et al. "Mediated Moderator and Moderated Mediator." *Acta Psychologica Sinica* 38, no. 3 (2006): 448–452.

[106] Bisseling D, Sobral F. "A Cross-Cultural Comparison of Intragroup Conflict in the Netherlands and Brazil." International Journal of Conflict Management 22, no. 2 (2011): 151–169.

[107] Milberg S, Margaret S C. "Moods and Compliance." *British Journal of Psychology* 27, (1988): 79–90.

[108] Liu Ning, Zhao Mei. "Coordination of the Relationship between Task and Relationship Conflict in Teams." *Science and Technology Management Research* 32, no. 5 (2012): 179–182.

[109] Lu Hui, Wang Fuqi et al. "The Management of Conflicts among Project Teams under Traditional Chinese Culture." *Science of Science and Management of S.&T.* no. 7 (2006): 161–164.

[110] M. Eysenck. *Psychology: An Integrated Approach*. Shanghai: East China Normal University Press, 2000.

[111] Zajonc R B. "Closing the Debate on the Primacy of Affect." In *Feeling and Thinking: The Role of Affect in Social Cognition*, J P Forgas (Eds.). New York: Cambridge University Press, 2000.

[112] Boyatzis R E. "From A Presentation to the Linkage Conference on Emotional Intelligence." Chicago, IL, September, 1999.

[113] Jordan P J. "Workgroup Emotional Intelligence: Scale Development and Relationship to Team Process Effectiveness and Goal Focus." *Human Resource Management Review* 12, no. 2 (2002): 195–214.

[114] Jacobs S L. "An Exploration of Group Emotional Intelligence Affect on Group Member Satisfaction." University of South Alabama, 2003.

[115] Zhang Huihua. "A Meta-Analysis of the Relationship between Emotional Intelligence and Work-related Variables: The Sample of Chinese Respondents." *Journal of Psychological Science* 35, no. 5 (2012): 1175–1184.

[116] Chen Quan. "The Influence of Emotional intelligence on TMT Conflict, Behavioral Integration and Performance of Strategic Decision." Doctor's thesis, Jiangsu University, 2013.

[117] Jordan P J, Troth A C. "Emotional Intelligence and Conflict Resolution: Implications for Human Resource Development." *Advances in Developing Human Resource* s4, no. 1 (2002): 62–79.

[118] Barsade S G. "The Ripple Effect: Emotional Contagion in Groups." *Administrative Science Quarterly* 47, no. 4 (2002): 644–675.

[119] George J M. "Affect Regulation in Groups and Teams." In *Emotions in the Workplace: Understanding the Structure and Role of Emotions in Organizational Behavior*, R.G. Lord, R J Klimoski(Eds.). San Francisco, CA: Jossey-Bass, 2002.

[120] Wolff S B, Anthony T P. "Emotional Intelligence as the Basis of Leadership Emergence in Self-Managing Teams." *The Leadership Quarterly* 13, (2002): 505–522.

[121] Hu Ruishan. "Discussion of Team Diversity, Action and Performance." Master's thesis, Taiwan: National Sun Yat-sen University, 2007.

[122] Wei Xuhua. "An Experimental Study on the Influence of Group Emotional Intelligence on Group Decision Making Process and Decision Outcome." Master's thesis, Central South University, 2008.

[123] Coleman J S. "Social Capital in the Creation of Human Capital." *American Journal of Sociology* 29, no. 3 (2011): 427–431.

[124] Wu Jiebing. "Industrial Clusters' Competitive Advantage as Explained by Inter-

firm Network Structure and Dynamic Capabilities." Doctor's thesis, Zhejiang University, 2006.

[125] Leenders R T A J. "Virtuality, Communication and New Product Team Creativity: A Social Network Perspective." *Journal of Engineering and Technology Management* 20, (2003): 69–92.

[126] Burt R. "Structural Holes and Good Ideas." *American Journal of Sociology* 110, no. 2 (2004): 349–399.

[127] Hamme C. "Group Emotional Intelligence: The Research and Development of An Assessment Instrument." Rutgers State University of New Jersey, 2003.

[128] Jordan P J, Lawrence S A. "Emotional Intelligence in Teams: Development and Initial Validation of the Short Version of the Workgroup Emotional Intelligence Profile (WEIP-S)." *Journal of Management & Organization* 5, (2009): 452–469.

[129] Liu Dong. "Build a Team with High EQ." *Enterprise Reform and Management*, no. 5 (2004): 38–39.

[130] Wang Liang, Zhao Lang et al. "A Discussion on the Emotional Quotient of Project Team and the Performance of Project Team." *Project Management Technology* 7, (2007): 28–30.

[131] Hackman J R. "The Design of Work Teams." In *Handbook of Organizational Behavior*, J. Lorsch (Ed.). Upper Saddle River, NJ: Prentice-Hall, 1987.

[132] Kirkman B, Rosen B. "Beyond Self-Management Antecedents and Consequences of Team Empowerment." *Academy of Management Journal* 42, (1999): 58–74.

[133] Wang Yanzi, Luo Jinlian et al. "A Study about the Influence of Social Network on Team Creativity." *Forcasting* 31, no. 4 (2012): 22–27.

[134] Weiner B. "Intrapersonal and Interpersonal Theories of Motivation from An Attributional Perspective." *Educational Psychology Review* 12, no. 1 (2000): 1–14.

[135] Goleman D. *Emotional intelligence*. New York: Random House LLC, 2006.